Costs and Benefits of Preventing Crime

CRIME and SOCIETY

Series Editor John Hagan

Costs and Benefits of Preventing Crime, edited by Brandon C. Welsh, David P. Farrington, and Lawrence W. Sherman

Breaking Away from Broken Windows: Baltimore Evidence and the Nationwide Fight Against Crime, Grime, Fear, and Decline, Ralph B. Taylor

Losing Legitimacy: Street Crime and the Decline of Social Institutions in America, Gary LaFree

Public Opinion, Crime, and Criminal Justice, Julian V. Roberts and Loretta Stalans

Whistleblowing at Work: Tough Choices in Exposing Fraud, Waste, and Abuse on the Job, Terance D. Miethe

Power, Politics and Crime, William J. Chambliss

The Community Justice Ideal, Todd Clear and David Karp

Casualties of Community Disorder: Women's Careers in Violent Crime, Deborah R. Baskin and Ira B. Sommers

Poverty, Ethnicity, and Violent Crime, James F. Short

Great Pretenders: Pursuits and Careers of Persistent Thieves, Neal Shover

Crime and Public Policy: Putting Theory to Work, edited by Hugh D. Barlow

Control Balance: Toward a General Theory of Deviance, Charles R. Tittle

Rape and Society: Readings on the Problems of Sexual Assault, edited by Patricia Searles and Ronald J. Berger

Inequality, Crime, and Social Control, George S. Bridges and Martha A. Myers

FORTHCOMING

Betrayal and Treason: Violations of Trust and Loyalty, Nachman Ben-Yehuda

Latino Homicide: A Five-City Study, Ramiro Martinez

Costs and Benefits of Preventing Crime

EDITED BY:

Brandon C. Welsh

DEPARTMENT OF CRIMINAL JUSTICE,
UNIVERSITY OF MASSACHUSETTS–LOWELL

David P. Farrington

INSTITUTE OF CRIMINOLOGY,
UNIVERSITY OF CAMBRIDGE

Lawrence W. Sherman

FELS CENTER OF GOVERNMENT,
UNIVERSITY OF PENNSYLVANIA

Westview Press
A Member of the Perseus Books Group

Crime and Society

Published in 2001 in the United States of America by Westview Press, 5500 Central Avenue, Boulder, Colorado 80301–2877, and in the United Kingdom by Westview Press, 12 Hid's Copse Road, Cumnor Hill, Oxford OX2 9JJ

Find us on the World Wide Web at www.westviewpress.com

A CIP catalog record of this book is available from the Library of Congress.
ISBN: 0-8133-9780-4

The paper used in this publication meets the requirements of the American National Standard for Permanence of Paper for Printed Library Materials Z39.48–1984.

10 9 8 7 6 5 4 3 2 1

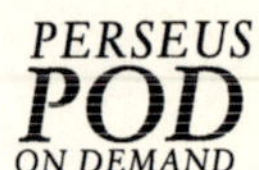

Contents

List of Tables and Figures

Tables

Figures

List of Acronyms

ABE	Adult Basic Education
ADP	Adolescent Diversion Project
AFDC	Aid for Dependent Children
AIC	Australian Institute of Criminology
ART	Aggression Replacement Training
ASI	Addiction Severity Index
BBBSA	Big Brothers/Big Sisters of America
CBA	cost-benefit analysis
CCTV	closed circuit television
CEA	cost-effectiveness analysis
CJS	criminal justice system
CPC	Child-Parent Center
CPPOA	Cost → Procedure → Process → Outcome Analysis
CRP	Crime Reduction Programme
DATOS	Drug Abuse Treatment Outcome Study
FDRP	Family Development Research Program
FFT	Functional Family Therapy
GDP	gross domestic product
HATTS	HIDTA Automated Treatment Tracking System
HIDTA	High Intensity Drug Trafficking Areas
ICPC	International Centre for the Prevention of Crime
ISI	Institute for Scientific Information
ISP	Intensive Supervision Programs
MRT	Moral Reconation Therapy
MST	Multisystemic Therapy
MTFC	Multidimensional Treatment Foster Care
MTROI	months-to-return-on-investment
NCP	National Crime Prevention
NCVS	National Crime Victimization Survey
NIDA	National Institute on Drug Abuse
NIJ	National Institute of Justice
NOAA	National Oceanic and Atmospheric Administration
NSWDP	National Supported Work Demonstration Project
OJJDP	Office of Juvenile Justice and Delinquency Prevention

ONDCP	Office of National Drug Control Policy
PEIP	Prenatal–Early Infancy Project
QOP	Quantum Opportunities Program
R&R	Reasoning and Rehabilitation
SES	socioeconomic status
SSDP	Seattle Social Development Project
TAB	Totalizator Agency Board
TC	Therapeutic Community
WTA	willingness to accept
WTP	willingness to pay

Foreword

Crime is costly not just for the immediate victims, but for all of us. The prices of consumer goods are inflated by shoplifting, employee theft, embezzlement, antitrust violations, and extortion of legitimate businesses by organized crime. Our tax bills reflect the pervasive crimes of income-tax evasion and government program fraud, as well as the necessity of supporting law-enforcement and criminal justice systems. The fear of predatory crime adds to our anxieties about our children while motivating an expensive and sometimes isolating quest for safety. In short, crime is a tax on our standard of living, imposing both tangible and intangible costs.

This perspective has not been much recognized or developed in the crime-control literature. As far back as 1967 the President's Commission on Law Enforcement and the Administration of Justice hazarded an estimate of the total dollar cost of crime (3 percent of the gross national product), and there have been occasional efforts to place a monetary value on the crime-prevention benefits of specific programs. Far more common, however, have been program evaluations that assess effects on criminal behavior but stop short of estimating the associated costs and benefits. As a result we know more about *what works* than about *what's worthwhile.* Until we incorporate a more systematic approach to the "value" aspect of "evaluation," the policy implications will remain unclear.

A good beginning is to recognize that public programs to prevent crime absorb scarce resources that have alternative uses. If you were crime-control czar and the taxpayers handed you an extra $1 billion, how should you spend it? More generally, could you make a good case for spending that extra $1 billion on crime prevention, rather than environmental cleanup or debt reduction or tax relief? The answer to the first question requires cost-effectiveness analysis, whereas the second requires a cost-benefit analysis.

This sort of analysis is made difficult, even in principle, by the fact that much of the benefit of crime reduction is not measured in any market transaction or accounting entry, but rather must be imputed. What, for example, is the value of rapes or gunshot wounds that are forestalled through crime-prevention efforts? And the evaluation problem is not limited to the benefit side—the *costs* of crime prevention may also have intangible elements that are as important or more so than the accounting costs in the relevant agencies. For example, the true social cost of incarcerating 2 million criminals and defendants in this country goes far beyond the tens of billions of dollars spent running the prisons and jails; it also includes the more-difficult-to-estimate value of lost freedom to those who are locked up and to those who care about them.

Estimating costs and benefits is difficult even for a crime like income-tax evasion, which at first glance appears to be all about recorded financial transactions—expenditure on collection and enforcement versus revenues collected. Yet, if that's all that matters, why isn't the Internal Revenue Service given a larger enforcement budget? It is well established that every additional million budgeted for the IRS is repaid many times over by the resulting addition to tax revenues. The answer is that the costs of securing tax compliance are not limited to those reflected in the IRS budget (as anyone who has been subjected to an audit will agree), and the social benefit of additional compliance may well be less than the extra dollars collected (since that money is lost to private use).

We see, then, that the business of assessing costs and benefits requires a considerable investment in the conceptual framework as well as in estimation technique. This book provides an important beginning on both. The return to this effort will someday be realized in the form of improved resource allocation to crime prevention efforts. And meeting the intellectual challenges along the way has its own rewards.

Philip J. Cook
Duke University

Preface

What are the cost savings from preventing a typical burglary, robbery, assault, or even a criminal career? Who benefits from these savings? How often do the benefits from preventing crime or criminal behavior exceed the resources spent on preventing or controlling crime? Is it more cost-effective to invest in early-childhood programs or juvenile boot camps to reduce criminal offending? These are some of the important questions that face policymakers in crime and justice today. Answering them is no easy task. Nevertheless, it is important to provide answers in order to ensure that the dollars devoted to crime reduction are spent as efficiently as possible.

The principal aim of this book is to report on and assess the current state of knowledge on the monetary costs and benefits of crime prevention programs. Remarkably, this crucial topic has rarely been studied up to the present. This book examines key methodological issues, reports on the most up-to-date research findings, discusses international policy perspectives, and presents an agenda for future research and policy development on the economic analysis of crime prevention. Throughout, it addresses the important question of how governments should be allocating scarce resources to make crime prevention policy and practice more effective and to produce the greatest economic benefits to society. The book brings together research results and perspectives from across North America, Europe, and Australia.

This book originated from a two-day meeting and workshop on the costs and benefits of preventing crime, held at the University of Maryland at College Park in March 1999. Convened by the University of Maryland's Department of Criminology and Criminal Justice and sponsored by the Jerry Lee Foundation and an anonymous foundation, the conference brought together leading researchers in the fields of crime prevention, experimental criminology, welfare economics, and operations research to discuss the state of knowledge on the benefit-cost analysis of crime prevention programs and to identify priorities for future research and policy development. Papers were presented and discussed on substantive issues relating to methods, findings, and policy developments. Subsequently, the papers were revised in the light of editorial comments, and they are now presented here.

The meeting and workshop, and hence this volume, would not have been possible without the generous financial support of the Jerry Lee Foundation and an anonymous foundation. This volume also benefited from comments by the presenters and participants at the two-day conference, and the urging (and gentle pushing) of some of those in attendance to publish these important papers. Over and above the presenters (i.e., the authors in this volume), we would like to thank the following individuals for their valuable contributions as participants: Michael Buckley, Shawn Bushway, Jerry Lee, Spencer De Li, Rolf Loeber, Doris Mackenzie, Carol Petrie, Winnie Reed, Andromachi Tseloni, and David Wilson. Last but by no means least, we wish to thank Mary West, Executive Assistant to the Chair of the Department of Criminology and Criminal Justice, who organized a superbly run and highly productive event and made sure an enjoyable time was had by all.

We are also very grateful for the support we have received from Westview Press, from John Hagan's warm reception of our initial idea for the present volume to the guidance of Andrew Day (formerly of Westview Press) and David McBride, our present editor, in shaping this book into what we hope will be an important contribution to the fields of criminology and criminal justice policy.

Brandon C. Welsh
David P. Farrington
Lawrence W. Sherman

PART ONE

Introduction

Assessing the Economic Costs and Benefits of Crime Prevention

BRANDON C. WELSH
DAVID P. FARRINGTON

The economic costs and benefits of crime prevention programs and policies are very important topics nationally and internationally, but they remain relatively neglected as areas of research. In recent years in the United States, Canada, the United Kingdom, and other industrialized countries, there has been a growing interest on the part of governments and other stakeholders in identifying the monetary value of crime prevention actions through the use of economic evaluation techniques, such as benefit-cost (or cost-benefit) analysis. Many of these countries have begun to reorient their crime prevention (and criminal justice) policies around an evidence- and efficiency-based model, looking to put in place programs with demonstrated effectiveness and cost savings. This has occurred for many reasons, including rising criminal justice costs—particularly in the area of prisons (Maguire and Pastore 1998)—evidence of the magnitude of the financial costs of crime and victimization to society (Miller, Cohen, and Wiersema 1996; Cook et al. 1999), governmental fiscal restraints, a movement toward general efficiency practices in government (Waller and Welsh 1999), and growing evidence of the effectiveness of alternative, noncriminal justice approaches to preventing crime (Tremblay and Craig 1995; Wasserman and Miller 1998).

Arguments such as "for every dollar spent, seven dollars are saved in the long run" (Schweinhart, Barnes, and Weikart 1993) have proved very powerful. Indeed, benefit-cost studies conducted over the last twenty years demonstrate that many different crime prevention strategies, such as early childhood intervention, situational prevention, and offender treatment, hold much promise in reducing the monetary costs associated with crime and paying back public and private investments in prevention programs (Welsh and Farrington 2000b).

Discussions of the economic efficiency of crime prevention programs can be very persuasive and have gained wide appeal in political, policy, and, more recently, academic settings. In many ways, the interest in attaching dollar values to crime prevention programs can be seen as an outgrowth of the focus on "what works" in preventing crime. *Efficiency, performance measures,* and *targeting resources* (among other terms) have become the common currency of discussions about crime prevention. However, compared to the number of outcome evaluation studies of crime prevention programs, which themselves are relatively few (Sherman et al. 1997, 1998), there is a dearth of benefit-cost analysis studies in this area. This is also true in many other prevention and intervention areas such as child and adolescent mental health (Knapp 1997) and substance abuse (Plotnick 1994; Rajkumar and French 1997; Bukoski and Evans 1998).

The lack of research on the economics of crime prevention underscores the need for caution in making general claims of cost savings or cost-effectiveness. Present critiques of research on the costs of crime and economic analysis of crime prevention programs and policies (e.g., Zimring and Hawkins 1995) have drawn attention to the ease with which the readily understood metric of dollars has been used, especially at the political level, to advance the policy or legislative agenda of the day. In the United States, for example, this has involved claims that the benefits of prisons and their primary aim of incapacitation far outweigh the costs of constructing facilities and housing and supervising offenders (Zedlewski 1987; DiIulio and Piehl 1991). Often missing from these claims have been rigorous and comprehensive benefit-cost analyses that are needed to describe accurately the economic contribution made by these programs to taxpayers and society at large.

The principal aim of this book is to report on and assess the present state of knowledge on the economic costs and benefits of crime prevention. The book examines key methodological issues, reports on the most up-to-date research findings, discusses international policy perspectives, and presents an agenda for future research and policy development on the economic analysis of crime prevention. Throughout, it addresses the important question of how governments should be allocating scarce resources to make crime prevention policy and practice more effective and to produce the greatest economic returns to society. It brings together research results and perspectives from across North America, Europe, and Australia.

This book comprises ten chapters, and there are four main parts: methods and perspectives of economic analysis, economic analysis findings, international policy perspectives on the economics of preventing crime, and future directions for research and policy development.

Methods and Perspectives of Economic Analysis

Chapters 1 and 2 deal specifically with methodological perspectives in performing economic analyses of crime prevention programs. Many of the chapters in Parts III and IV of this book also report on important methodological features of economic analysis, but chapters in these two parts are principally concerned with findings of economic analyses and international policy perspectives on the economics of preventing crime, respectively. For readers unfamiliar with the technical jargon and methodology of economic analysis, the present section will serve as a useful background.

An economic analysis can be described as a tool that allows choices to be made between alternative uses of resources or alternative distributions of services (Knapp 1997, 11). Many criteria may be used in economic analysis. The most common is efficiency, which is the focus throughout this book. Efficiency is essentially about achieving maximum outcomes from minimum inputs.

Benefit-cost analysis and cost-effectiveness analysis are the two most widely used techniques of economic analysis. A cost-effectiveness analysis can be referred to as an incomplete benefit-cost analysis: No attempt is made to estimate the monetary value of program effects produced (benefits), only resources used (costs). Benefit-cost analysis, on the other hand, monetizes both costs and benefits and compares them. A cost-effectiveness analysis makes it possible to specify, for example, the number of crimes prevented per $1,000 expended on each program. Another way to think about how benefit-cost and cost-effectiveness analyses differ is that "cost-effectiveness analysis may help one decide among competing program models, but it cannot show that the total effect was worth the cost of the program" (Weinrott, Jones, and Howard 1982, 179), unlike benefit-cost analysis.

An economic analysis is a step-by-step process that follows a standard set of procedures: (1) define the scope of the analysis, (2) obtain estimates of program effects, (3) estimate the monetary value of costs and benefits, (4) calculate present value and assess profitability, (5) describe the distribution of costs and benefits (an assessment of who gains and who loses; e.g., program participant, government/taxpayer, crime victim), and (6) conduct sensitivity analyses (Barnett 1993, 143–48). In the case of benefit-cost analysis, all of the six steps are carried out; for cost-effectiveness analysis, the third and fifth steps are omitted.

Barnett (1993, 1996) and Barnett and Escobar (1987, 1990) have discussed the application of these steps in the context of early childhood intervention programs, and we adopt this useful methodology to discuss the application of benefit-cost analyses to crime prevention programs in general. By no means is the following meant to serve as a comprehensive guide to carrying out benefit-cost analyses. Comprehensive texts on benefit-cost analysis such as Layard and Glaister (1994) and Boardman et al. (1996) should be consulted.

Define the Scope of Analysis

This step can be divided into two parts: First, define the alternatives to be compared (e.g., participation in a program versus nonparticipation); second, identify the limits of the comparison (Barnett 1993, 144). A determination is made at this stage about the perspective the economic analysis will take. The "public" (government/taxpayer and crime victim) and the "society" (government/taxpayer, crime victim, and program participant) are the two most common perspectives used in economic analyses of crime prevention programs. Other perspectives can include the government agency funding the program (e.g., probation, social services), participants of the program, or crime victims. (See Chapter 10 for a discussion of benefits according to the different perspectives.)

Another important element at this stage is the decision about what program outcomes are to be measured. Administrative issues (e.g., resources, time) or parameters of the study may limit the number of outcomes that can be measured. The best approach is to attempt to measure all of the relevant outcomes and, later, to estimate their monetary value independently (see the step on estimating monetary value).

Estimate Program Effects

Determining that a program prevented crimes requires an estimate of how many crimes would have been committed in the absence of the program and a disentangling of program effects on crime from all the other possible influences on crime. Program effects can be measured in different ways, with differing degrees of statistical power.

In practical terms, a benefit-cost analysis or any other type of economic analysis is an extension of an outcome evaluation, and is only as defensible as the evaluation upon which it is based. Weimer and Friedman recommend that benefit-cost analyses be limited to programs that have been evaluated with an "experimental or strong quasi-experimental design" (1979, 264). The most convincing method of evaluating crime prevention programs is the randomized experiment (Farrington 1983), which is often referred to as the "gold standard" of evaluation designs. The key feature of randomized experiments is that the experimental and control groups are equated before the experimental intervention on all possible extraneous variables. Hence, any subsequent differences between them must be attributable to the intervention.

However, the randomized experiment is the most convincing method of evaluation only if a sufficiently large number of units is randomly assigned to ensure that the program group is equivalent to the control group on all possible extraneous variables (within the limits of statistical fluctuation). As a rule of thumb, at least fifty units in each category are needed (Farrington 1997). This number is relatively easy to achieve with individuals but very difficult to achieve with larger units such as areas, schools, or prisons. For larger units such as areas, the best and most feasible design usually involves before-and-after measures in experimental and control areas, together with statistical control of extraneous variables. Nonrandomized experiments and before-after designs without a control group are less convincing methods of evaluating crime prevention programs.

In Chapter 2, Faye Taxman and Brian Yates report on the design of planned benefit-cost and cost-effectiveness analyses of a randomized controlled experiment comparing seamless integration of criminal justice and psychological services (e.g., coerced treatment with testing and sanctions) to traditional criminal justice services (e.g., supervision with testing) for drug-abusing offenders. Their approach goes beyond the usual focus of economic analyses on outcomes by systematically analyzing the relationships among costs, treatment procedures, psychological and related processes, and outcomes (Cost → Procedure → Process → Outcome Analysis, or CPPOA). This allows for a detailed examination of how relationships between program resources (costs) and outcomes produced by programs (benefits) may be enhanced or diminished by a variety of programmatic, community, interpersonal, and psychological variables. This is a rare but extremely valuable application of economic analysis techniques to assessing alternative crime prevention programs.

Estimate Monetary Value

The estimation of the monetary value of program resources used (costs) and effects produced (benefits) is the most important step in an economic analysis. As described by Barnett, "This step makes it possible to put all program consequences on an equal footing, so program costs, various positive outcomes, and any negative outcomes can be aggregated to provide a single measure of the program's impact on society and on particular sub-groups of society" (1993, 145). It is also the step that distinguishes a benefit-cost analysis from a cost-effectiveness analysis, which does not attempt to estimate the monetary value of program effects. Estimating the monetary value of costs is considered less complex than benefits, but no less important.

The most crucial issue involved in carrying out benefit-cost analyses is deciding what program resources used and effects produced should have dollar figures attached. No prescribed formula exists for what to include (or exclude). Prest and Turvey note that benefit-cost analysis "implies the enumeration and evaluation of all the relevant costs and benefits" (1965, 683). Estimating the monetary value of program benefits requires a great deal of ingenuity on the part of the evaluator. Unlike program costs, which can most often be broken down into operating (e.g., overhead, administration) and capital (e.g., rental of facilities), program benefits are disparate and involve a number of assumptions in order to arrive at reasonable estimates of monetary value. Program benefits often consist of costs avoided. This book's conclusion, Chapter 10, discusses the need for the development of a standard list of costs and benefits that should be measured as part of benefit-cost analyses of crime prevention programs.

Other important issues that must be addressed at this stage of an economic analysis include the use of average or marginal costs and benefits, accounting for the borrowing of money to pay for large-scale capital intensive projects, the inclusion of intangible victimization costs (e.g., pain, suffering, lost quality of life), and social versus external costs.

In the context of program resources used, "Marginal costs describe how the total cost of an operation changes as the unit of activity changes by a small amount," while "[a]verage costs are derived by simply dividing total costs by total workload in a given period of time" (Aos 1998, 13). The main limitation of average costs, as noted by Aos, is that "some of those costs . . . are fixed and do not change when workload changes" (1998, 13).

The borrowing of money to pay for a program often occurs in situational crime prevention programs that undertake large-scale capital intensive projects (e.g., installation of technical hardware, such as closed circuit television cameras). A key question is how best to account for the payments on the capital expenditure and debt charges on the loan in calculating the costs of the program. In assessing the economic efficiency of a program that lasts for only a short period of time, it might be unreasonable to include the total capital expenditure, which might dwarf any benefits accrued over this period. The Safe Neighbourhoods Unit recommends spreading the payments and the debt charges over the life expectancy of the program, but not beyond the loan repayment period, and using this "period as the basis for estimating a more realistic annual capital costs figure" (1993, 145).

One of the more controversial issues of benefit-cost analyses of crime prevention programs is the valuation of intangible victimization costs. This controversy stems from two major sources: First, the large estimates that have been produced for victim costs (Cohen 1988, 1998; Miller, Cohen, and Rossman 1993; Cohen, Miller, and Rossman 1994; Miller, Cohen, and Wiersema 1996); and second, the methodology used. Intangible victim costs are typically estimated on the basis of what a civil court would pay crime victims (jury compensation method) or what the public would willingly pay for additional safety (willingness-to-pay method).[1] Zimring and Hawkins are critical of the jury compensation method, contending, "Pain and suffering damages for personal injury in Anglo-American law are notorious for both their arbitrariness and their inflated size" (1995, 139). In defense of the jury compensation method, Cohen notes, "Jury awards exhibit identifiable patterns that can be distilled from a large sample of cases through regression analysis that controls for factors such as the involvement of the plaintiff, deep pocket of the defendant, etc." (1998, 8). In fact, both methods have been endorsed by various U.S. government agencies (e.g., the Consumer Product Safety Commission) and are used in benefit-cost studies (Cohen 1998, 8). Chapter 1 by Mark Cohen discusses the methods behind these different approaches and the importance of monetizing intangible and tangible (e.g., property loss, medical care) crime costs in benefit-cost analyses of crime prevention programs.

Another contentious issue in economic analysis is social versus external costs of crime. In Chapter 1, Cohen defines *external cost* as "the cost imposed by one person on another, where the latter person does not voluntarily accept this negative consequence." *Social cost* is defined as a cost that reduces the "aggregate well-being of society." The use of either of these terms has important implications for a program's economic efficiency.

Calculate Present Value and Profitability

Present value is concerned with making all monetary costs and benefits of a program comparable over time. The time value of money is best understood by the following: "A dollar today is worth more than a dollar next year because today's dollar can be invested to yield a dollar plus interest next year" (Barnett and Escobar 1987, 390). If a program's costs and benefits are confined to one year, then the calculation of present value is unnecessary.

Two separate steps must be carried out to adjust for differences in the value of money over time. First, the effect of inflation is removed by "translating nominal dollars from each year into dollars of equal purchasing power, or *real dollars*." This is achieved by the application of a price index to the nominal monetary units, which more or less cancels out the effect of inflation. Second, the time value of money is taken into account "by calculating the *present value* of real dollars from each year" (Barnett 1993, 146; emphases in original). For this to be achieved, real monetary units from different years must be discounted using a real or inflation-adjusted discount rate (typically between 3 percent and 7 percent per annum in the United States) to their "common value at the beginning of a program (or earliest program if two are compared)" (Barnett and Escobar 1987, 390). One of the limitations of not calculating present value is that benefits will be slightly larger than they should be. The reason is that the calculation of present value very often reduces future benefits more than present costs, because benefits tend to come later than costs (Barnett 1993, 147).

Once present value has been calculated an assessment can be made of the program's profitability or economic efficiency. From a benefit-cost analysis, the economic efficiency of a program can be reported in the form of the benefit-cost ratio (benefits divided by costs) or net value (benefits minus costs). Interpreting these measures is straightforward: A benefit-cost ratio greater than 1.0 and a plus sign for net value mean that the program is economically efficient.

Describe the Distribution

Describing the distribution of program costs and benefits involves identifying who gained and who lost from the program; for example, the program participant, funding agency, or taxpayer in general. This is an assessment of equity or fairness in the distribution of program costs and benefits. For a program that achieved a desirable benefit-cost ratio or net benefit, future funding may also depend on which parties received the benefits.

Conduct Sensitivity Analyses

This step is used to check the validity and to test the effects of variations in assumptions made in an economic analysis. For example, a typical sensitivity analysis involves the use of a range of discount rates in the calculation of present value. Barnett and Escobar note, "Sensitivity analysis can be used to indicate the range of values within which assumptions can be safely ignored or the specific conditions that must be found or produced if a policy or program is to yield the desired results" (1987, 391).

Economic Analysis Findings

Chapters 3, 4, and 5 present the most up-to-date information on the independent and comparative economic efficiency from benefit-cost analyses of programs spanning a broad range of crime prevention strategies, including developmental (e.g., early childhood, family), situational (e.g., reducing opportunities for crime), and correctional intervention (e.g., rehabilitation in community and institutional settings and with juveniles and adults).

Our previous efforts to bring together and assess the existing evidence on the economic costs and benefits of different crime prevention strategies (for developmental prevention, see Welsh 2000; for situational prevention, see Welsh and Farrington 1999; for correctional intervention, see Welsh and Farrington 2000a) and crime prevention programs in general (Welsh and Farrington 2000b) reveal that it is difficult to claim with any certainty that one type of program is more economically efficient than another. This is because of the small number of studies and the difficulty of comparing them. For example, despite finding that correctional (rehabilitative) intervention shows promise as an economically efficient crime prevention strategy, we were not able to address the important issue of whether treatment in community or institutional settings is the better investment of taxpayer dollars (Welsh and Farrington 2000a).

However, in recent years, there has been a steady growth of economic evaluation research in the crime prevention area, with efforts directed at investigating such important policy issues. Benefit-cost analysis is only one type of approach that has been used to assess the economic efficiency of different crime prevention programs and policies. Cost-effectiveness analysis and sophisticated mathematical modeling techniques such as simulation models,[2] which attempt to imitate the effects of real-life events through the modeling of behaviors and systems, have also contributed to the knowledge base in the crime prevention area. Leading studies include a number by the RAND Corporation that have explored the cost implications and crime reduction effectiveness of California's three-strikes law (Greenwood et al. 1994), the cost-effectiveness of early intervention versus incarceration (Rydell 1986; Greenwood et al. 1996), the cost-effectiveness of mandatory minimum sentences and alternative policies for reducing illicit drug use and crime (Caulkins et al. 1997, 1998), and the comparative cost-effectiveness of school-based drug prevention programs and different enforcement and treatment approaches to reduce cocaine use (Caulkins et al. 1999); the Dutch Ministry of Justice's policy simulation model comparing the cost-effectiveness of four alternative crime prevention strategies (van Dijk 1996, 1997); the Washington State Institute for Public Policy's comparative benefit-cost analysis of different crime prevention programs (see below; Aos, Barnoski, and Lieb 1998; Aos et al. 1999); and Donohue and Siegelman's assessment of the costs and benefits of allocating existing resources spent on prisons to early childhood programs to reduce future crimes (1998). (For a summary of the main findings of most of these studies, see Welsh and Farrington, 2000b.)

Costs and Benefits of Specific Programs

As noted above, a benefit-cost analysis allows for a determination of whether the total effect of a program (e.g., the monetary value of crimes avoided) is worth the resources expended on it. In other words, a benefit-cost analysis of a specific program provides a measure of its economic efficiency. Benefit-cost analyses of crime prevention programs are typically of this form, as opposed to a comparative benefit-cost analysis of two similar programs, which could also provide a measure of comparative economic efficiency. Chapters 3 and 4 summarize the economic efficiency of crime prevention programs.

In Chapter 3 we review the existing research evidence on the monetary value of crime prevention programs, focusing specifically on benefit-cost analyses of real-life programs, that is, programs that employed research designs with the capacity to control for threats to internal and external validity such as experimental and quasi-experimental designs. Using Tonry and Farrington's (1995) classification scheme, Chapter 3 organizes studies around three of the four major strategies of crime prevention: developmental prevention, situational prevention, and criminal justice prevention (correctional intervention); community prevention, the fourth strategy, was not included because only one study was identified. For each crime prevention strategy, benefit-cost results are summarized and a selected study is reviewed in detail.

Three key findings emerge from the review. First, each of the three crime prevention strategies provides value for money. Second, for situational prevention and correctional intervention programs it appears more likely that benefits will exceed costs in the short-term, while for (early childhood) developmental prevention programs there is a greater chance that benefits will not begin to surpass costs until the medium- to long-term. Third, developmental prevention and, to a lesser extent, correctional intervention were found to provide important monetary benefits beyond reduced crime. These monetary benefits can take the form of, for example, increased tax revenues from higher earnings, savings from reduced usage of social services, and savings from less health care utilization. The benefits of situational prevention, on the other hand, appear to be largely confined to reduced crime.

Chapter 4 by Peter Greenwood and his colleagues at the RAND Corporation summarizes their recent research on the economic costs and benefits of early childhood prevention programs (Karoly et al. 1998). Two leading programs are the focus of the study: the Elmira Prenatal–Early Infancy Project (Olds et al. 1997) and the Perry Preschool project (Schweinhart, Barnes, and Weikart 1993). Following the identification of those program effects that potentially accrue to the government (for

Elmira: health, employment, welfare, and crime; for Perry: education, employment, welfare, and crime), a benefit-cost analysis is carried out to enable a determination of whether, for each program and subsample (Elmira was divided into lower- and higher-risk families), benefits outweigh costs. The authors also calculate the potential benefits for future years (beyond the most recent follow-up) to allow for an assessment of the relationship between program costs and benefits over time (e.g., how long after the program ends governments can expect to realize a return on investment).

Chapter 4 presents a number of key findings on the monetary value of early childhood programs in preventing delinquency and later offending. It was found that benefits outweighed costs for Perry and the higher-risk families (unmarried and low socioeconomic status [SES]) of Elmira at twenty-two and thirteen years' postintervention, respectively, while for the lower-risk families (two-parent or higher SES) of Elmira costs exceeded benefits at thirteen years' postintervention. Also, monetary benefits to the government—in the form of savings to the criminal justice system and reduced reliance on welfare, for example—continued to accumulate for a long period of time after the interventions had ended, but not for Elmira's lower-risk families.

Comparative Economic Efficiency

Chapter 5 by Steve Aos and his colleagues at the Washington State Institute for Public Policy reports on the first research study, using a standard methodology to measure program costs and benefits, to assess the independent and comparative monetary costs and benefits of different crime prevention programs. The research aims to "identify interventions that reduce crime *and* lower total costs to taxpayers and crime victims" (Aos, Barnoski, and Lieb 1998, 1; emphasis in original). The authors refer to their methodological approach as a "bottom line" financial analysis, which they consider parallel to the approach used by investors to study rates of return on various financial investments. A comprehensive analytical model was developed to describe the economic contribution—from government and crime victim perspectives—of twenty-five published crime prevention programs, ranging from early childhood intervention to juvenile and adult offender treatment. Most of the programs used high-quality experimental research designs to evaluate program effects, thereby increasing confidence in the benefit-cost findings.

Two overall conclusions came out of the research: First, some prevention and intervention programs lower criminal activity, and some do not; second, some programs not only work, but also save more money than they cost. Of the twenty-five programs assessed, only seven did not produce a desirable benefit-cost ratio when criminal justice and crime victim benefits were measured. Furthermore, almost all of the juvenile offender treatment programs produced substantial benefits per dollar of cost.

International Policy Perspectives

Chapters 6, 7, and 8 discuss international policy perspectives on the economics of preventing crime. Chapters 6 and 7 report on current policy developments with respect to economic analysis of crime prevention in the United Kingdom and Australia, respectively. Chapter 8 discusses the recent evolution of governmental crime prevention strategies in Western countries and the increasing importance of an evidence- and efficiency-based approach in the development of national crime prevention policy.

A growing list of industrialized countries has begun to reorient crime prevention (and criminal justice) policies around an evidence- and efficiency-based model, aiming to put in place programs with demonstrated effectiveness and economic efficiency. As discussed above, this has occurred for many reasons, including rising criminal justice costs—particularly in the area of prisons—evidence of the magnitude of the financial costs of crime and victimization to society, governmental fiscal restraints, a movement toward general efficiency practices in government, and growing evidence of the effectiveness of alternative, noncriminal justice approaches to preventing crime.

Chapter 6 by Sanjay Dhiri and his colleagues at the Home Office in the United Kingdom reports on the government's "Crime Reduction Programme" and its focus on promoting economic evaluation research of crime prevention programs. The Crime Reduction Programme, a three-year, £250 million ($400 million) initiative begun in April 1999, aims to contribute to "reversing the long term growth rate in crime by ensuring . . . the greatest impact for the money spent" (Home Office 1999, 3). One of the program's core objectives is the improvement of the state of knowledge on the effectiveness and economic efficiency of crime prevention efforts so as to enable funding decisions to be based on the best-available evidence. This chapter discusses in detail the policy guidelines developed to aid researchers in conducting economic analyses of crime prevention programs and the Home Office's efforts to compile and utilize this information to assess value for money and inform national policy.

Chapter 7 by John Chisholm of the Australian Institute of Criminology in Canberra presents the findings of a number of leading economic analysis studies of crime prevention programs, focusing in particular on implications for the Australian situation and on Australian programs.

Chapter 8 by Daniel Sansfaçon and Irvin Waller of the International Centre for the Prevention of Crime in Montreal, Canada, is a fitting concluding chapter to this part of the book. In North America, Europe, and other regions of the world, federal and central governments have been forced to find ways to reduce expenditures, restructure departments, and identify investments that will best meet the needs of their citizens. Major reforms have been implemented in such areas as health care and education; for crime prevention, the strategic issues are only just beginning to be faced. The authors' examination of the recent evolution of national crime prevention strategies in leading industrialized countries such as Belgium, Canada, France, the Netherlands, the United Kingdom, and the United States, and the increasing importance of an evidence- and efficiency-based approach in the development of such strategies, points to a (potentially) promising future for preventing crime and building safer communities internationally.

Future Directions

Chapters 9 and 10, the concluding chapters, report on future directions for research and policy development on the economic analysis of crime prevention programs. Chapter 9 by Daniel Nagin of Carnegie Mellon University focuses on the important issue of the measurement of economic benefits in benefit-cost analyses of developmental prevention programs. He proposes that developmental prevention should be evaluated from the perspective of saving a human life, and accordingly makes a number of recommendations for assessing the value of developmental prevention programs.

Chapter 10 by ourselves and Lawrence Sherman brings together the main conclusions on the economic costs and benefits of crime prevention from the chapters in Parts II, III, and IV, and identifies gaps in knowledge and priorities for policy development and research. Significantly, it builds on the key points raised in Chapter 9. Central to Chapter 10 is a discussion of the key issues that need to be addressed in working toward a standard manual for carrying out benefit-cost analyses of crime prevention programs.

Promoting increased outcome evaluation research in the crime prevention area and the use of higher-quality (experimental and quasi-experimental) research designs to evaluate program effects is the first step needed in advancing a program of research on the economic evaluation of crime prevention. This needs to be followed by rigorous and comprehensive (prospective) economic analyses, preferably benefit-cost analyses, which should become a standard feature in evaluating crime prevention programs. Future research on the economic evaluation of crime prevention should also be concerned with standardizing the measurements of costs and benefits. Advancing knowledge in this area with the goal of improving confidence in what works in preventing crime and saves money for government, taxpayers, and society at large offers to yield important benefits.

Notes

1. See Rajkumar and French (1997) for a review of different methods for estimating both tangible and intangible victim costs.
2. These models utilize benefit-cost and cost-effectiveness analysis techniques.

References

Aos, S. 1998. Costs and benefits: Estimating the "bottom line" for crime prevention and intervention programs. A description of the cost-benefit model, version 2.0. Unpublished paper. Olympia: Washington State Institute for Public Policy.

Aos, S., Barnoski, R., and Lieb, R. 1998. Preventive programs for young offenders effective and cost-effective. *Overcrowded Times* 9, no. 2: 1, 7–11.

Aos, S., Phipps, P., Barnoski, R., and Lieb, R. 1999. *The comparative costs and benefits of programs to reduce crime: A review of national research findings with implications for Washington State: Version 3.0.* Olympia: Washington State Institute for Public Policy.

Barnett, W. S. 1993. Cost-benefit analysis. In L. J. Schweinhart, H. V. Barnes, and D. P. Weikart, *Significant benefits: The High/Scope Perry Preschool study through age 27*, 142–73. Ypsilanti, Mich.: High/Scope Press.

______. 1996. *Lives in the balance: Age–27 benefit-cost analysis of the High/Scope Perry Preschool program.* Ypsilanti, Mich.: High/Scope Press.

Barnett, W. S., and Escobar, C. M. 1987. The economics of early educational intervention: A review. *Review of Educational Research* 57: 387–414.

______. 1990. Economic costs and benefits of early intervention. In S. J. Meisels and J. P. Shonkoff, eds., *Handbook of early childhood intervention*, 560–82. Cambridge: Cambridge University Press.

Boardman, A. E., Greenberg, D. H., Vining, A. R., and Weimer, D. L. 1996. *Cost-benefit analysis: Concepts and practice.* Englewood Cliffs, N.J.: Prentice-Hall.

Bukoski, W. J., and Evans, R. I., eds. 1998. *Cost-benefit/cost-effectiveness research of drug abuse prevention: Implications for programming and policy.* NIDA Research Monograph 176. Washington, D.C.: National Institute on Drug Abuse.

Caulkins, J. P., Rydell, C. P., Everingham, S. S., Chiesa, J., and Bushway, S. D. 1999. *An ounce of prevention, a pound of uncertainty: The cost-effectiveness of school-based drug prevention programs.* Santa Monica, Calif.: RAND.

Caulkins, J. P., Rydell, C. P., Schwabe, W., and Chiesa, J. 1997. *Mandatory minimum drug sentences: Throwing away the key or the taxpayers' money?* Santa Monica, Calif.: RAND.

______. 1998. Are mandatory minimum drug sentences cost-effective? *Corrections Management Quarterly* 2: 62–73.

Cohen, M. A. 1988. Pain, suffering, and jury awards: A study of the cost of crime to victims. *Law and Society Review* 22: 537–55.

______. 1998. The monetary value of saving a high-risk youth. *Journal of Quantitative Criminology* 14: 5–33.

Cohen, M. A., Miller, T. R., and Rossman, S. B. 1994. The costs and consequences of violent behavior in the United States. In A. J. Reiss, Jr., and J. A. Roth, eds., *Understanding and preventing violence.* Vol. 4 of *Consequences and control,* 66–167. Washington, D.C.: National Academy Press.

Cook, P. J., Lawrence, B. A., Ludwig, J., and Miller, T. R. 1999. The medical costs of gunshot injuries in the United States. *Journal of the American Medical Association* 282: 447–54.

DiIulio, J. J., and Piehl, A. M. 1991. Does prison pay? The stormy national debate over the cost-effectiveness of imprisonment. *Brookings Review* (Fall): 28–35.

Donohue, J. J., and Siegelman, P. 1998. Allocating resources among prisons and social programs in the battle against crime. *Journal of Legal Studies* 27: 1–43.

Farrington, D. P. 1983. Randomized experiments on crime and justice. In M. Tonry and N. Morris, eds., *Crime and justice: A review of research,* 4: 257–308. Chicago: University of Chicago Press.

______. 1997. Evaluating a community crime prevention program. *Evaluation* 3: 157–73.

Greenwood, P. W., Model, K. E., Rydell, C. P., and Chiesa, J. 1996. *Diverting children from a life of crime: Measuring costs and benefits.* Santa Monica, Calif.: RAND.

Greenwood, P. W., Rydell, C. P., Abrahamse, A. F., Caulkins, J. P., Chiesa, J., Model, K. E., and Klein, S. P. 1994. *Three strikes and you're out: Estimated benefits and costs of California's new mandatory-sentencing law.* Santa Monica, Calif.: RAND.

Home Office 1999. *Reducing crime and tackling its causes: A briefing note on the Crime Reduction Programme.* London: Home Office Communications Directorate.

Karoly, L. A., Greenwood, P. W., Everingham, S. S., Houbé, J., Kilburn, M. R., Rydell, C. P., Sanders, M., and Chiesa, J. 1998. *Investing in our children: What we know and don't know about the costs and benefits of early childhood interventions.* Santa Monica, Calif.: RAND.

Knapp, M. 1997. Economic evaluations and interventions for children and adolescents with mental health problems. *Journal of Child Psychology and Psychiatry* 38: 3–25.

Layard, R., and Glaister, S., eds. 1994. *Cost-benefit analysis.* 2d ed. Cambridge: Cambridge University Press.

Maguire, K., and Pastore, A. L., eds. 1998. *Sourcebook of criminal justice statistics 1997.* Washington, D.C.: Bureau of Justice Statistics, U.S. Department of Justice.

Miller, T. R., Cohen, M. A., and Rossman, S. B. 1993. Victim costs of violent crime and resulting injuries. *Health Affairs* 12: 186–97.

Miller, T. R., Cohen, M. A., and Wiersema, B. 1996. *Victim costs and consequences: A new look.* Washington, D.C.: National Institute of Justice, U.S. Department of Justice.

Olds, D. L., Eckenrode, J., Henderson, C. R., Kitzman, H., Powers, J., Cole, R., Sidora, K., Morris, P., Pettitt, L. M., and Luckey, D. 1997. Long-term effects of home visitation on maternal life course and child abuse and neglect: Fifteen-year follow-up of a randomized trial. *Journal of the American Medical Association* 278: 637–43.

Plotnick, R. D. 1994. Applying benefit-cost analysis to substance use prevention programs. *International Journal of the Addictions* 29: 339–59.

Prest, A. R., and Turvey, R. 1965. Cost-benefit analysis: A survey. *Economic Journal* 75: 683–735.

Rajkumar, A. S., and French, M. T. 1997. Drug abuse, crime costs, and the economic benefits of treatment. *Journal of Quantitative Criminology* 13: 291–323.

Rydell, C. P. 1986. The economics of early intervention versus later incarceration. In P. W. Greenwood, ed., *Intervention strategies for chronic juvenile offenders: Some new perspectives*, 235–58. New York: Greenwood Press.

Safe Neighbourhoods Unit 1993. *Crime prevention on council estates.* London: Her Majesty's Stationery Office.

Schweinhart, L. J., Barnes, H. V., and Weikart, D. P. 1993. *Significant benefits: The High/Scope Perry Preschool study through age 27.* Ypsilanti, Mich.: High/Scope Press.

Sherman, L. W., Gottfredson, D. C., MacKenzie, D. L., Eck, J. E., Reuter, P., and Bushway, S. D. 1997. *Preventing crime: What works, what doesn't, what's promising.* Washington, D.C.: National Institute of Justice, U.S. Department of Justice.

______. 1998. Preventing crime: What works, what doesn't, what's promising. *Research in Brief* (July). Washington, D.C.: National Institute of Justice, U.S. Department of Justice.

Tonry, M., and Farrington, D. P. 1995. Strategic approaches to crime prevention. In M. Tonry and D. P. Farrington, eds., *Building a safer society: Strategic approaches to crime prevention.* Vol. 19 of *Crime and justice: A review of research*, 1–20. Chicago: University of Chicago Press.

Tremblay, R. E., and Craig, W. M. 1995. Developmental crime prevention. In M. Tonry and D. P. Farrington, eds., *Building a safer society: Strategic approaches to crime prevention.* Vol. 19 of *Crime and justice: A review of research*, 151–236. Chicago: University of Chicago Press.

van Dijk, J. J. M. 1996. Assessing the costs and benefits of crime control strategies. Unpublished paper. The Hague: Ministry of Justice.

______. 1997. Towards a research-based crime reduction policy: Crime prevention as a cost-effective policy option. *European Journal on Criminal Policy and Research* 5: 13–27.

Waller, I., and Welsh, B. C. 1999. International trends in crime prevention: Cost-effective ways to reduce victimization. In G. Newman, ed., *Global report on crime and justice*, 191–220. New York: Oxford University Press.

Wasserman, G. A., and Miller, L. S. 1998. The prevention of serious and violent juvenile offending. In R. Loeber and D. P. Farrington, eds., *Serious and violent juvenile offenders: Risk factors and successful interventions*, 197–247. Thousand Oaks, Calif.: Sage.

Weimer, D. L., and Friedman, L. S. 1979. Efficiency considerations in criminal rehabilitation research: Costs and consequences. In L. Sechrest, S. O. White, and

E. D. Brown, eds., *The rehabilitation of criminal offenders: Problems and prospects,* 251–72. Washington, D.C.: National Academy of Sciences.

Weinrott, M. R., Jones, R. R., and Howard, J. R. 1982. Cost-effectiveness of teaching family programs for delinquents: Results of a national evaluation. *Evaluation Review* 6: 173–201.

Welsh, B. C. 2000. Economic costs and benefits of primary prevention of delinquency and later offending: A review of the research. In D. P. Farrington and J. W. Coid, eds., *Early prevention of adult antisocial behavior.* Cambridge: Cambridge University Press, in press.

Welsh, B. C., and Farrington, D. P. 1999. Value for money? A review of the costs and benefits of situational crime prevention. *British Journal of Criminology* 39: 345–68.

______. 2000a. Correctional intervention programs and cost-benefit analysis. *Criminal Justice and Behavior* 27: 115–33.

______. 2000b. Monetary costs and benefits of crime prevention programs. In M. Tonry, ed., *Crime and justice: A review of research,* 27: 305–61. Chicago: University of Chicago Press.

Zedlewski, E. W. 1987. Making confinement decisions. *Research in Brief* (July). Washington, D.C.: National Institute of Justice, U.S. Department of Justice.

Zimring, F. E., and Hawkins, G. 1995. *Incapacitation: Penal confinement and the restraint of crime.* New York: Oxford University Press.

PART TWO

Methods and Perspectives of Economic Analysis

1

The Crime Victim's Perspective in Cost-Benefit Analysis

The Importance of Monetizing Tangible and Intangible Crime Costs

MARK A. COHEN

The most significant (and controversial) portion of a criminal justice policy benefit-cost analysis is likely to be the cost of criminal victimization—in particular, the valuation of intangible losses such as pain, suffering, and lost quality of life. This chapter reviews the methodologies employed by economists in estimating the cost of crime to victims and provides a basic understanding of the value and pitfalls of placing monetary values on crime.

Public policy analysts have conducted benefit-cost analyses for many years.[1] Programs as diverse as environmental regulations, highway construction, land use regulations, welfare benefits, job training programs, and immunization policies have all been analyzed in this manner. Schools of public policy and departments of economics teach courses devoted solely to the intricacies of benefit-cost analyses. Since the early 1980s, federal government regulatory agencies have been required to conduct benefit-cost analyses on major regulatory initiatives. These requirements have been adopted through Executive Order and implemented by the Office of Management and Budget.[2] Recent proposals in Congress would legislatively mandate similar requirements.[3] Thus, benefit-cost analyses have become a routine tool in the development of environmental, health, and safety regulations.

Despite its widespread use elsewhere, benefit-cost analysis has not been a staple of the criminal justice policy analyst's tool kit. This is rapidly changing in response to both increasing public demand for accountability of government agencies and the availability of new data and techniques of analysis for identifying the costs and benefits of criminal justice policies. Ultimately, benefit-cost analyses might be required for newly proposed criminal justice policies. Because the academic literature now contains methodologies for doing benefit-cost analysis in the criminal justice arena, the next generation of criminal justice students will soon be learning about these tools in courses on criminology and criminal justice policy.

This chapter is organized as follows: Section 1 discusses the conceptual underpinnings of this line of research, asking questions such as, Why put dollar values on the intangible costs of crime? Whose costs and whose benefits are relevant? And what criticisms have been offered against the economic approach to placing dollar values on the intangible impact of crime? Section 2 reviews alternative methodologies to measure the intangible costs of crime to victims. Section 3 reviews the existing empirical literature, whereas section 4 concludes with a research agenda for future studies.

Conceptual Issues in Costs and Benefits of Criminal Justice Policy

This section reviews several important theoretical issues concerning the propriety of placing dollar values on crime. I first consider why measuring the costs and benefits of crime and criminal justice policies is a worthwhile exercise. Second, I discuss the difficulty of defining "social costs" and introduce the notion of the "external costs" imposed by crime. Third, I examine *whose* costs and benefits should be considered in conducting benefit-cost analysis of a criminal justice policy. Fourth, I discuss the difference among average, marginal, and aggregate costs of crime. Finally, I consider some of the criticisms that have been articulated against the use of this methodology, both in general and in the context of criminal justice programs.

Why Should We Measure the Monetary Costs of Crime?

The idea of measuring the monetary costs of crime has been around for many years. Gray (1979) reviews the history of the cost of crime and reports that several governmental commissions have been called upon to report on the cost of crime. Although these reports noted the difficulty and lack of progress over the years in adequately capturing the full costs of crime, they also acknowledged the importance of continuing this line of research.

To most economists, there is no question that crime costs should be estimated. Economics involves the allocation of scarce resources in society. Criminal justice policy decisions always involve choices between two or more alternatives, each having their own costs and benefits. The enumeration of those costs and benefits puts the various alternatives on a level playing field and can help policymakers make more informed decisions that enhance society's well-being. Of course, if the enumerated costs and benefits are inaccurate, there is a risk that more information can lead to worse decisions. Further, many noneconomists would argue that there is neither a moral justification nor an adequate empirical basis for placing dollar values on intangible factors such as pain, suffering, and lost quality of life. I will return to these issues later in this section. For now, I assume that such intangibles can be measured and consider three important policy-relevant purposes of measuring costs and benefits: (1) comparison of the relative harm caused by type of crime, (2) comparison of the aggregate harm from crime to other social ills, and (3) benefit-cost analysis of alternative crime control policies. Martin and Bradley (1964) provide a more detailed discussion of the importance of identifying and quantifying the costs of crime.

Relative harm by type of crime. Policymakers are often interested in comparing the harm caused by different types of crime. For example, most advocates of sentencing guidelines rely on victim harm as one component of their sentencing structure. Those who subscribe to a "just deserts" philosophy combine harm with culpability, whereas those who advocate a utilitarian approach combine harm with detectability and deterability. Although one can tally the various harms associated with each type of crime (e.g., value of property stolen, frequency of injuries by type of injury, mental health–related injuries), without a common metric such as dollars, it is difficult to objectively compare these harms.

A few nonmonetary metrics have been proposed for comparing harms—such as the number of days for a victim to recoup from the financial loss or the number of years of potential life lost (see e.g., Maltz 1975). These are primarily designed to overcome the perceived unfairness of valuing harms according to the wealth of the individual being harmed.[4] However, these proposals also suffer from not having a common metric. One is still unable to compare ten lost workdays to one lost life year.

Absent a common metric to compare harms, the generally accepted approach to rank the severity of crimes has been to survey the public (see Wolfgang et al. 1985; Cullen et al. 1982; Rossi et al. 1974; and Rossi and Berk 1997). These surveys ask respondents to rank the seriousness of various crimes and result in relatively consistent rankings over time and across populations. However, they are based on subjective public perceptions concerning the severity of crimes—which may include misperceptions about the frequency of injuries in typical criminal events. For example, Cohen (1988a) argued that public perception surveys tend to underestimate the harm associated with violent crimes relative to property crimes. Thus, whereas public perception surveys are useful for determining the public's attitudes toward crime, they are limited in their ability to objectively measure and compare the seriousness of crimes.

Aggregate costs and benefits. One of the most common—yet probably least important—reasons for estimating the costs of crime is to tally the aggregate cost to society. Multibillion-dollar cost estimates can easily make their way into the popular press and political debate. There are two basic problems with tallying the costs of intentional injury. First, having been told that crime costs the United States $450 billion per year, what are we to do with this information? If we are successful in fully estimating the aggregate cost of crime, we can compare this total cost estimate to that of other social problems (e.g., cancer, auto crashes, homelessness). Whether one agrees that this is a useful exercise or not, various advocacy groups do compare "cost of crime" estimates to the cost of other social ills in an effort to affect policy decisions. Unfortunately, misuses of these data occur on both sides of the political debate.

Until recently, most estimates of the cost of crime (including estimates published by the Bureau of Justice Statistics) have significantly missed the mark. For example, Irwin and Austin (1994) use the "official" estimates of $19 billion to illustrate that crime is less of a problem than other social ills and to argue against increased prison sentences. A more comprehensive cost study sponsored by the National Institute of Justice reports the annual cost of crime to victims to be $450 billion (Miller, Cohen, and Wiersema 1996). An article reporting on that study in the *New York Times* quoted a Republican representative as saying the report "demonstrates that the cost of building prisons and adding police are justified" (Butterfield 1996). Despite the rhetoric, neither small nor large "cost of crime" numbers demonstrate that the cost of building more prisons is justified or that alternatives to incarceration are better than more prisons.

Even if properly measured, one cannot simply compare aggregate cost estimates of crime with estimates of the cost of other social ills to arrive at policy recommendations for future public spending priorities. Suppose, for example, that the cost of crime in the United States was estimated to exceed the cost of auto crashes. This does not necessarily mean that society should increase expenditures on crime prevention relative to prevention of auto crashes. If the current expenditures on "preventing" crimes and auto crashes are factored into the equation, it might be found that society is already spending too much on the former and not enough on the latter. The more relevant question is how much additional reduction in crimes (or auto crashes) would we observe if we spent more on prevention. This can be answered only if we know such things as the deterrent and incapacitative effects of various sanctions, increased police patrols, and so on.

Subject to the above caveat, comparing cost estimates of crime with other social ills can provide a basis of comparison on a common metric. For example, a study by Streff et al. (1992) estimated that the total cost of traffic crashes in Michigan was about three times as much as the total cost of crime in that state. Although no immediate policy implications should be drawn from this comparison, it does help begin the process of identifying public policy priorities and puts crime into its proper perspective. Over time, it might also be possible to quantify the magnitude of any change in crime rates by comparing costs from year to year.

A second problem with tallying the costs of crime is that the true cost of crime is more than the sum total of its parts. If there were no robbers or rapists in this world, hitchhiking would probably be a way of life for a huge portion of the population. If violence was totally eliminated from society, organized crime might evaporate (as it depends on the threat of violence for its survival), and the standard of living of many inner-city residents would increase as businesses returned to previously abandoned storefronts. These massive changes in social structure could come about only with equally impressive changes in social behavior. Thus, any aggregate estimates of the cost of crime would need to account for these factors.

Cost-effectiveness and benefit-cost analysis of crime control policies. Perhaps the most important—and controversial—use of monetary estimates of the cost of crime is to compare the benefits and costs of alternative crime control policies. There is no shortage of crime prevention and crime reduction programs and proposals that would benefit from government funding. However, the government can fund only so many of these programs. One of the benefits of using dollars as a common metric for analyzing criminal justice policy is that society spends dollars to try to prevent crime from occurring in the first place. Society's ability to control criminal behavior and reduce the incidence of victimization is limited by its ability to pay for police, courts, corrections, and prevention programs.

In an effort to reduce crime and the severity of its consequences, society has undertaken many criminal justice experiments, including intensive probation, electronic monitoring of offenders, shock incarceration, targeted and community police, spouse arrest programs for domestic violence, and so on. As new policies are tested and policy options are considered, one must be able to apply objective evaluation techniques.[5] If two options have identical crime control effects but differing costs, the choice is simple. Unfortunately, few policy alternatives are so easily compared. In a more realistic case where a new policy reduces crime at some additional expense (or increases cost at a savings), one of the key questions is whether that reduced (increased) crime is worth its cost. Only by monetizing the cost of criminal victimization can one begin to answer that question.

In cases where a program passes a benefit-cost test using only tangible costs, the need for monetizing intangible losses is less obvious. For example, Prentky and Burgess (1990) show that the cost of incarcerated sex offender treatment is less than the tangible benefits from lower recidivism rates (e.g., lower reprocessing costs of recidivists and lower victim costs). No intangible benefits need to be estimated because the program already passes a benefit-cost test. However, a similar study of early release programs in Illinois by Austin (1986) concluded the benefits (reduced prison costs) exceeded costs (tangible costs associated with increased crime due to recidivists). As I show in Cohen (1988a), if the cost of recidivism includes the intangible cost of crime to victims, the benefit-cost ratio goes the other way, and Illinois residents are better off building more prisons or finding another less costly but equally effective alternative. To let these prisoners out early saves taxpayers money—but at the expense of future crime victims.

One of the most compelling reasons to monetize the costs and benefits of crime control programs—and to attempt a benefit-cost analysis—is the consequence of not doing so. Whenever a criminal justice or prevention program is adopted or not adopted, society is implicitly conducting such an analysis and placing dollar values on crimes. For example, suppose one program costs $1 million and ultimately will prevent one hundred burglaries from occurring. Whether made explicit or not, the policymaker adopting that program has determined that it is worth spending at least $10,000 to reduce each burglary ($1 million divided by one hundred burglaries). If another $1 million program that was not funded would have prevented fifty serious physical assaults from occurring, the policymaker is implicitly determining that each assault is worth less than $20,000 ($1 million divided by fifty). Thus, even the policymaker who has ethical concerns about placing dollar values on crime and conducting benefit-cost analyses implicitly makes a value judgment about the monetary value of crime.

Social Versus External Costs of Crime

One of the most confusing and misunderstood concepts in the cost-of-crime literature is the difference between "social costs" and "external costs." Many authors ignore this distinction or otherwise sweep it under the rug, thus making it difficult for the reader to know how to compare different estimates. This is not surprising, because there is no real agreement on which crime costs are social costs. Neither is there full agreement on whether or not social costs should be the relevant criteria for assessing the monetary cost or seriousness of crime. I argue that the relevant concept for analysis of crime control programs is "external" cost, not social cost.

An "external cost" is the cost imposed by one person on another, where the latter person does not voluntarily accept this negative consequence. For example, the external costs associated with a mugging include stolen property, medical costs, lost wages, as well as pain and suffering endured by the victim. The victim neither asked for nor voluntarily accepted compensation for enduring these losses. Moreover, society has deemed that imposing these external costs is morally wrong and against the law.

The concepts of social costs and external costs are closely related but not identical. "Social costs" are costs that reduce the aggregate well-being of society. Although pain and suffering costs are not actual commodities or services exchanged in the marketplace, individuals are willing to pay real dollars and expend real resources in order to avoid the pain, suffering, and lost quality of life associated with becoming a crime victim. Thus, to the extent that society cares about the well-being of crime victims, these costs should also be considered social costs of victimization.

The value of the stolen property is more problematic. Some economists have argued that stolen property is an "external" but not technically a "social" cost, because the offender can enjoy the use of the property. For example, Cook (1983, 374) argues that the relevant concept should be the "social cost"—which would exclude transfers of money or property. However, Cook notes that he "presumes that the criminal is properly viewed as a member of society." In contrast, Trumbull (1990) argues that those who violate the criminal law are not entitled to have their utility counted in the social welfare function, that is, their gain or loss is to be ignored. This example highlights the fact that "social cost" is a normative concept based on a subjective evaluation of whether an activity is socially harmful.

Regardless of whether one considers stolen property a transfer, there are other social costs associated with theft. Consider the case of an auto theft where the auto is never recovered, and the thieves use the car for their own private benefits. Although technically a "transfer," the fact that cars are stolen forces potential victims to buy security systems, park in secure lots, and take other preventive measures. If the car or some of its contents are "fenced," resources devoted to the fencing operations are considered a social cost as they are diverted from socially productive uses. Thus, the value of stolen property might be used as a proxy for these lost resources, and are thus a measure of social cost (Becker 1968, 171 n. 3). It is important to note that it would be "double-counting" to include both the value of stolen property and all collateral costs of the theft in an estimate of the "social cost" of theft.

Regardless of whether stolen property is considered a social cost, society has an interest in enforcing property rights and has determined it is a crime to steal. There will be less productive investment—and therefore less social wealth—in a society where property rights are not enforced. The value of the stolen car must certainly be considered a cost of crime. For that reason, many economists who study the cost of crime rely on an "external cost" approach, including all costs imposed by a criminal on external parties—whether they are technically considered "social costs" or not.

Even the "external cost" notion of crime has pitfalls, however. Consider the "victimless" crime of drug abuse, which is not by itself an external cost if the user voluntarily purchases drugs and reaps the full benefits and costs associated with their use. Nevertheless, drug abuse imposes many external costs: Drug users might be less productive in the workforce and might commit crimes to support their drug habits, dealers might forego socially productive work activities, and society might be burdened with additional medical costs in treating drug addicts.[6] Some of these costs (such as crime committed to support a drug habit and medical costs associated with drug overdoses) are clearly external or social costs (or both) irrespective of whether drug use is illegal. However, some costs are only social costs because society has deemed drug use illegal. For example, economists generally consider the foregone legitimate earnings of a person in the illegal drug trade to be a social cost due to the socially valuable resources that are wasted. However, because illegal drug sales are voluntary transactions between two parties, these resources would not be considered social costs if drugs were made legal.

Another complicating factor in conceptualizing social and external costs is that many crimes are allegedly committed as a form of self-help based on the perpetrator's sense of being wronged by the victim (Black 1998). Examples of this might be collecting on a bad debt, an original owner who steals back his property, and assaults committed in response to violent behavior committed by the ultimate victim. Although motives such as revenge or "self-help" do not justify criminal activity, they do raise the question of who is being harmed and whether those harms are "external" or "social" costs society wishes to prevent.

From Whose Perspective Are These Costs and Benefits to Be Measured?

One of the most significant costs of crime is the pain, suffering, and lost quality of life endured by victims. Economists have long noted that "psychic" benefits and costs are part of individual utility and hence social welfare. Individuals are willing to trade tangible goods and services in exchange for some of these psychic benefits. Thus, they represent real social costs and benefits. Similarly, individuals who experience the pain, suffering, and lost quality of life from becoming a crime victim would be willing to pay real dollars to reduce those psychic costs.

Although lost productivity of incarcerated offenders is normally included in estimates of the cost of crime, noticeably missing is the lost quality of life to offenders while behind bars. When an offender is locked up and unable to be gainfully employed, not only does the offender lose wages, but society loses the value of those hours of work. Hence, the offender's lost productivity is generally included as a social cost. However, the pain, suffering, and lost quality of life to the offender in prison are not considered either an external or a social cost of crime, because the offender is the only one who suffers. Not all would agree with this approach, however, as antiprison activists might care very much about the treatment of imprisoned offenders. They might also care about the monetary and psychic costs to the family of the offender. The latter are more properly considered both external and social costs, to the extent that the family of the offender did not participate in the crime. As this example illustrates, benefit-cost analysis is not a value-free concept, but instead involves definitions and explicit boundaries in order to determine whose costs and benefits matter.

Critiques of Benefit-Cost Analysis and Monetizing Crime Costs

Although few would disagree with the fact that enumerating costs and benefits is a worthwhile exercise, there is less agreement on whether costs and benefits should be measured, and if so, how much weight benefit-cost analysis should be given in policy analysis. At one extreme, many economists would argue that virtually any cost and any benefit can be measured—albeit with some uncertainty and often using indirect methods. Some economists might even argue that benefit-cost analysis should be the primary criteria used in making policy decisions. At the other extreme, some authors argue that not only is it difficult or impossible to measure some costs and benefits, but in any case benefit-cost analysis is inappropriate for use in many policy discussions. Various objections to benefit-cost analysis or monetizing intangible victim costs (or both) have been raised. This section considers three of the most important issues raised by critics: (1) philosophical and ethical concerns, (2) lack of a consistent theoretical basis for estimating crime costs, and (3) disparities between public perception and objective measures of crime severity.

Philosophical and ethical objections. Kelman (1981) articulates several concerns over the use of benefit-cost analysis on ethical and philosophical grounds. He argues that some things simply cannot be valued, such as free speech, pollution, or safety.[7] He also argues that benefit-cost analysis assumes that economic efficiency is the goal—at the expense of other socially desirable goals such as equity or fairness. This is not a criticism of the methodology—only of those who want to impose benefit-cost analysis as the sole criteria for public decisionmaking. Benefit-cost analysis does not discriminate on the basis of socioeconomic status. A $1,000 medical cost is valued at $1,000 regardless of whether the person being injured is rich or poor. Thus, the tool is politically neutral and can (and will) be overridden when other policy goals come into conflict. Instead, when viewed as one tool available to policymakers, benefit-cost analysis itself has many benefits and only limited costs. Indeed, most texts on benefit-cost methodology include an analysis of the "incidence" of costs and benefits—that is, who bears the costs and who reaps the benefits—as an integral part of benefit-cost analysis. The policymaker is presented with the evidence and left to determine how to weigh the differing goals of economic efficiency and equity.

A more subtle concern is the fact that the methodology itself may incorporate inequities in society. For example, if one is measuring lost wages to victims of crime—and those victims tend to be in the lower-income quartiles—the benefits of a crime prevention program will be skewed downward based on the victim's income. If one were to compare a crime reduction program to another program that targets airline safety, for example, the typical wage rate might be higher for the airline accident victim than the crime victim. Further, if one were to conduct a survey of potential victims to determine their willingness to pay for crime reduction programs, the value one elicits is likely to be highly dependent on the wealth (i.e., ability to pay) of the respondent. Thus, from a public policy standpoint, benefit-cost analysis does indeed discriminate against the less wealthy in society. If society deems this unfair, the analyst needs to make adjustments in the estimated costs and benefits to "neutralize" the effect of wealth on the estimated costs and benefits. This has been done to some extent in some of the empirical studies of the cost of crime. For example, the methodology developed in Cohen (1988a) is based on the statistical "value of life" of the typical individual in the United States—not the typical crime victim. However, wage losses and reported short-term medical costs are necessarily taken from crime victim surveys.

Theoretical concerns. Zimring and Hawkins (1995) are highly critical of recent attempts to monetize the cost of crime. They argue that the "state of the art" in economics has not developed to the point where we can adequately characterize the social costs and benefits. Thus, economists have problems both in defining the social cost of crime and in measuring it in any meaningful way.[8] Although there is some validity in both concerns, there is also much confusion about the proper role benefit-cost analysis can play in policy debates.

Zimring and Hawkins note that recent attempts to estimate the monetary costs of crime fail to articulate a coherent theory underlying their cost estimates. Those who attempt to estimate the cost of crime have perpetuated much of the confusion; indeed, my writings in this area are partly to blame by not thoroughly explaining the underlying theory. Part of the problem is a misunderstanding of the difference between social costs and external costs, a subject that was discussed at length above. As an example, Zimring and Hawkins (1995, 141) cite the theft of a $50,000 Mercedes in which the owner failed to take relatively inexpensive antitheft precautions. Noting that this might be a $50,000 personal loss to the owner, they wonder what the social cost is. As discussed earlier, although there might be some disagreement about whether the $50,000 theft is technically a "social cost," there is no doubt that it is an "external cost" that society has an interest in preventing. Because society has laws making it a crime voluntarily to appropriate the property of others, and the harm to the victim is clearly related to the value of the item stolen, $50,000 is a good estimate of the external cost of the crime.

Next, Zimring and Hawkins raise the concern that "any public expenditure to prevent it up to $49,999 would be justified on a cost-benefit basis." On the contrary, I would *not* argue that society should spend up to $49,999 to prevent this theft. Although a simple benefit-cost analysis comparing the theft to a proposal requiring an expenditure of $49,999 to prevent the theft would conclude that benefits exceed costs, if alternative measures could prevent the theft at a lower cost, those alternatives would be preferred and *they* would be economically efficient. To spend $49,999 to prevent a theft that could be prevented for $200 is economically *inefficient*. This example has important policy implications. It is *not* appropriate to examine only one policy option. Instead, policy analysts should examine many alternatives to find the one that has the highest benefit-cost ratio or the most "bang for your buck." Indeed, regulatory agencies are often required by law to consider all technically feasible alternatives to proposed regulations.

The distinction between social and external costs is most apparent for "victimless crimes" such as drug abuse, prostitution, and gambling. Although economists are often chided for their arguments that these crimes impose no social costs and ought to be legalized, that is a simplistic view of the economic arguments. It is true that there is no direct social cost associated with many of these crimes, as they are voluntarily supplied and demanded, and the individuals who consume these illegal products incur both the direct cost and the direct benefit of these products. However, society *has* made them illegal for some reason—often because of the collateral consequences that are socially undesirable, including medical or health concerns, external costs imposed on children or other family members, and so on. To the extent that these *external* costs can be identified and measured, they should be included as the cost of victimless crimes. (Chapters 8 and 9 of Hellman 1980 provide a useful discussion of the economics of victimless crimes.)

Zimring and Hawkins raise another objection to the use of "cost of crime" estimates that include intangible costs such as pain, suffering, and lost quality of life. They note, for example, that the intangible cost of a murder is estimated to be approximately $2 million. If all deaths in the United States were valued at that level, they note, the "cost" of all deaths in the United States would exceed the gross national product! Following their logic, if one uses intangible costs to determine how much society should spend to prevent a social ill such as crime, we should be willing to spend our entire wealth on preventing death and ignore all other aspects of life. The fallacy in this line of thinking, however, is forgetting the fact that, for policy purposes, these estimates are only of value in making marginal decisions. In other words, they can be used to compare the benefits and costs of a particular policy proposal that will have a relatively small impact on crime and does not have a significant "wealth" effect on society. If we were to spend hundreds of billions of dollars fighting crime, the marginal benefit of crime control would decrease dramatically relative to the benefit of placing attention on other social ills. Thus, the real concern raised by the Zimring and Hawkins critique is that, for policy purposes, we must keep in mind that the cost estimates are based on current levels of crime and current levels of health, well-being, and wealth in society.

Public perception versus objective measures of risk. Perhaps one of the most difficult issues that needs to be confronted, as these methods are developed further and implemented in policy analysis, is the fact that the public's perception of the risk of crime may not be the same as the actual risk. Indeed, it has long been noted that, as crime rates have been declining over the past decade, the public's concern about crime only grows. There are many possible explanations for this disparity that are beyond the scope of this chapter (see Warr forthcoming). Furthermore, any method that asks the public for their willingness to pay for reduced crime inherently must confront the fact that the public might be misinformed about the risk and severity of crime. Thus, public expenditures on crime prevention might be too high relative to what the public would demand if they were fully informed. The reverse is also true, of course, so that any "objective" measure of crime severity will ignore public perception and fear.

Methodologies for Measuring the Intangible Costs of Crime

There are many methods for estimating the intangible or nonmonetary costs of crime. Broadly, these methods can be described as either "direct" or "indirect." Direct methods use primary sources such as crime victim surveys. Indirect methods use secondary sources such as property values or jury awards. This section reviews the state-of-the-art techniques for identifying and measuring the intangible costs of crime. Although even tangible costs are often difficult to measure accurately, this chapter focuses on the more controversial intangible costs.

Victims, potential victims, and communities all incur intangible costs of crime. Crime victims incur pain, suffering, and lost quality of life following the physical injury or psychological trauma (or both) associated with victimization. Potential victims might have increased fear, manifested as psychological anxiety or actual averting behavior (e.g., staying home at night, walking longer distances to avoid certain streets). Communities and businesses might suffer from reduced tourism and retail sales as outsiders perceive the community to be a high crime area. High crime rates might also inhibit economic development as employers and potential employees shun certain communities.

Several different approaches have been utilized to estimate the monetary value of these intangible costs. Perhaps the earliest indirect method was to infer property owners' willingness to pay for a safer neighborhood through higher property values. To the extent that risk of victimization is capitalized in housing prices, we expect higher-crime neighborhoods to have lower housing prices controlling for all other factors that affect house prices (Thaler 1978). Testing this requires detailed location-specific housing characteristics (square feet, number of rooms, age, and the like), housing prices, crime rates, and other location-specific amenities (e.g., tax rates, school quality, distance to center city, and so on). Multiple regression analysis isolates the effect of crime on housing prices. The coefficient on the crime variable is then interpreted as the marginal willingness to pay for a reduction in the crime rate. Note that this is a marginal valuation, based on the current crime rate and small changes around that rate.

Property value studies necessarily rely on important assumptions about the competitiveness of the housing market and consumer information about neighborhood crime rates. They also ignore the effect that location-specific amenities—including crime—have on local wage rates. A few researchers have estimated both a housing and a wage equation in order to capture both effects (see, for example, Hoehn, Berger, and Blomquist 1987). Although these models use two equations, they have yet to estimate simultaneous models taking account of the interaction between housing prices and wages. Data limitations have prevented most property value studies from isolating the cost of any individual crime type. Instead, studies generally estimate the cost of an aggregate measure of crime such as the crime index. Bartley (1999) estimated the cost of rape, robbery, assault, burglary, and larceny using the approach developed by Hoehn, Berger, and Blomquist (1987), although he was only moderately successful in disentangling these costs.

One of the positive features of the property value studies of crime is that they rely upon actual market transactions. Although economists tend to favor market-based approaches where actual market transactions (housing prices) are used, any market-based approach necessarily takes into account the wealth and income of the buyer. Thus, the fact that less-wealthy individuals necessarily buy less-expensive homes leads to an estimate of the value of crime that is based on "ability to pay."

The housing market is not the only place affected by crime rates. People buy handguns and security alarms, take cabs instead of walk, and take other precautions to avoid crime. Although all of these expenditures can be considered part of the cost of society's response to crime, they might also be used in estimating the cost of crime itself. For example, a study of the purchase of security alarms might allow us to infer the value that consumers place on a particular reduction in the probability of being victimized.

Another method of estimating the intangible costs of crime is to infer society's willingness to pay for reductions in crime from noncrime studies of society's willingness to pay for safety. Although there are several approaches, this growing literature primarily estimates wage rate differentials for risky jobs (Viscusi 1993). Thus, for example, if there is an additional fifty-dollar wage rate premium for accepting an increased risk of death of 1 in 500,000, that is interpreted to mean that the collective "value of life" is $25 million (fifty dollars x 500,000). There is now an extensive literature on the "value of life," which should *not* be interpreted as the value of any one particular life, but instead is society's value of saving a "statistical" life. Philips and Votey (1981) combined "value of life" estimates and out-of-pocket costs of crime with society's perception of the seriousness of crime to arrive at crime-specific monetary estimates. However, their methodology was unable to account for the risk of injury and death for many crimes.

Cohen (1988a) attempted to overcome these data limitations by combining estimates of the "value of life" with monetary estimates of the pain, suffering, and lost quality of life for nonfatal injuries. The approach used in Cohen (1988a) is a hybrid of direct and indirect cost estimation. Tangible costs are taken primarily from victim surveys and include medical bills and lost wages. Intangible costs include the "value of life" for fatal crimes and pain, suffering, and the lost quality of life for nonfatal injuries. These intangible costs are estimated using indirect techniques. Risk of death is calculated directly from FBI data identifying the underlying crime in homicide cases. Risk-of-death probabilities are multiplied by the "value of life" to arrive at an estimate of the value of the risk of death component of each crime type.

The innovative—and most controversial—methodology introduced by Cohen (1988a) was the use of jury award data to estimate the monetary value of pain, suffering, and lost quality of life for *nonfatal* injuries. At the time, Cohen relied upon jury awards in traditional tort cases and matched the type and severity of injury (e.g., broken bones) with crime victim data in the National Crime Victimization Survey (NCVS). This approach implicitly assumes that identical injuries are valued the same whether caused by an auto accident or an assault. However, crime victims might endure more pain and suffering due to the psychological trauma and fear of repeat victimization. More recently, Miller, Cohen, and Wiersema (1996) obtained data on jury awards to victims of physical and sexual assault and estimated crime costs using these cases.[9] These data were unavailable previously, because civil lawsuits by crime victims are a relatively new phenomenon that has grown to the point where adequate data exist. These lawsuits are seldom against perpetrators who lack resources to pay for the damage they have caused. Instead, they are generally against third parties alleging inadequate security, such as a parking lot owner who did not provide adequate lighting or an apartment owner who did not adequately secure a building.

The reason that the jury award approach is controversial is primarily the popular notion that jury awards in the United States are unpredictable or unreasonably high or both. Theoretically, juries are asked to make the victim "whole," by compensating the victim for all out-of-pocket losses plus pain, suffering, and lost quality of life. Punitive damages are meant to punish the tortfeasor, not to compensate the victim; hence, they are excluded from the pain, suffering, and lost quality of life estimates. Despite popular beliefs to the contrary, considerable evidence exists that jury awards are predictable in a large sample of cases. Popular press articles and calls for tort reform often focus on the outliers and punitive damage awards. The more common cases, however, are quite predictable, and jury awards are used as a measure of pain and suffering in other contexts, including government regulatory agencies (e.g., the Consumer Product Safety Commission). Perhaps the most compelling argument, however, is that our society has placed its tort system in the hands of juries and has decided that these awards are "just compensation."

Despite my defense of the use of jury awards to measure victim compensation for intangible harms, this approach is theoretically *not* the most appropriate one for purposes of estimating willingness-to-pay to reduce the risk of crime. Jury awards are *ex post* compensation designed to make a person whole. For policy purposes, the more relevant question is the "willingness to pay" (WTP) to reduce crime, which is an *ex ante* concept. The property value studies described above are *ex ante* WTP approaches, because they are based on actual market transactions taking into account the prospective risk of criminal victimization. The WTP for reduced crime is likely to be lower than the amount juries would award as compensation for an injury after the fact (see Cohen, Miller, and Rossman 1994, 73–74).

Regardless of the theoretical concerns, Cohen (1990) finds that the jury award method yields estimates of the cost of an index crime that are consistent with the property value studies. Cohen and Miller (1999b) find that jury awards are consistent with the value of a life year implied by the "value of life" studies based on worker wage rate differentials.

An alternative approach to estimating the *ex ante* WTP for reduced crime is to survey the public directly (i.e., potential victims). This approach, often called "contingent valuation," is a methodology developed in the environmental economics literature and has been used extensively to place dollar values on nonmarket goods such as improvements in air quality or saving endangered species. There have been literally hundreds of contingent valuation studies, metanalyses, and textbooks written on the subject (Mitchell and Carson 1989). Although there is some disagreement on the reliability of these surveys, they are continually used in benefit-cost analysis and natural resource–damages litigation, and for other purposes. A distinguished panel of social scientists, chaired by two Nobel laureates in economics (Arrow et al. 1993) were commissioned by the National Oceanic and Atmospheric Administration (NOAA) to assess the contingent valuation methodology. The panel concluded that this is a valid approach and provided a set of guidelines for conducting a reliable contingent valuation survey. Thus, if done properly, contingent valuation surveys can be useful policy tools. Although used in many different policy contexts, contingent valuation is only beginning to be employed in criminal justice research.[10]

Finally, economists often rely upon indirect measurement techniques by appealing to the notions of *opportunity cost* and *revealed preference*. In some instances, this is as straightforward as identifying foregone productive opportunities, such as the time an offender spends in prison or the time a victim spends out of work while dealing with the criminal justice process. In other instances, the costs are subtler. If consumers are rational and maximize utility, we can learn many useful things from their behavior—such as their "revealed preference" for one choice over another. Thus, the fact that individuals choose a leisure activity over working another hour provides us with a lower-bound estimate of the value of that leisure activity—it must be at least as much as the opportunity cost of the time involved. This notion can be used to value the cost of many preventive or avoidance activities that people take to reduce their likelihood of victimization. Examples of these time costs include the time people take to lock and unlock cars and homes and taking a longer route home to avoid a bad neighborhood.

Some crimes with very large intangible costs, such as treason or crimes that betray the public trust, may never be monetized. However, that does not invalidate the theory that would identify the social cost of treason to be the risk of harm to our national security or the social cost of a public betrayal of trust to be a diminution of public trust and moral behavior.

Review of Empirical Estimates of the Cost of Crime

This section reviews the empirical literature estimating the costs of crime. The purpose of this review is to provide the most recent estimates available. However, because some older studies used different methodologies, they are included for comparison purposes. Where *intangible* costs have been estimated, studies that limit themselves to the *tangible* costs of crime are excluded.[11] Most crime cost studies to date have focused on traditional index crimes, with some recent attempts being made to estimate drunk driving and child abuse.

Traditional Index Crimes

Table 1.1 contains the most recent estimates of the cost of crime to victims (Miller, Cohen, and Wiersema 1996), using the approach originally developed by Cohen (1988a)—combining out-of-pocket losses, the risk of death as measured by the "value of life," and jury awards for nonfatal injuries. Table 1.1 provides estimates of the cost per criminal victimization, which ranges from a low of $370 for larceny to $2.9 million for murder (1993 dollars). These figures include attempted crimes that are unsuccessful and are averaged over all crimes—whether or not injury occurs. They include the cost of victim services provided by government and nonprofit agencies and the initial emergency police response (but not follow-up expenses to catch the offender). They exclude the risk of death, because crimes resulting in death are included as a separate crime category.

The estimates of tangible victim costs in Table 1.1 are considerably higher than in comparable government estimates derived from victim surveys. For example, Klaus (1994) estimates that the average cost per rape in the NCVS is $234. Respondents in the NCVS are asked only for short-term costs, and some categories (e.g., mental health) are excluded altogether. Thus, Miller, Cohen, and Wiersema (1996) estimate tangible rape victim costs to be $5,100—including $2,200 in lost productivity and $2,200 in mental health care (Cohen and Miller 1998). Generally, the largest component of crime costs is "quality of life" or "intangible" costs. However, the ratio of intangible to tangible costs varies considerably by crime, with burglary being on the low end (intangibles being about one-third of tangibles) and rape being at the high end (intangibles being fifteen times greater than tangible losses).

Note that Table 1.1 is based on the cost per *victimization*, not the cost per *victim*. Some crimes—particularly physical and sexual assaults—are often repeated against the same victim. Although little research has been conducted on the effect of multiple incidents on victims, Miller, Cohen, and Wiersema (1996) also provide preliminary estimates of the cost per victim.

Table 1.2 aggregates victim crime costs based on the number of victimizations in the United States between 1987 and 1990, resulting in aggregate annual costs of $450 billion in 1993 dollars. This estimate includes only the cost of crime to victims and services provided to victims of crime. It excludes the cost of prevention and the criminal justice system. Of this amount, tangible costs are estimated to be $105 billion, or about 25 percent of the total. The crime-specific estimates in Table 1.2 *exclude* the risk of death, because a category already exists for fatal crimes. To include the risk of death in aggregate crime cost data would be double-counting. Although it would be tempting to update this figure to current dollars, this is not a straightforward exercise. Because crime has been steadily declining in the United States since 1990, updating national crime costs requires recent data on victimization rates. It also requires recent data on the distribution of injuries and severity of injuries in order to

TABLE 1.1 Losses per Criminal Victimization (Including Attempts)

	Productivity	*Medical Care/ Ambulance*	*Mental Health Care*	*Police/ Fire Services*	*Social/ Victim Services*	*Property Loss/ Damage*	*Subtotal: Tangible Losses*	*Quality of Life*	*TOTAL*
Fatal Crime									
Rape, Assault, and so on	$1,000,000	$16,300	$4,800	$1,300	$0	$120	$1,030,000	$1,910,000	$2,940,000
Arson Deaths	724,000	17,600	4,800	1,900	0	21,600	770,000	1,970,000	2,740,000
DWI	1,150,000	18,300	4,800	740	0	9,700	1,180,000	1,995,000	3,180,000
Child Abuse	**2,200**	**430**	**2,500**	**29**	**1,800**	**10**	**7,931**	**52,371**	**60,000**
Sexual Abuse (including rape)	2,100	490	5,800	56	1,100	0	9,500	89,800	99,000
Emotional Abuse	900	0	2,700	20	2,100	0	5,700	21,100	27,000
Rape and Sexual Assault (excluding Child Abuse)	**2,200**	**500**	**2,200**	**37**	**27**	**100**	**5,100**	**81,400**	**87,000**
Other Assault or Attempt	**950**	**425**	**76**	**60**	**16**	**26**	**1,550**	**7,800**	**9,400**
NCVS with Injury	3,100	1,470	97	84	46	39	4,800	19,300	24,000
Age 0-11 with Injury	2,800	1,470	100	84	46	39	4,600	28,100	33,000
Non-NCVS Domestic	760	310	81	0	0	39	1,200	10,000	11,000
No Injury	70	0	65	69	9	15	200	1,700	2,000
Robbery or Attempt	**950**	**370**	**66**	**130**	**25**	**750**	**2,300**	**5,700**	**8,000**
With Injury	2,500	1,000	65	160	44	1,400	5,200	13,800	19,000
No Injury	75	0	66	110	15	400	700	1,300	2,000
Drunk Driving	**2,800**	**1,400**	**82**	**40**	**?**	**1,600**	**6,000**	**11,900**	**18,000**
With Injury	12,100	6,400	82	120	?	3,600	22,300	48,400	71,000
No Injury	170	0	82	17	0	1,000	1,300	1,400	2,700
Arson	**1,750**	**1,100**	**18**	**1,000**	**?**	**15,500**	**19,500**	**18,000**	**37,500**
With Injury	15,400	10,000	24	1,000	?	22,400	49,000	153,000	202,000
No Injury	8	0	18	1,000	0	14,600	16,000	500	16,000
Larceny or Attempt	**8**	**0**	**6**	**80**	**1**	**270**	**370**	**0**	**370**
Burglary or Attempt	**12**	**0**	**5**	**130**	**5**	**970**	**1,100**	**300**	**1,400**
Motor Vehicle Theft or Attempt	**45**	**0**	**5**	**140**	**0**	**3,300**	**3,500**	**300**	**3,700**

SOURCE: Miller, Cohen, and Wiersema (1996, Table 2).

NOTES: All estimates in 1993 dollars. Totals may not add due to rounding. Major categories are in bold, subcategories listed under bold headings. Risk of death is excluded. ?=unknown

TABLE 1.2 Aggregate Annual Costs of Criminal Victimization (Millions of 1993 Dollars)

	Tangible	*Quality of Life*	*TOTAL*
Fatal Crime (1990)	**$33,000**	**$60,000**	**$93,000**
Rape/Robbery/Abuse/Neglect/Assault	25,000	46,000	71,000
Arson Deaths	600	1,700	2,000
Drunk Driving Deaths (DWI)	7,200	12,300	20,000
Child Abuse	**7,300**	**48,000**	**56,000**
Rape	900	8,000	9,000
Sexual Abuse	1,400	12,800	14,000
Physical Abuse	3,200	20,400	24,000
Emotional Abuse	1,900	7,100	9,000
Rape and Sexual Abuse	**7,500**	**119,000**	**127,000**
Other Assault or Attempt	**15,000**	**77,000**	**93,000**
NCVS with Injury	11,000	44,900	56,000
Age 0-11 with Injury	600	3,900	5,000
Non-NCVS Domestic	2,200	19,100	21,000
No Injury	1,300	9,500	11,000
Robbery or Attempt	**3,100**	**8,000**	**11,000**
With Injury	2,500	6,600	9,000
No Injury	600	1,100	2,000
Drunk Driving	**13,400**	**27,000**	**41,000**
With Nonfatal Injury	11,300	24,600	36,000
No Injury	2,400	2,500	5,000
Arson	**2,700**	**2,400**	**5,000**
With Nonfatal Injury	750	2,400	3,000
No Injury	1,900	65	2,000
Larceny or Attempt	**9,000**	**0**	**9,000**
Burglary or Attempt	**7,000**	**1,800**	**9,000**
Motor Vehicle Theft or Attempt	**6,300**	**500**	**7,000**
TOTAL	**$105,000**	**$345,000**	**$450,000**

SOURCE: Miller, Cohen, and Wiersema (1996, Table 4).
NOTES: Totals computed before rounding. "No Injury" cases involve no physical injury, but may involve psychological injury. NCVS fatal crimes = all crime deaths except drunk driving and arson. Personal fraud/attempt is excluded to prevent possible double-counting with larceny.

determine if this has changed significantly since the 1987–90 period in which the Miller, Cohen, and Wiersema (1996) estimates were based.

Drunk driving is a special category of crime that has some unique measurement issues. It is a crime (and a risk to society) every time someone drives drunk. Yet, many drunk driving incidents occur without any collisions, and thus there is no harm to victims. In other crime categories, "attempted" offenses are included as they might involve some property loss, fear, anxiety, and trauma. No comparable data exist on drunk driving incidents that do not result in collisions. In addition, not all collisions where the driver was drunk are "caused" by drunk driving. Some of those accidents might have occurred regardless. Thus, some method of attributing collisions to their "cause" is necessary.

Drug Abuse

A series of reports have been commissioned by U.S. government agencies to determine the economic costs of alcohol and drug abuse in the United States. The 1998 study by Harwood, Fountain, and Livermore estimates the total cost of drug abuse to be $98 billion in 1992. The bulk of these costs ($69 billion) is productivity losses to drug abusers, including premature death, reduced productivity while at work, career criminals who do not enter the legitimate labor market, and crime related costs such as victim losses and time spent by offenders who are incarcerated. About $10 billion is estimated to be spent on drug abuse services and health care for drug related illnesses. The remaining $18 billion is estimated to be the cost of crime committed by drug abusers. Harwood, Fountain, and Livermore (1998) include only tangible costs and ignore intangible costs to victims, families of drug abusers, and so on. Because a significant portion of these costs is associated with victims of crime, there is some overlap between these estimates and those reported in Miller, Cohen, and Wiersema (1996).

The Harwood, Fountain, and Livermore (1998) report illustrates the difficulty of preparing credible estimates of the cost of drug abuse. First, the empirical evidence on the causal connection between drug abuse and crime is limited and largely unresolved (Miczek et al. 1994). Thus, the authors necessarily rely on assumptions that are based on a few limited studies. In addition, they assume that average productivity losses for incarcerated drug offenders are the same as average in the population, about $39,000 per year (see Cohen 1999). Yet, we know that the typical incarcerated offender is not as productive as the average person in the population (Cohen, Miller, and Rossman 1994) and that those engaged in street level drug dealing have been found to have relatively low legitimate wage earning potential (Reuter, MacCoun, and Murphy 1990).

The actual cost of purchasing illegal drugs is not included in the Harwood, Fountain, and Livermore (1998) study. According to a study by Abt Associates (1995), about $53 billion was spent on illegal drugs in 1992.[12] Heavy cocaine users are estimated to spend about $9,000 to $10,000 per year on cocaine, and heroin addicts spend about $17,000 per year on heroin. However, adding these costs would largely result in double-counting. Drug users buying drugs transfer wealth from themselves to the seller, which is a voluntary transaction not resulting in direct external costs. However, the external and social costs do result from the *activities* surrounding the purchase and consumption of drugs (i.e., theft to support a drug habit, medical costs associated with drug induced illness, and the like). Cohen (1998, 19) argues that one could use the cost of drugs as a proxy for the opportunity cost of resources devoted to drug distribution. However, there is a significant risk premium associated with selling drugs, which presumably is reflected in the price of drugs. Because the Reuter, MacCoun, and Murphy (1990) study of street level drug dealers finds legitimate hourly earnings to be about 25 percent of hourly earnings from drug sales, I assumed as a first approximation that only 25 percent of the price of drugs represents a social cost—the lost productivity due to a drug dealer not working in legitimate activities. The remainder represents a risk premium paid to dealers who must face a higher risk of being killed on the job.

Economic Crimes

Although fraud is not generally considered a "street crime" and is not included in the list of index crimes, it appears to be a significant cost to victims. Table 1.3 lists various estimates of the cost of white collar or economic crimes. For example, estimates of employee theft and fraud amount to $435 billion—about equal to the cost of all street crime combined (including intangible costs). Titus, Heinzelmann, and Boyle (1995) conducted a national survey of the U.S. population to identify victims of personal fraud, and estimated the annual tangible costs to be $45 billion. However, some of the fraud definitions include incidents that may not be considered criminal.

Studies to date have assumed that the tangible losses for fraud are limited to the dollar value of the fraud. Anecdotal evidence suggests that losses can be significantly greater in certain cases. For example, some frauds prey on the elderly and uneducated poor. To the extent that these victims lose their home, are unable to afford health care, and so on, the costs may far exceed the dollar value of the fraud. Whether these losses are common or significant in the aggregate is unknown. Moreover, I am unaware of any study that attempts to quantify the intangible costs of fraud.

Concluding Remarks

Benefit-cost analysis and placing dollar values on the intangible costs of crime have arrived in the criminal justice policy arena, and they will not go away. Increased scrutiny of government spending programs, coupled

TABLE 1.3 The Cost of Criminal Fraud

Industry	*Fraud Type*	*Cost ($ billions)*	*Year*	*Source*
All Firms	Employee theft and fraud	$435	1996	(1)
Telecommunications	Theft of services	$3.7–$5.0	1995	(2)
Health care	Overcharge, services not rendered, kickbacks, and so on	$70	1992	(3)
Insurance	False Claims	$120	1995	(4)
Entertainment	Bootlegging	$23	1995	(5)
Telemarketing	Con artists, sweepstakes, phone scams	up to $40	1995	(6)
All consumers	Fraud in general	$45	1991	(7)

SOURCES:

(1) Association of Certified Fraud Examiners. *Report to the Nation on Occupational Fraud and Abuse*, 1995.

(2) Communications Fraud Association. Private communication.

(3) U.S. General Accounting Office. *Health Insurance: Vulnerable Payers Lose Billions to Fraud and Abuse.* May 1992.

(4) Insurance Information Institute. *Insurance Issues Update.* September 1996.

(5) Recording Industry Association of America, as cited in "Music and Performer Groups Act to Curb Piracy." Reuter European Business Report. London, September 26,1996.

(6) Federal Trade Commission. 1995–1996 Report; Staff Summary of Federal Trade Commission Activities Affecting Older Americans, http://www.ftc.gov/os/1998/9803/aging98.rpt.htm.

(7) Titus, Richard M., Fred Heinzelmann, and John M. Boyle. Victimization of Persons by Fraud. *Crime and Delinquency* 41 (1995): 54-72.

with new evidence that certain targeted prevention and rehabilitation programs work, provides the impetus for both new, innovative criminal justice policies and fierce public debate over their merits. This chapter provides a framework for the future analysis of criminal justice policy.

It should become clear from reading this chapter, however, that we are far from the point where benefit-cost methods can be applied to criminal justice programs on a wholesale basis. There is much more work to do on many of the components of estimating the cost of crime. In many cases, these same problems exist in other program areas that value lives and other intangibles. Among the issues that would benefit most from further work are: refinement and agreement on the "statistical value of life," studies that directly elicit the public's WTP for reduced crime (especially for property crimes where intangible losses are difficult to estimate), a better understanding of how to incorporate public perceptions into policy decisions, agreement on the proper discount rate for policy analysis involving long-term benefits, and measures of community well-being that go beyond individual crime victims.

My purpose in writing this chapter was twofold. First, because I am obviously in favor of encouraging the use of empirical tools in analyzing alternative criminal justice or crime prevention policies, I hope this chapter will encourage policy analysts to experiment with these tools and thereby improve their policy decisions. Although the techniques described in this chapter have been used for many years in other areas of public policy, they are just beginning to penetrate the criminal justice policy arena. The technique is not "ideological," but instead can be an important tool in the public policy debate. Both the hard-line view of "three strikes and you're out" and the more compassionate view of focusing on prevention instead of punishment can be subjected to rigorous cost-benefit analyses in addition to political rhetoric.

The second goal, however, is to encourage other researchers to devote serious time and energy to further improving the empirical evidence on the costs of crime and the benefits of crime prevention strategies. The criminal justice literature is far behind other areas of public policy that affect the health and well-being of our society—such as environmental protection and health care. Literally hundreds of studies, peer-reviewed journal articles, conferences, and actual regulatory analyses have been conducted in these areas. It is time for the criminal justice research community to catch up.

Notes

I would like to acknowledge support from the Dean's Fund for Summer Research, Owen Graduate School of Management, Vanderbilt University. This chapter is based partly on Cohen, M. A. (forthcoming). Measuring the costs and benefits of crime and justice. *Measurement and analysis of crime and justice.* Vol. 4 of *Criminal justice 2000*. Washington, D.C.: National Institute of Justice.

1. Gramlich (1981) contains a historical overview of benefit-cost analysis as well as a textbook treatment of the fundamentals of this technique. See also Mishan (1988) for a standard textbook on benefit-cost analysis.

2. President Reagan promulgated the first such requirement in 1981, Executive Order 12291 (46 Federal Register 13193). In 1993, President Clinton issued Executive Order 12866 (58 Federal Register 51735). Although these Executive Orders cannot supersede statutory provisions, they have had a dramatic effect on the manner in which regulatory agencies draft and analyze proposed rules.

3. For example, see Senate Bill 981, 105th Congress (1997), which would require all major rules to be accompanied by a benefit-cost analysis.

4. As discussed later in the chapter, there are methods that can be adopted to deal with the effect of wage inequality in estimating the cost of crime. In short, the analyst might adopt "average" wage rates in the United States in estimating the cost of lost wages. This puts all crime victims on an equal footing—regardless of their wealth.

5. See Sherman et al. (1997) for a comprehensive examination of the effectiveness of alternative programs.

6. French, Rachal, and Hubbard (1991) contain a useful discussion of the distinction among private, social, and external costs and provide a conceptual framework for estimating the costs of drug abuse.

7. See Zerbe and Dively for a detailed discussion of the Kelman article and opposing views in support of the use of benefit-cost analysis (1994, 263–70).

8. This section addresses theoretical concerns with monetizing crime. Section 2, which reviews the methodologies used to estimate crime costs, discusses the main concerns of Zimring and Hawkins—the use of jury awards in monetizing pain and suffering.

9. Details can be found in Cohen and Miller (1999a).

10. The National Institute of Justice recently funded a more comprehensive public survey on attitudes toward sentencing and parole decisions that includes a significant contingent valuation component to it, "Measuring Public Perception of Appropriate Prison Sentences," NIJ #1999-CE-VX–0001. For further details, contact the author, who is project manager. The only study I am aware of that employs a similar technique in the context of violence is Ludwig and Cook (1999), which examines the public's willingness to pay for reduced gun violence.

11. Cohen (forthcoming) contains a more comprehensive discussion of empirical studies (including the costs of white-collar crime and the cost of the criminal justice system).

12. See Caulkins (forthcoming) for a discussion of the difficulty with measuring drug costs.

References

Abt Associates, Inc. 1995. *What America's users spend on illegal drugs, 1988–1993.* Cambridge, Mass.: Abt Associates, Inc.

Anderson, D. A. 1999. The aggregate burden of crime. *Journal of Law and Economics* 42: 611–42.

Arrow, K., R. Solow, P. R. Portney, E. E. Leamer, R. Radner, and H. Schuman. 1993. Report of the NOAA Panel on contingent valuation. *Federal Register* 58: 4601–14.

Austin, J. 1986. Using early release to relieve prison crowding: A dilemma in public policy. *Crime and Delinquency* 32: 404–502.

Bartley, W. A. 1999. A valuation of specific crime rates. Ph.D. diss., Vanderbilt University.

Becker, G. 1968. Crime and punishment: An economic approach. *Journal of Political Economy* 78: 169–217.

Black, D. J. 1998. *The social structure of right and wrong.* San Diego: Academic Press.
Butterfield, F. 1996. Study reveals high cost of crime in U.S. *New York Times* (April 22).
Caulkins, J. P. Forthcoming. Measuring the costs and benefits of crime and justice. *Measurement and analysis of crime and justice.* Vol. 4 of *Criminal justice 2000.* Washington, D.C.: National Institute of Justice.
Cohen, M. A. 1988a. Pain, suffering, and jury awards: A study of the cost of crime to victims. *Law and Society Review* 22: 538–55.
______. 1988b. Some new evidence on the seriousness of crime. *Criminology* 26: 343–53.
______. 1990. A note on the cost of crime to victims. *Urban Studies* 27: 125–32.
______. 1998. The monetary value of saving a high-risk youth. *Journal of Quantitative Criminology* 14: 5–33.
______. 1999. Alcohol, drugs, and crime: Is "crime" really one-third of the problem? *Addiction* 94: 636–39.
______. Forthcoming. Measuring the costs and benefits of crime and justice. *Measurement and analysis of crime and justice.* Vol. 4 of *Criminal justice 2000.* Washington, D.C.: National Institute of Justice.
Cohen, M. A., and Miller, T. R. 1998. The cost of mental health care for victims of crime. *Journal of Interpersonal Violence* 13: 93–100.
______. 1999a. The monetary value of pain and suffering due to criminal victimization: Evidence from jury awards. Working paper (rev.).
______. 1999b. Willingness to award nonmonetary damages and the implied value of life from jury awards. Working paper (rev.).
Cohen, M. A., Miller, T. R., and S. B. Rossman. 1994. The costs and consequences of violent behavior in the United States. In A. J. Reiss Jr. and J. A. Roth, eds., *Understanding and preventing violence.* Vol. 4 of *Consequences and control,* 67–166. Washington, D.C.: National Academy Press.
Cook, P. J. 1983. Costs of crime. In S. H. Kadish, ed., *Encyclopedia of crime and justice,* 373–38. New York: Free Press.
Cullen, F. T., B. G. Link, and C. W. Polanzi. 1982. The seriousness of crime revisited. *Criminology* 20: 83–102.
French, M. T., J. V. Rachal, and R. L. Hubbard. 1991. Conceptual framework for estimating the social cost of drug abuse. *Journal of Health and Social Policy* 2: 1–22.
Gramlich, E. M. 1981. *Benefit-cost analysis of government programs.* Englewood Cliffs, N.J.: Prentice-Hall.
Gray, C. M., ed. 1979. *The costs of crime.* Beverly Hills, Calif.: Sage Publications.
Harwood, H. J., D. Fountain, and G. Livermore. 1998. *The economic costs of alcohol and drug abuse in the United States, 1992.* Washington, D.C.: U.S. Department of Health and Human Services, National Institutes of Health.
Hellman, D. A. 1980. *The economics of crime.* New York: St. Martin's Press.
Hoehn, J. P., M. C. Berger, and G. C. Blomquist. 1987. A hedonic model of interregional wages, rents, and amenity values. *Journal of Regional Science* 27: 605–20.
Irwin, J., and J. Austin. 1994. *It's about time: America's imprisonment binge.* Belmont, Calif.: Wadsworth.

Kelman, S. 1981. Cost-benefit analysis: An ethical critique. *Regulation* (Jan.-Feb.).

Klaus, P. A. 1994. *The cost of crime to victims*. Washington, D.C.: U.S. Department of Justice, Bureau of Justice Statistics.

Ludwig, J., and P. J. Cook. 1999. The benefits of reducing gun violence: Evidence from contingent-valuation survey data. National Bureau of Economic Research Working Paper 7166 (June).

Maltz, M. D. 1975. Measures of effectiveness for crime reduction programs. *Operations Research* 23: 452–74.

Martin, J. P., and J. Bradley. 1964. Design of a study of the cost of crime. *British Journal of Criminology* 4: 591–603.

Miczek, K. A., J. F. DeBold, M. Haney, J. Tidey, J. Vivian, and E. M. Weerts. 1994. Alcohol, drugs of abuse, aggression, and violence. In A. J. Reiss Jr. and J. A. Roth, eds., *Understanding and preventing violence.* Vol. 3 of *Social influences.* Washington, D.C.: National Academy Press.

Miller, T. R., M. A. Cohen, and B. Wiersema. 1996. *Victim costs and consequences: A new look.* Washington, D.C.: U.S. Department of Justice, National Institute of Justice.

Mishan, E. J. 1988. *Cost-benefit analysis: An informal introduction.* 4th ed. London: Unwin Hyman.

Mitchell, R. C., and R. T. Carson. 1989. *Using surveys to value public goods.* Washington, D.C.: Resources for the Future.

Philips, L., and H. L. Votey Jr. 1981. *The economics of crime control.* Beverly Hills, Calif.: Sage Publications.

Prentky, R., and A. W. Burgess. 1990. Rehabilitation of child molesters: A cost-benefit analysis. *American Journal of Orthopsychiatry* 60: 108–17.

Reuter, P., R. MacCoun, and P. Murphy. 1990. *Money from crime: A study of the economics of drug dealing in Washington, D.C.* Santa Monica, Calif.: RAND.

Rossi, P. H., and R. A. Berk. 1997. *Just punishments: Federal guidelines and public views compared.* New York: De Gruyter.

Rossi, P. H., E. Waite, C. E. Boise, and R. A. Berk. 1974. The seriousness of crimes: Normative structure and individual differences. *American Sociological Review* 39: 224–37.

Sherman, L. W., D. C. Gottfredson, D. L. MacKenzie, J. Eck, P. Reuter, and S. D. Bushway. 1997. *Preventing crime: What works, what doesn't, what's promising.* Washington, D.C.: U.S. Department of Justice, National Institute of Justice.

Streff, F. M., L. J. Molnar, M. A. Cohen, T. R. Miller, and S. B. Rossman. 1992. Measuring costs of traffic crashes and crime: Tools for informed decision making. *Journal of Public Health Policy* 13: 451–71.

Thaler, R. 1978. A note on the value of crime control: Evidence from the property market. *Journal of Urban Economics* 5: 137–45.

Titus, R. M., F. Heinzelmann, and J. M. Boyle. 1995. Victimization of persons by fraud. *Crime and Delinquency* 41: 54–72.

Trumbull, W. N. 1990. Who has standing in cost-benefit analysis? *Journal of Policy Analysis and Management* 9: 201–18.

Viscusi, W. K. 1993. The value of risks to life and health. *Journal of Economic Literature* 31: 1912–46.

Warr, M. Forthcoming. Fear of crime in the United States: Avenues for research and policy. *Measurement and analysis of crime and justice.* Vol. 4 of *Criminal justice 2000*. Washington, D.C.: U.S. Department of Justice, National Institute of Justice.

Wolfgang, M. E., R. M. Figlio, P. E. Tracy, and S. I. Singer. 1985. *The national survey of crime severity*. Washington, D.C.: U.S. Department of Justice, Bureau of Justice Statistics.

Zerbe, R. O., Jr., and D. D. Divey. 1994. *Benefit-cost analysis in theory and practice.* New York: HarperCollins.

Zimring, F. E., and G. Hawkins. 1995. *Incapacitation: Penal confinement and the restraint of crime.* New York: Oxford University Press.

2

Quantitative Exploration of the Pandora's Box of Treatment and Supervision

What Goes on Between Costs In and Outcomes Out

FAYE S. TAXMAN
BRIAN T. YATES

Evaluations of drug treatment and criminal justice supervision programs rarely examine what goes on between consumption of the resources by a program and the outcomes produced. Resources ranging from counseling services to facilities, drug testing, medication, and staff/participants' time are invested in treatment and supervision. Positive and permanent changes in the lives of participants are produced by treatment, we hope, along with future reductions in use of health, mental health, and criminal justice services. The same is true with criminal justice supervision—very little is understood about the costs and outcomes generated from the services.

Whereas the procedures of treatment and supervision are often specified, compliance varies widely depending on the individual offender, the nature of the program and services, and the staff. All too often, however, there is no independent assessment of the extent to which treatment and supervision services are actually implemented as planned, and the impact of the variation in the usage of designated services on costs, benefits, and outcomes. Finally, it is unfortunately quite unusual for a program to monitor with any regularity the supposed linkages among the procedures of treatment and supervision and the desired outcomes of treatment and supervision.

The aim of this research on traditional supervision and the coerced treatment model of supervision for substance abusing offenders is to measure, report regularly, and analyze relationships among:

1. *costs* of resources used in treatment and criminal justice supervision,
2. *procedures* implemented in treatment and criminal justice supervision,
3. psychological and related *processes* that are supposed to change within clients as a result of treatment and criminal justice supervision procedure implementation, and
4. *outcomes* targeted by treatment and supervision (including changes in specific effectiveness variables as well as accumulation of specific benefits).

The present study takes advantage of an existing clinical trial examining the effectiveness of different treatment and supervision conditions for drug involved offenders. Using longitudinal interviews, urinalyses, and clinical and criminal justice databases, this study examines the impact of two different approaches to treatment and supervision on internal processes and client outcomes such as drug test positive rates, rearrest rates, and employment rates. This chapter explains the methodology that will be used in the study to estimate costs and benefits as well as to understand variations in individual rates.

Addressing Unanswered Questions

Although many researchers, policymakers, and practitioners continue to affirm the potential effectiveness of drug abuse treatment in reducing recidivism among offenders (Anglin and Hser 1990; Gerstein et al. 1994; Hubbard et al. 1989; Leukefeld and Tims 1988, 1990; Lipton 1995; Petersilia and Turner 1993; Visher 1990), an uneasiness exists about the services available for offenders. Many of the correctional interventions (e.g., boot camps, intensive supervision) that have been considered as "treatment" do not actually provide clinical substance abuse treatment. Petersilia and Turner (1993) note that few intensive supervision offenders receive drug treatment services, although those offenders who do tend to have better outcomes. This study and others highlight the need for understanding the actual context of services to achieve better clinical and crime-reduction outcomes. An emerging comprehensive approach to services for offenders includes (Taxman 1998):

1. *case management* of criminal justice offenders to ensure better treatment and criminal justice outcomes (Pendergast, Anglin, and Wellisch 1994; Scarpitti, Inciardi, and Martin 1994; Siegal and Cole 1993),
2. *continuum of care* with multiple service units instead of episodic treatment experiences (Hubbard et al. 1989; Lipton 1995; Taxman and Spinner 1997; Wexler, Lipton, and Johnson 1988), and
3. *complementary supervision and monitoring services,* including drug testing and sanctions to modulate behavior (Taxman and Lockwood 1996; Belenko, Fagan, and Dumanovsky 1994; Harrell and Cavanaugh 1996).

The scientific base for guiding policy is scanty and characterized by few clinical trials or well-designed studies (Sherman et al. 1997). A review of the literature reveals how the proposed research will address the following gaps in our knowledge base.

Lack of High-Quality Experiments

There is a notable lack of high-quality experiments, especially those using random assignment to conditions and sample sizes sufficient to achieve adequate power to detect differences in program outcomes. Debate over whether correctional treatment for substance abusers "works" (and, if so, which treatment works best) has been fueled by contradictory findings from research on the effectiveness of intensive supervision programs (Byrne 1990; Petersilia and Turner 1993), boot camps (Cowles, Castellano, and Gransky 1995; MacKenzie and Souryal 1994; MacKenzie 1997), jail-based drug treatment (Peters 1993; Peters et al. 1992; Peters and May 1992), and day reporting centers (Parent et al. 1995). Typically, findings range from "nothing works" (Martinson 1974; Whitehead and Lab 1989) to "something works but not very well" and, finally, "the new stuff doesn't work any better than what we were doing before" (Andrews et al. 1990a; Lipsey 1990; Palmer 1992; Sherman et al. 1997; Tonry and Will 1988).

There is a paucity of credible research on the effectiveness of correctional treatment programs (Andrews et al. 1990; Martinson 1974; Sherman et al. 1997; Whitehead and Lab 1989). The evaluations that have been performed frequently lack random assignment to treatment and control groups, and sometimes include no comparison group at all. Also, when drug abusing offenders are assigned to traditional or experimental treatments, the common finding of no significant difference in recidivism or substance use seems to be due to low statistical power, small samples, lack of treatment integrity, poor implementation of treatment procedures, or a combination of these problems. The field needs sound experimental studies with random assignment and sufficiently large sample sizes to determine the maximum effectiveness of possible substance abuse treatment services (Sherman et al. 1997; Weisburd 1993).

Lack of Treatment Integrity

Even if a treatment has high efficacy, its actual effectiveness may be determined largely by the thoroughness of the crucial components of the treatment. Adequate implementation of treatment protocols (treatment *integrity*, sometimes also called *fidelity* of adherence to a program model) is a particular problem in contemporary research and practice. Poor treatment integrity may dilute the potential effectiveness of treatment and other services. Numerous treatment integrity issues cited in the literature generally are attributed to a lack of theory behind the program and insufficient amounts of services, use of inappropriate services (Andrews et al. 1990a), short duration of treatment programs (Pendergast, Anglin, and Wellisch 1994), lack of staffing training (Gustafon 1991), and lack of essential program components (Gendreau 1996). The failure to provide a minimum level of service has left many approaches without an empirical basis for continuation. In fact, it is critical to understand some of the minimum service levels needed to achieve outcomes.

Clarifying the Nature of Treatment and Other Program Procedures

Case management has been promoted as a critical component of any treatment system (Anglin et al. 1999). It involves outreach, assessment, care planning, reassessment, coordination, treatment planning, brokering services, treatment monitoring, discharge planning, advocacy, and sometime actual clinical interventions (Anglin et al. 1996; Martin and Inciardi 1996; Metja et al. 1994a). The actual context and nature of case management practices varies considerably (Anglin et al. 1996) with tremendous uncertainty as to the actual functions performed by case managers (Shwartz et al. 1997). A series of studies on the effectiveness of case management have generated inconclusive and occasionally negative findings (e.g., Anglin et al. 1996; Martin et al. in press), due in part to the large variance in services regarded as part of "case management practices." As it is most often implemented, case management relies on the individual manager to make informed decisions and scramble for the needed resources and services. Unfortunately, the case manager typically is not a power broker, and lacks the authority and resources to handle all pertinent decisions about a client. Understanding the nature of the services provided to the client is critical in trying to estimate the costs and outcomes from supervision and treatment experiences.

Failure to Tailor Treatment Procedures to Client Characteristics

Client characteristics that appear to be crucial to consider when deciding what mixture and sequence of services to administer are *risk* (e.g., probability of reoffending) and *needs* (e.g., psychosocial factors affecting relapse; cf. Andrews and Bonta 1994; Andrews et al. 1990a; McLellan and Alterman 1991). McLellan et al. (1983) found that matching clients to services according to empirically determined rules may save more than $53 per day per patient or approximately $3,700 per patient. Yet, in practice the tendency is to place the client in the first available treatment slot (Duffee and Carlson 1996). Research has not fully validated the variables that are important in tailoring treatment procedures to client characteristics or the expected results.

Failure to Use Leverage to Achieve Treatment Goals

Nearly half of all offenders drop out of treatment (Simpson, Joe, and Brown 1997). The leverage of the criminal justice system can be an important means of reducing dropouts by establishing credible punitive contingencies. Supervision and monitoring can augment the treatment to enhance treatment goals and pursue long-term outcomes. The use of criminal justice sanctions for offenders has been discussed, and recent results from a drug court evaluation demonstrate that offenders who receive sanctions are four times less likely to continue drug use than those who receive typical supervision (Harrell and Cavanaugh 1996). The question that remains is how to bring the contingencies possible via the criminal justice system to bear in a manner that facilitates achievement of treatment goals.

Failure to Measure Costs, Cost-Effectiveness, and Cost-Benefit

A dramatically increased interest in research on the cost as well as the effectiveness of substance abuse treatment procedures was spurred by the 1991 publication of a National Institute on Drug Abuse (NIDA) monograph, "Economic costs, cost-effectiveness, financing, and community-based drug treatment" (Cartwright and Kaple 1991). The entire monograph was devoted to educating substance abuse researchers and policymakers about basic issues in cost-effectiveness analysis and cost-benefit analysis (see also Alfano, Thurstin, and Nerviano 1987; Apsler and Harding 1991; Hubbard and French 1991). More recently, standards for assessing the cost, effectiveness, and the cost-effectiveness of treatment procedures for medical problems have been set by a committee of health economists (Gold et al. 1996). These standards are potentially applicable to assessments of the cost, cost-effectiveness, and cost-benefit of substance abuse treatment procedures as well as criminal justice procedures. Two instruments for estimating costs of substance abuse treatment have been developed and applied in several case studies by French et al. (1997).

Isolation of Costs of Specific Treatment Procedures

A recent, promising trend in the substance abuse field is isolation of the costs of adding specific components to a substance abuse treatment program. For example, French et al. (1994) developed a detailed financing flowchart and cost analysis framework to measure the marginal cost of adding training and employment services to methadone maintenance (see also Bradley, French, and Rachal 1994). The cost of specific procedures that compose different forms of substance abuse treatment have also been assessed and contrasted statistically by Anderson et al. (in press). Relatively few studies have analyzed the relationship between treatment costs and treatment outcomes, however—whether those outcomes are measured in the usual units (e.g., drug free days, criminal behavior) or in monetary units (e.g., cost of services not expended per drug-free day, costs borne by victims and society as a result of criminal behavior; cf. Cohen 1998; Cohen and Miller 1998). Only a few substance abuse researchers have pursued the intertwined issues of cost and outcomes for a significant period (cf. Harwood et al. 1988; Hayashida et al. 1989; Rufener, Rachal, and Cruze 1977). This approach has only just begun to be applied, and it does not encompass the costs from services that the treatment program of interest causes to be used, such as through referrals. In an integrated service delivery system, it is critical to measure the costs of all services whether they are primary or secondary.

Aggregate, not Individual-Level, Analyses of Costs and Outcomes

In the seminal work on criminal justice costs, Cohen (1998) uses aggregate data to estimate the cost of saving a high-risk youth. The process of using aggregate information from national surveys and cross-sectional studies, however, results in estimates that do not consider the full range of costs that may occur from varying levels of individual experience, and the impact of these costs on benefits and outcomes. Furthermore, the costs do not reflect the actual conditions under which the person may be treated but reflect simulations of various treatment combinations and estimates of their total costs. In addition, the model does not lend itself to examining the impact of various individual experiences on the ability of the client when interactions occur among program procedures, client characteristics, and service availability.

Calls are mounting for comprehensive research that examines how the resources consumed in treatment and supervision can be related in a meaningful fashion to maximize outcomes and affect the resulting processes occurring largely inside clients (Donovan 1990; Schuster 1991). Because many of the treatment services also include job training, drug testing, supervision, and other related services, a complete assessment of treatment costs must include the costs of these services. Little research has examined the possibility that sufficiently detailed data on costs, procedures, processes, and outcomes could be analyzed to decide how best to apply current treatment and criminal justice procedures to maximize effectiveness for individual clients, overall effectiveness of entire programs, and monetary benefits for clients and programs within budget constraints (Yates 1994).

The Cost → Procedure → Process → Outcome Analysis (CPPOA) Model

Whereas cost-effectiveness analysis (CEA) and cost-benefit analysis (CBA) have traditionally provided summative evaluations designed to support policy and funding decisions (Gerstein et al. 1994), *formative* CEA and CBA can incorporate research findings to understand better how treatment resources are allocated to match treatment needs and achieve desired outcomes (Yates 1980, 1985, 1996, 1997a). One approach to assessing cost-effectiveness and cost-benefit has been to adopt a scientist-manager-practitioner role (DeMuth, Yates, and Coates 1984) and collect data in preparation for conducting operations research to optimize cost-effectiveness and cost-benefit for the program. This approach is termed Cost → Procedure → Process → Outcome Analysis or CPPOA (Yates 1995). The CPPOA model incorporates traditional health economics but extends them to also include analyses of how the specific amounts of different resources make possible different treatment procedures that in turn foster changes in the psychosocial processes that determine the outcomes of substance abuse treatment for criminal offenders.

CPPOA collects information on and analyzes relationships among four major classes of variables and examines how a fifth—client characteristics—may moderate these relationships. The first class of variables is *resources* used in the services; in our research these resources are those that are used to implement two different types of service delivery models—the seamless system and traditional criminal justice processes. Resources include staff time (both treatment and criminal justice), client time, space, equipment, supplies, services, drug testing, laboratory technicians, and court proceedings. The second category is *procedures* performed as part of the protocol. For the treatment group, this will include therapy groups (both individual and group), aftercare, medication, education, supervision services (e.g., face-to-face services, collateral contacts, and so on), drug testing, and graduated sanctions. For the control group, the services will include face-to-face and collateral contacts, drug testing, and graduated sanctions. The third category of CPPOA refers to internal *processes* (e.g., anxiety, depression, physiological addiction, psychological urges to use a drug, expectancies that sanctioning contingencies will be implemented by treatment and criminal justice personnel, relapse prevention skills, criminal proclivities, etc.) affected by the protocols. Finally, the model includes the *outcomes* resulting from the interventions. In this case, the outcome variables include criminal activity, employment, and substance abuse including opiate, cocaine, and crack use; alcohol abuse; and (as hypothesized, reduced) use of health care, social services, and future criminal justice services.

Cost and outcome data collected as part of CPPOA also allow traditional cost-effectiveness and cost-benefit analyses to be conducted to describe program performance. We will use data collected for CPPOA to compare the seamless and traditional delivery systems for substance abuse treatment in terms of cost, effectiveness, monetary benefits, cost-effectiveness, and cost-benefit analysis. Additional data collected in CPPOA should allow us to isolate the program procedures and psychosocial processes responsible for the differences we find among delivery systems in cost, effectiveness, benefits, cost-effectiveness, and cost-benefit analysis. We then will be able to recommend how to streamline the seamless delivery system so that effectiveness and benefits are the maximum possible within cost constraints.

To accomplish these goals, reliable and valid data are collected on all substantial costs, procedures, processes (including demographics), and outcomes for each client in both experimental goals. Figure 2.1 lists the variables and the source of the information for the clinical trial. Criminal justice data collection sources and instruments will be used to gather data on the needed variables to determine service unit costs in both the seamless system and traditional services (control group) as well as the different interim and long-term outcomes.

FIGURE 2.1 Cost → Procedure → Process → Outcome Analysis Matrix for HIDTA Experiment

Costs (Values of Resources Used)	→	Program Procedures	→	Psychosocial Processes	→	Interim Outcomes (during treatment)	→	Long-Term Outcomes • Immediate Post • 1-Year Post • 2-Year Post
Temporal • Direct service *Paid* *Volunteer* • Administrative • Other indirect • MIS Material • Equipment *Direct service* *Administrative* • Supplies *Psychometrics* *Office supplies* Spatial • Direct service • Administrative • Other indirect Transportation Communications Financing		Seamless Psychosocial Treatment System • Assessment • Continuum of care • Supervision • Compliance measures and graduated sanctions • Self-help groups Traditional Criminal Justice System • Regular urinalysis • Probation • Self-help groups		Reduced Mental Disturbance • Somatization • Obsessive-compulsive • Interpersonal sensitivity • Depression • Anxiety • Hostility • Phobic anxiety • Paranoid ideation • Psychoticism • General severity Improved Relationships with Family Readiness to Change Self-Efficacy Expectancy for Relapse Prevention		Reduced HIV Transmission Behaviors Increased appropriate use of: • Social services • Public health services • Employment and vocational training services Improved Family Living Situation Reduced Substance Abuse		Continuation of Interim Outcomes Reduced Criminal Activity Reduced Substance Abuse Employment (licit) Cost savings in: • Private, public health services • Mental health services • Welfare • Employee assistance • Program use • Training of new employees • Incarceration (jail/prison) • Probation/parole services • Drug treatment services

Randomized Experiment of Two Metaprocedures

Our research examines the impact of two *metaprocedures*—traditional and seamless systems—on the effectiveness and costs of substance abuse treatment to criminal offenders. In a *traditional* criminal justice system, offenders receive only supervision services, that is, face-to-face contact, drug testing, and collateral contacts. The *seamless* system of care uses systemic case management to organize and integrate treatment and criminal justice procedures for maximum impact on effectiveness (Taxman 1998; Taxman, Kubu, and DeFastno 1999). It is built on principles of boundary spanning across the criminal justice and treatment agencies where the systems of care are predefined (Moore 1992; Taxman and Lockwood 1996). The seamless system protocol defines the exact units of care that the client will receive, removing the often arbitrary discretion of any individual treatment staff, case manager, or supervision agent to determine the components of a treatment plan. Instead, the seamless system ensures that the offender receives coordinated services including:

1. a minimum of nine months of treatment in two different levels of care (i.e., *continuum of care*),
2. *drug testing* during the period of supervision,
3. *specialized supervision* by agents trained in treatment issues, and
4. *graduated sanctions* (accountability measures) to ensure compliance with treatment and supervision conditions.

Our study is the first empirical study of the effectiveness, and cost, of the seamless system approach or, more specifically, a coerced treatment model for offenders compared to traditional supervision services. The seamless system approach provides an organization and management to the delivery of treatment and complementary supervision services across two major systems—treatment and criminal justice. It removes the barriers of coordination by providing the necessary policy guidance and resources to allow probation and treatment staff to deliver treatment, supervision, and drug testing services. Through graduated sanctions, agencies have predefined similar goals of crime reduction. If effective, the approach offers a refreshing protocol for providing treatment services to offenders in an environment where treatment is often considered a secondary goal to punishment (Petersilia 1999; Zimring and Hawkins 1995). The existing models of coordinating services tend to occur at the client level (brokerage) model. Findings from this evaluation will be critical in defining new organizational structures to deliver treatment services to an offender population.

Setting

The seamless service system involved in this CPPOA is a project funded by the Office of National Drug Control Policy (ONDCP) as part of that group's High Intensity Drug Trafficking Areas (HIDTA) program in the Washington, D.C.–Baltimore corridor. The National Institute of Justice (NIJ) funds a one-year evaluation of the program focused on outcomes (e.g., criminal activity and substance abuse outcomes). Two jurisdictions have been selected to conduct the longitudinal study based on the strong integrity of the implementation of the seamless system. Our research, funded by a NIDA grant, augments the existing evaluation research with posttreatment follow-ups to examine the impacts on recidivism, substance abuse, and social adjustment. The NIDA grant includes funds for assessing the costs of service delivery systems and for using CPPOA to measure and pinpoint methods of optimizing the empirical observed relationships among costs and outcomes in the seamless and traditional service systems.

In the present study, the randomized block experimental design will occur in two jurisdictions (Alexandria City, Virginia, and Montgomery County, Maryland). The two sites were selected not only because they have seamless and traditional systems in place, but also because they provide different organizational and structural contexts that may moderate differences found in costs, procedures, processes, and outcomes for traditional and seamless programs. Alexandria City is relatively small in both population (about 100,000) and area, and has one probation office and one treatment site. The treatment services are offered at the criminal justice agency, and aftercare services are offered at the treatment center that is less than three miles away. In contrast, Montgomery County is a considerably larger jurisdiction in a different state, with more than 757,000 residents, three probation offices, and more than ten contractual treatment programs and one centralized county program. Montgomery County also has a central intake unit that all treatment clients must use before entering the treatment system. These differences will allow our research to examine the impact of system features on the implementation of the seamless system and system reform components in diverse settings.

Recruitment of Individual Participants and Assignment to Conditions

As summarized in Figure 2.2, a random assignment protocol is employed in each site at the point the criminal justice system refers clients for treatment. For the sites included in the proposed study, probation is the inter-

FIGURE 2.2 Randomized Assignment Process

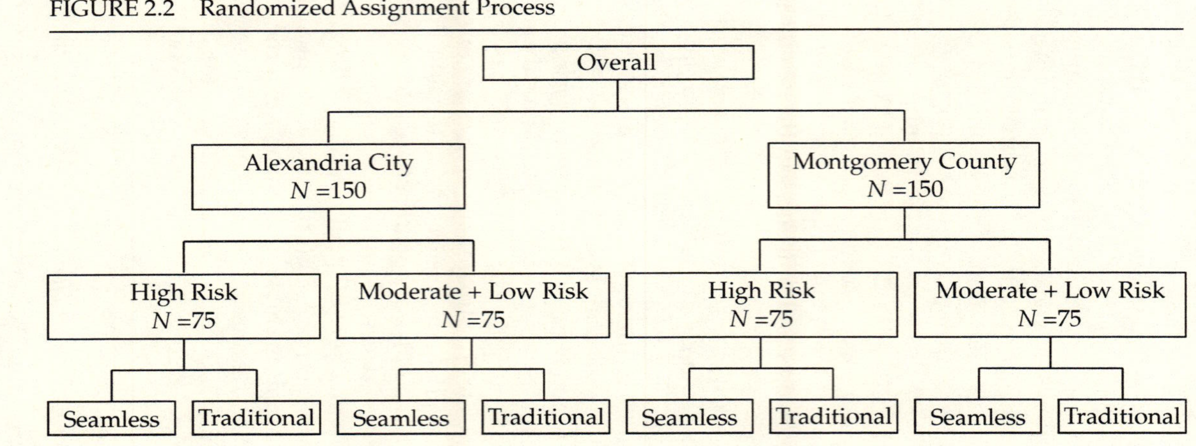

face between criminal justice and treatment. Probation staff conduct preliminary assessments of all offenders to include the traditional probation risk and needs screening that categorize offenders into different levels of risk or potential harm to the community. The traditional assessment also indicates whether the offender has a serious conviction and exhibits behavior driven by substance abuse (the eligibility criteria for HIDTA treatment services). In each site, sex offenders and offenders with violent histories are excluded from the eligible population. The pool for random assignment consists of offenders that are typical drug abusers who are involved in property and drug crimes as a means of funding their substance abuse habits.

Mechanics of Randomization

The existing eligibility and screening process will be used to assign offenders to the seamless system and traditional criminal justice processing (surveillance model). This assignment process relies on the existing resource utilization model employed in the study sites, which means that random assignment will be based on the number of available treatment slots. This process ensures that the randomization does not provide unfair access to treatment services or leave unfilled treatment slots. Randomization will not impact the screening or assessment of eligible offenders but will provide for a fair, systematic process of assignment to treatment. The randomization process will depend on the number of treatment slots available on a first-come, first-served basis. For example, in any given week the treatment system will alert the researchers to the number of slots available for treatment. Randomization will occur by risk category based on the number of interviews and the number of available slots. Separate random tables are for high- and moderate-risk clients.

Participation in the proposed research study must, of course, have the voluntary and informed consent of subjects. Eligible offenders will be contacted by research staff before assignment to seamless or traditional conditions. Offenders will be asked to participate in a study during the time they are under supervision of the criminal justice agency. These recruitment procedures will be implemented until 150 research respondents (75 for seamless system, 75 in control group) in each site agree to participate in the research study. The recruitment period will be up to two years per site. All eligible offenders entering the intensive probation unit during the recruitment period will be recruited for the study and randomly assigned to an intervention by the research team.

Stratification of Subjects

Offender risk level is a major concern for criminal justice programs. Some researchers and criminal justice policymakers posit that the apparent effectiveness of treatment programs for offenders is due to assignment of lower-risk offenders (i.e., first offenders or those with lower probability of recidivating) to available treatment slots (Andrews et al. 1990a; Andrews and Bonta 1994). Certainly the risk level of the offender is important to examine because it allows us to investigate the potential moderating effects of offender history and other client characteristics on the effectiveness and benefits of the seamless versus traditional systems. From a policy perspective, it also provides the opportunity to determine how different types of offenders perform in different interventions. For example, if we find that high-risk offenders do the same or better than moderate-risk offenders, this provides policymakers and practitioners with important information about the effectiveness of treatment interventions as compared to incarceration-based interventions for "hardcore" offenders.

To allow experimental examination of the impact of risk level on the success of the seamless system, our experiment will block subjects into two risk categories before assignment: high and moderate risk. This process, defined by experimental statisticians as *stratification* or *blocking*, is commonly used in experimental studies in medicine and psychology (Fleiss 1986; Lipsey 1990; Pocock and Lagakos 1982). In block randomized experiments, subjects are first placed into stratified groups and then randomly assigned into treatment and control conditions (Sherman and Weisburd 1995; Weisburd 1993; Weisburd and Green 1995). This provides a more precise comparison among the treatment and control conditions (Brown 1980; Zelen 1975). Also, blocking allows us to examine, within our experimental design, the interaction between risk level and treatment.

Cost, Procedure, Process, and Outcome Variables Selected

This section explains why we selected particular cost, procedure, process, and outcome variables for the CPPOA model contrasting traditional and seamless programs, and describes the nature of these variables and, briefly, how we will collect data on their values for offenders in our study.

Cost (Resource Utilization) Variables

Data being collected on per-person costs include the amounts, types, and values of resources used to implement the seamless system for both criminal justice supervision and substance abuse treatment services. Costs will be assessed from both programmatic and societal (comprehensive) perspectives (e.g., Siegert and Yates 1980; Yates, Haven, and Thoresen 1979; cf. Yates 1980), and in three basic steps:

1. *resource utilization assessment* for each direct service procedure for each client,
2. *monetization* of resources used in direct services, and
3. *distribution* of overhead personnel and other program resources over clients.

Cost assessment will begin by constructing a *cost → procedure* matrix listing in columns all treatment services (procedures) provided and in rows all resources (costs) used directly by one or more treatment procedures (see Table 2.1). As part of the process of determining costs, it will be necessary to observe randomly selected treatment and control interventions to get estimates of time spent on certain activities. At both sites, research assistants will collect data on frequencies and durations of treatment groups, supervision contacts, drug testing, conferences with treatment and supervision staff, and all other key program procedures. The assistants will also collect data on characteristics of nonpersonnel resources, including the size of the office used in sessions, time spent by the offender in transit to and from the session, and the cost of that transportation. Data on service procedures then will be validated against corresponding information available in the Alexandria City and Montgomery County databases, and from the reimbursement system used by the treatment providers.

If data produced by researcher observations approximate closely the service cost information available from program databases, those databases will be used for cost data collection. If not, the observational methods will be improved to capture occurrence of service delivery with greater accuracy. We will determine how variable the expenditure of resources is for different episodes of delivering the same procedure to the same client, and to different clients. If justified, a modal duration will be found for individual service procedures, and that will be multiplied by frequency of delivery of the service to each client to calculate the costs of each service procedure each month at the client level (cf. Yates 1996; see also French et al. 1997).

Procedure Variables: What Is "Seamless" and Why Treatment?

Based on research on the treatment and supervision field, the components of the seamless system have been identified as affecting everyday

TABLE 2.1 Cost Procedure Table

	Procedures			
	Seamless Service Integration			*Traditional Service Administration*
		Psychological Treatment		*Criminal Justice*
	• *Assessment* • *Continuum of Care* • *Supervision*	• *Urinalysis* • *Compliance Measures and Graduated Sanctions* • *Self-Help Groups*		• *Regular Urinalysis* • *Supervision*
Costs (Resources Used)	*Continuum of Care, Level I* *Restricted Facility* *Cognitive Behavior Therapy (20–30 hours/week)*	*Continuum of Care, Level II* *Intensive Outpatient Treatment* *Cognitive Behavior Therapy (20–30 hours/week)* *Self-Help Groups*	*Continuum of Care, Level III* *Outpatient Treatment* *Weekly Support Group and Outpatient Treatment* *Self-Help Groups*	
Personnel				
Therapists				
Administrtors				
Clerical staff				
Medical (nurses, physicians)				
Criminal justice supervision				
Criminal justice (police, prosecutors, judges, sheriff)				
Other				

Facilities	
Residential	
Outpatient	
Incarceration	
Other	
Equipment	
Restriction equipment	
Supplies	
Urinalysis	
Other	

decisions in the management of any client in referral, in placement, in transition, and in discharge. The seamless components provide a structured manner of delivering services based on systemic processes, whereas the traditional (control group) relies on more fragmented approaches. The components, which will be used in the CPPOA model, are:

Assessment. Treatment placement requires the consideration of the needs of the client. For the criminal justice client, risk or propensity to commit crimes is also variable in determining the appropriate treatment and supervision placement. The literature describes how a needs/risk classification can be used to choose the appropriate mix of service for the offender population to achieve better outcomes (Andrews and Bonta 1994; Andrews et al. 1990), but research in this area is minimal (Palmer 1992). Furthermore, researchers have recently posited that most treatment resources are expended on clients who will not benefit from those services as much as others, particularly higher-risk offenders (Andrews et al. 1990a; Gendreau 1996; Palmer 1995). Assessments, using the Addiction Severity Index, will be used to ascertain the severity of substance abuse and the public safety risk that the client presents.

Continuum of care. The *continuum of care* moves the client through the treatment delivery system consistent with their progress in changing their behavior, and offers services to different clients that match their needs. Responding to pressures to shorten time spent in programs (Etheridge et al. 1997), despite demonstrations that length of time in treatment is a factor in the positive outcomes (Condelli and Hubbard 1994; Hubbard et al. 1989; Simpson, Joe, and Brown 1997), programs offering a continuum of care now typically require the offender to participate in a more intense service, followed by less intensive aftercare or counseling. The continuum of care concept also uses assessments of the offender's risk level to guide treatment placement decisions regarding the amount of control and structure needed to achieve treatment and criminal justice goals (Andrews et al. 1990a, 1990b). For example, higher-risk offenders may need a residential setting or day or evening programs for a year because of their propensity to engage in criminal activity. The residential or day or evening setting provides external controls on the offenders' behavior by limiting the amount of unsupervised time. As the offender demonstrates progress and personal development—for example, by cooperating fully with treatment procedures and contributing to the residential community or intermediate care setting—he or she is moved gradually to less restrictive and more therapeutic services.

Supervision. Monitoring and oversight can facilitate the treatment process by enforcing treatment conditions, and verifying and validating the progress of the client. Essentially, this supervision consists of *case management* (Moore 1990, 1992), including collateral contacts (to identify potential problems in the community); *face-to-face contacts* (to observe and discuss treatment progress and compliance with general court conditions); and *changes in services based on progress*. Although these restrictions on freedoms are punitive, they also serve therapeutic functions by supporting the development of responsibility and structure in the offender.

Urinalysis. Urinalysis serves both therapeutic and monitoring functions. The technology allows for immediate determination of the offender's continued abstinence from substance use. Frequency of drug testing can be varied depending on the behavior of the offender. Thus, it is a popular treatment and supervision tool to monitor offender compliance (Visher 1990; Wish and Gropper 1990). Since drug testing is used by both systems, it is important that the drug testing information be shared and used to support mutual treatment and public safety goals.

Compliance assessment and graduated sanctions. Both treatment and supervision agencies have a common problem of compliance with program requirements. Dropout rates are high in most public health treatment programs. In the recent Drug Abuse Treatment Outcome Study (DATOS) data, Simpson, Joe, and Brown (1997) report that more than half of the clients do not complete drug treatment programs. Taxman and Byrne (1994) estimate that at least half of the offenders do not comply with basic supervision requirements: One or more technical violations were found for 30 to 80 percent of offenders. Noncompliance with probation requirements constitutes the largest growth of prison admissions. The use and application of sanctioning or the leverage of the criminal justice system tend to vary considerably in practice, in both the treatment and the criminal justice arenas.

Recent advancements in the field have promoted the use of behavior modification approaches, referred to as *graduated sanctions* in the criminal justice literature, to provide swift, certain, and appropriate responses to compliance problems (Taxman, Soule, and Gelb 1999; Harrell and Cavanaugh 1996; Kleiman 1997). Similar to contingency management, graduated sanctions hold clients accountable for their behavior through a series of known consequences to common noncompliant behavior. The responses are set at gradations where more punitive and stringent sanctions are imposed with increased and continued noncompliance. In a recent evaluation of the Washington, D.C., Superior Drug Court, which used graduated sanctions for positive urinalysis results, clients were four times *less* likely to test positive for drugs than when no sanctions were employed (Harrell and Cavanaugh 1996). These findings provide theoretical support for the use of accountability measures to affect client behavior change.

Program completion. Program completion will refer to successfully completing the treatment program or supervision or both. For clients assigned to the seamless treatment condition, completion of the treatment continuum of care (the stated treatment plan for the offender) will be determined by whether the offender completed the agreed-upon plan or modifications of the plan. For clients assigned to traditional processing, completion of probation will be determined by whether the offender completed the conditions of probation or modifications of this plan within the study period. Program completion will then be used to measure retention in the treatment or probation system of care. From the research perspective, a *success* will be defined as an individual who completed the treatment and supervision regime with no more than three graduated sanctions during the supervision period. The programs have agreed that offenders in either the seamless or the traditional systems will have *technically violated* their program if they have more than three noncompliant incidents where graduated sanctions were used but no change in behavior was evidenced.

Outcome Variables

Drug use. Drug use will be measured by urinalyses as well as self-report during interviews that precede the urinalyses. Within each site, both the treatment and the control groups will be tested at the same rate—for Montgomery County, testing will be twice a week, and for Alexandria City, three times a month. Different frequencies of drug testing in Alexandria City and Montgomery County reflect the different sociopolitical environments delivering services and the capacity of the existing system to enhance monitoring through drug testing. Drug test results will be available for the months the offender is under supervision; offenders will be asked to give a urine sample during each follow-up interview as well. Relapse will be measured as the proportion of positive urinalysis results. We will also examine the types of drugs tested positive and the patterns of testing positive. Self-report data will also be used during the follow-up period to determine use of drugs while the offender is being tested and after testing ceases.

Social adjustment. Social adjustment refers to changes in the offender's lifestyle during the follow-up period. The changes will be examined in the following areas: employment, living situation, risk behaviors, HIV/AIDS status, mental health status, and general physical health. The Life Events Survey (e.g., criminal and life functioning calendars) and HIV/AIDS instrument will be used to obtain consistent information on the offender's social adjustment during the follow-up period.[1] Measures will be constructed to determine prosocial changes. For example, if the offender was unemployed at baseline but employed at follow-up, an employment measure will be constructed from existing items in the Life Events Survey. The survey also has sufficient items to allow construction of measures on stable living arrangement (e.g., maintained a residence) and stable family situation (e.g., maintained consistency). Researchers will use this information to determine changes in behavior during this period using analyses of variance repeated measures.

Benefit assessment. In addition to the usual outcome variables of drug abuse, criminal behavior, and mental and physical health status, we will collect data on potential monetary *benefits* of traditional and seamless treatment. Cost-savings benefits include (hoped-for) reductions in hospitalization, emergency room visits, and outpatient medical services, as well as in social services such as housing and income support. Direct benefits include income generated by employment and volunteering to serve in community and other public efforts. In addition to real income generated by clients in the two conditions, reported on the Life Events Survey, the monetary value of changes (reductions, we hope) in criminal behaviors and of changes (again, it is hoped, reductions) in use of a variety of social services can be estimated and summed to arrive at the monetary benefit of treatment for each client. We will examine estimates developed by researchers such as Ball and Ross (1991), Gerstein et al. (1994), and Langenbucher et al. (1993), as well as costs attributed by local criminal justice and social service officials to changes in specific behaviors. Sensitivity analysis will be used to examine the effects of low, medium, and high assumptions about the monetary value of reduction in different behaviors and in utilization of different services. These benefits will be examined in statistical analysis in the same manner as other outcome measures.

Data Sources and Collection Schedule

Data will be obtained from two types of data sources: official records and interview surveys. Official records include criminal justice records, treatment program records, and police records. All respondents, regardless of research group assignment, are expected to be under probation supervision for at least two years. As part of this project, the sites have started using an automated tracking system called HIDTA Automated Treatment Tracking System (HATTS) supplemented by manual case files. HATTS contains information on treatment services, criminal justice services, drug testing, graduated sanctions, and discharge from treatment (Taxman and Sherman 1998). Montgomery County is currently using the system; Alexandria City is currently using the drug testing component of the system. HATTS is the major source of information about services received supplemented by case files.

At each of the follow-up interviews, respondents will provide information for the period since the last interview. We will compensate interviewees twenty-five dollars at the follow-up since the interviews are likely to be three to four hours in duration.

Planned Analyses: Exploring Pandora's Box

CPPOA

The CPPOA model will be used in conjunction with state-of-the-art cost assessment procedures (French et al. 1997; cf. Gold et al. 1996) to measure cost-effectiveness and cost-benefit relationships for each major component of the seamless and traditional programs, as well as for each program overall. The CPPOA model conceptualizes human services as systems that consume a variety of measurable resources to implement specific treatment procedures. These procedures are selected by service providers to operate on preexisting psychosocial processes in clients and environments to produce specific outcomes, such as cessation of illicit drug use and criminal behavior. The CPPOA model provides the methodology to understand more comprehensively the types and amounts of resources utilized in providing treatment and supervision services. Essentially, CPPOA

1. measures the *cost* of each HIDTA service *procedure* (e.g., seamless system, supervision services, drug testing, sanctioning, and the like) that was received by each offender in the two experimental conditions (*cost → procedure analysis*),
2. examines how the presence, absence, and amount of different services received is associated with *client characteristics* such as high versus moderate risk, prior criminal history, and prior treatment history,
3. evaluates how service procedures affect *outcomes* such as reductions in criminal arrests and drug use and contribution to society

through employment (*procedure → outcome analysis* and *process → outcome analysis*),

4. discovers how much the relationships among service procedures and outcomes may be moderated (facilitated or inhibited) by *processes* such as changes in mental health, changes in physical health, and psychosocial phenomena related to risk level, ethnicity, gender, age, and presence or absence of significant prior criminal activity, and
5. describes the relationships found among costs and outcomes for different procedures via path analysis (*cost → outcome analysis*), measuring outcomes both as effectiveness (i.e., in their given units, e.g., days drug-free, reduction in number of arrests, reduction in the use of social and health care services) and as benefits (i.e., effectiveness transformed in monetary units, such as dollars saved due to reduced drug use, reduced use of social and health care services, and reduced criminal involvement; cf. Yates 1995, 1996).

A major advance in the criminal justice field will be the development of per-person cost measures that include the array of supervision related services including supervision, drug testing, collateral contacts, and so on. Thus far, very little is available on supervision costs.

The CPPOA model allows us to identify treatment and criminal justice services that produce maximum outcomes for a given cost budget. Linear programming and other operations research analyses will be used to identify optimal service levels that produce outputs (cf. Yates 1980, 1997b). Results from the experimental design will be particularly useful in determining the maximum outcomes for a given cost with a model that includes different treatment services, different criminal justice services, drug testing, graduated sanctions, risk level of the offender, and demographic characteristics (e.g., age, prior criminal history, and so forth). By using similar analyses, the minimum cost of achieving set levels of outcomes will be obtained (cf. Yates 1980).

Procedure → Outcome Analyses

We anticipate that, compared to traditional supervision, the seamless system will reduce recidivism and substance abuse among offenders and improve social adjustment. Offenders participating in the seamless system should have improved psychological functioning, take longer to recidivate, consume fewer drugs, and have better employment than offenders participating in traditional supervision.

Since we are using an experimental research design, we do not need to control for covariates in our analyses of study outcomes. Factors beside treatment are assumed to be equivalent in both the experimental and the control conditions (Farrington 1983). However, the stratification process by risk levels basically requires us to use mixed model analyses that take into account the independent impact of risk level and the potential interaction between risk level and treatment. These analyses will also allow us to adjust degrees of freedom for significance levels in our study as required by the randomization. Using the mixed model approach, we will take into account several factors in each of the analyses we conduct. One factor will reflect the main effects of treatment. A second will adjust for the impact of risk level. A third factor will reflect the possible moderating effects of small versus large site implementation. The final factor will control for the interactions that are possible among risk level and treatment, risk level and site, and site and treatment.

Cost → Outcome Analyses

Data from the randomized experimental design will be used to compare the statistical significance, as well as describe the magnitude of costs, monetary benefits, cost-effectiveness, and cost-benefit, in the two components of treatment and supervision. Average and median costs, benefits, cost-effectiveness, and cost-benefit will be calculated per client as well as for groups of clients with high and moderate levels of pretreatment risk and for the two sites separately. Differences in costs, benefits, cost-effectiveness, and cost-benefit will also be examined for each risk group at each site, and for different periods of implementation of the seamless system.

More specifically, a summative cost-effectiveness analysis will contrast the additional (marginal) cost of the seamless service system to the increment in nonmonetary program outcomes. A summative cost-benefit analysis will estimate the monetary value of changes in measures of program effectiveness, and will contrast marginal cost with marginal benefit for seamless service administration. Both the cost-effectiveness and cost-benefit analyses will be conducted using actual data collected for each person assigned to the seamless and traditional service systems. Statistical analyses will test the significance and measure the effect size of hypothesized differences in costs, effectiveness, benefits, cost-effectiveness indices, and net benefit. Formative cost-effectiveness analyses will attempt to trace back from specific indices of effectiveness the processes, procedures, and resources that are critical to achieving the increment in effectiveness hypothesized for seamless system administration. This formative cost-effectiveness analysis will use linear programming to find the least-expensive combination of resources needed to achieve the observed levels of program effectiveness and program benefits.

The seamless system approach is expected to devote more resources to the offender in the short run with the expectations that over time these resources will reduce recycling through the system. If the seamless system keeps offenders off drugs and away from criminal behavior for a longer period of time, however, the total value of resources expended on offenders during their lifetime will actually be less than what would have been spent in the traditional cycle of punitive measures (incarceration), probation, and return to substance use and criminal behavior. This total "career cost" can be measured only by following a former drug user and offender for the rest of his or her life, of course. Using the prediction methods currently available, it is difficult reliably to infer "career cost" per client or offender from follow-up assessments of program outcomes even one or two years after treatment.

As a first approximation to contrasting the likely increment in seamless service system costs with the hoped-for decrement in career costs of drug treatment and related services, we will measure effectiveness and benefits through these follow-ups. We will examine how closely any additional benefits generated by the seamless system approach the additional costs of the seamless system (if, in fact, the seamless system costs more than the traditional system). The proposed research should contribute a highly detailed account of how an integrated seamless approach to helping the criminal substance abuser differs from the traditional criminal justice response to the criminal substance abuser. The research will employ traditional cost measures as well as analyze per unit costs and benefits. The cost savings that are anticipated should begin accruing shortly after treatment completion and should mount in seven through twelve months following completion.

Cost-effectiveness analysis, cost-benefit analysis, CPPOA. The CPPOA model uses a series of multiple regression analyses to find the significant paths from resources through procedures and processes to outcomes. We will also compare the cost and benefit results for the HIDTA seamless system group, different risk levels, and interaction of group and risk. Once the specific costs have been measured for each major treatment procedure and supervision services for each client, and placed in *cost → procedure* matrices (see Table 2.1), the costs can be summed: 1) for each resource separately across procedures, to find the amount of resources used for each client and for each service delivery condition overall; and 2) for each procedure separately across resources, to find the cost of administering each procedure and the cost of the two service administration conditions. This will allow us to create a per-unit cost for the procedure.

We then will analyze *cost* → *outcome* relationships using data on intervening and moderating variables to predict how outcomes could be maximized within cost constraints, or how costs could be minimized for the attainment of specific desirable outcomes (Yates 1996). Costs can be described in increasing degrees of comprehensiveness with:

1. *ratios* of total program cost (for all clients combined) compared to program-level measures of effectiveness (i.e., total program cost ÷ number of clients achieving criterion levels of negative urinalyses for targeted drugs; total program costs ÷ number of clients completing the program),
2. *ratios* of total program cost for individual clients to separate measures of effectiveness for individual clients (i.e., cost per drug-free day summarized with means, medians, and modes, and examined for their variability as well as the nature of their distribution, e.g., normal versus Poisson distributions),
3. *net benefit* of the program as a whole and for individual clients, which subtracts costs from benefits,
4. *time to payback* of program costs by program benefits, again for the program as a whole and for individual clients, and
5. *graphs* of total program cost for individual clients versus specific effectiveness measures for the same clients, showing the relationship among the amount of resources invested and the outcomes attained.

The above methods of describing cost-effectiveness and cost-benefit relationships provide the basis for comparing statistically the difference between seamless and traditional approaches. Ratios, in particular, can be used in statistical comparisons of the two approaches to services to examine mean differences in outcomes. To take into account the effects that program scale can have on relationships of cost to effectiveness and cost to benefit, we will examine possible economies-of-scale and related effects by graphing costs against effectiveness and costs against benefits for individual clients, distinguishing among clients from the different treatment programs and from the different sites.

Findings on the costs and outcomes of specific treatment procedures and service conditions will then be used in linear programming to find the combination of procedures and service administration method that maximize outcomes for different client populations within cost constraints. A cost → procedure process → outcome path diagram will be constructed from the data collected above to construct a model of simultaneous equations that describes the production process in criminal justice supervision, with or without treatment (Yates 1980, 1996). The models can be manipulated mathematically to maximize outcomes within cost constraints or minimize costs of producing outcomes at set criterion levels (Yates 1980, 1997b). For example, the model may determine that the seamless system of two levels of treatment for a total of nine months, graduated sanctions, and drug testing are more cost-effective for high-risk offenders than moderate-risk offenders. This will then produce the different service levels that optimize the desired outcomes.

Net benefit and time to return on investment. The cost-outcome analysis will subtract total benefit from total cost for each client to compute the *net benefit* of the seamless system for that client. These net benefits will be compared statistically between the seamless and traditional service systems using repeated-measures analyses of variance. In addition, the potential moderating effects of participant risk level will be examined using multiple linear or logistic regression. Net benefit will be analyzed using the statistical procedures planned for outcome variables. A repeated-measures dimension will be included in these analyses. For repeated-measures analyses, net benefit will be computed for each follow-up separately, using the benefits and costs accrued for that client by that time. A final cost-outcome analysis will use as the dependent variable the number of months required for monetary benefits to exceed monetary costs. This analysis will use data only from the final follow-up. For clients whose benefits have not exceeded costs by the final follow-up, but for whom a graph of cumulative benefits and costs over follow-ups shows a narrowing gap between the two, a projection of months-to-return-on-investment (MTROI) will be made based on the rate of benefit-cost gap closure for other clients. For clients whose benefits have not exceeded costs, and do not seem likely to due to complete recidivism, MTROI will be set as the estimated lifetime of the client given their age, gender, and ethnicity.

Conclusion

The clinical trial provides a unique opportunity to examine the relative costs, benefits, and cost → outcomes for two different sentencing options—a coerced treatment model using a seamless system and traditional supervision with no clinical services. The randomized design will both enlighten policy and provide a comparative basis for understanding the relative costs and benefits of utilizing seamless versus traditional approaches to substance abuse treatment. The contrast of the likely additional costs of the seamless approach with its hoped-for increments in effectiveness and in monetary benefits will be explored; similarly, the long-term outcomes and costs of the traditional approach will be available to illustrate comparable differences. Although nearly half of the offenders drop out of treatment (Simpson, Joe, and Brown 1997), it seems possible that the leverage of the criminal justice system can be an important means of reducing dropouts by establishing credible punitive contingencies. Supervision and monitoring can augment treatment to enhance treatment goals and pursue long-term outcomes. This experiment and the use of the CPPOA will provide new analytical tools to understand what are the long-term benefits from different policy alternatives.

Notes

Work on this manuscript and the project described by it was conducted at both University of Maryland at College Park and American University in Washington, D.C. It was supported by National Institute of Drug Abuse grant R01DA10705, National Institute of Justice grant 96CEVS0017, and Office of National Drug Control Policy grant 16PWBP528.

Correspondence should be sent to Faye S. Taxman, Department of Criminology and Criminal Justice, 2220 LeFrak Hall, University of Maryland at College Park, College Park, Md.; phone: (301) 405–4781; e-mail: ftaxman@crim.umd.edu. Inquiries regarding Cost → Procedure → Process → Outcome Analysis should be addressed to Brian T. Yates, Department of Psychology, American University, 4400 Massachusetts Avenue, N.W., Washington, D.C. 20016–8062; phone: (202) 885–1727; e-mail: *BrianYates@email.msn.com*.

1. These instruments were developed for this project based on available instruments in the field. The Life Events Survey consists of composite-score questions from criminal calendar questions (Nurco et al. 1988) and life events (Horney et al. 1995).

References

Alfano, A. M., A. H. Thurstin, and V. J. Nerviano. 1987. Cost-benefit estimates from ongoing alcoholism outcome research: A working paper. *International Journal of the Addictions* 22: 861–68.

Anderson, D. W., B. J. Bowland, W. S. Cartwright, and G. Bassin. In press. Service-level costing of drug abuse treatment.

Andrews, D. A., and J. Bonta. 1994. *The psychology of criminal conduct*. Cincinnati: Anderson Publishing.

Andrews, D. A., J. Bonta, and R. D. Hoge. 1990. Classification for effective rehabilitation: Rediscovering psychology. *Criminal Justice and Behavior* 17: 19–52.

Andrews, D. A., I. Zinger, R. D. Hoge, J. Bonta, P. Gendreau, and F. T. Cullen. 1990a. Does correctional treatment work? A clinically relevant and psychologically informed meta-analysis. *Criminology* 28: 369–404.

______. 1990b. A human science approach or more punishment and pessimism: A rejoinder to Lab and Whitehead. *Criminology* 28: 419–29.

Anglin, M. D., and Y. Hser. 1990. Treatment of drug abuse. In *Drugs and crime*, ed. Michael Tonry and James Q. Wilson, 393–460. Chicago: University of Chicago Press.

Anglin, M. D., D. Longshore, and S. Turner, 1999. Treatment alternatives to street crime: An evaluation of five programs. *Criminal Justice and Behavior* 26, no. 2: 168–95.

Anglin, M. D., D. Longshore, S. Turner, D. McBride, J. Inciardi, and M. Pendergast. 1996. *Studies of the functioning and effectiveness of treatment alternatives to street crime (TASC) programs: Final report*. Los Angeles: UCLA Drug Abuse Research Center.

Apsler, R., and W. M. Harding. 1991. Cost-effectiveness analysis of drug abuse treatment: Current status and recommendations for future research. In *Drug abuse services research series no. 1: Background papers on drug abuse financing and services research*, 58–81. Rockville, Md.: U.S. Department of Health and Human Services.

Ball, J. C., and A. Ross. 1991. *The effectiveness of methadone maintenance treatment: Patients, programs, services, and outcomes*. New York: Springer-Verlag.

Belenko, S., J. A. Fagan, and T. Dumanovsky. 1994. Effects of legal sanctions on recidivism in special drug courts. *Justice System Journal* 17: 53–81.

Bradley, C. J., M. T. French, and J. V. Rachal. 1994. Financing and cost of standard and enhanced methadone treatment. *Journal of Substance Abuse Treatment* 11: 433–42.

Brown, B. W., Jr. 1980. Designing for cancer clinical trials: Selection of prognostic factors. *Cancer Treatment Reports* 64: 499–502.

Byrne, J. M. 1990. The future of intensive probation supervision and new intermediate sanctions. *Crime and Delinquency* 36: 6–41.

Cartwright, W. S., and J. M. Kaple, eds. 1991. *Economic costs, cost-effectiveness, financing, and community-based drug treatment*. Research Monograph Series, No. 113. Rockville, Md.: National Institute on Drug Abuse.

Cohen, M. A. 1998. The monetary value of saving a high-risk youth. *Journal of Quantitative Criminology* 14: 5–33.

Cohen, M. A., and T. R. Miller. 1998. The cost of mental health care for victims of crime. *Journal of Interpersonal Violence* 13: 93–100.

Condelli, W. S., and R. L. Hubbard. 1994. Relationship between time spent in treatment and client outcomes from therapeutic communities. *Journal of Substance Abuse Treatment* 11: 25–33.

Cowles, E. L., T. C. Castellano, and L. A. Gransky. 1995. *"Boot camp" drug treatment and aftercare interventions: An evaluation review*. Washington, D.C.: National Institute of Justice.

DeMuth, N. M., B. T. Yates, and T. Coates. 1984. Psychologists as managers: Old guilts, innovative applications, and pathways to being an effective managerial psychologist. *Professional Psychology* 15: 758–68.

Duffee, D., and B. Carlson. 1996. Competing value premises for the provision of drug treatment to probationers. *Crime and Delinquency* 42: 574–93.

Etheridge, R. M., R. L. Hubbard, J. Anderson, S. G. Craddock, and P. M. Flynn. 1997. Treatment structure and program services in the Drug Abuse Treatment Outcome Study (DATOS). *Psychology of Addictive Behaviors* 11: 244–60.

Falkin, G. 1993. *Coordinating drug treatment for offenders: A case study*. New York: National Development and Research Institutes, Inc.

Farrington, D. P. 1983. Randomized experiments on crime and justice. In *Crime and justice: An annual review of research volume 4*, ed. M. Tonry and N. Morris, 257–308. Chicago: University of Chicago Press.

Fleiss, J. L. 1986. *The design and analysis of clinical experiments*. New York: John Wiley and Sons.

French, M. T., C. J. Bradley, B. Calingaert, M. L. Dennis, and G. T. Karuntzos. 1994. Cost analysis of training and employment services in methadone treatment. *Evaluation and Program Planning* 17: 107–20.

French, M. T., L. J. Dunlap, G. A. Zarkin, K. A. McGeary, and T. A. McLellan. 1997. A structured instrument for estimating the economic cost of drug abuse treatment. *Journal of Substance Abuse Treatment* 14: 1–11.

Gendreau, P. 1996. Offender rehabilitation: What we know and what needs to be done. *Criminal Justice and Behavior* 23: 144–61.

Gerstein, D. R., R. A. Johnson, H. J. Harwood, D. Fountain, N. Suter, and K. Malloy. 1994. *Evaluating recovery services: The California Drug and Alcohol Treatment Assessment (CALDATA)*. Sacramento: State of California, Health and Welfare Agency, Department of Alcohol and Drug Programs.

Gold, M. R., J. E. Siegel, L. B. Russell, and M. C. Weinstein, eds. 1996. *Cost-effectiveness in health and medicine*. New York: Oxford University Press.

Gustafon, J. S. 1991. Do more and do it better: Staff related issues in the drug treatment field that affect quality and effectiveness of services. In *Improving drug abuse treatment*, ed. R. W. Pickens, C. G. Leukefeld, and C. R. Schuster, 53–62. Research Monograph Series, No. 106. Rockville, Md.: National Institute on Drug Abuse.

Harrell, A., and S. Cavanagh. 1996. *Preliminary results from the evaluation of the D.C. Superior Court drug intervention program for drug felony defendants*. Washington, D.C.: National Institute of Justice.

Harwood, H. J., R. L. Hubbard, J. J. Collins, and J. V. Rachal. 1988. The costs of crime and the benefits of drug abuse treatment: A cost-benefit analysis using TOPS data. In *Compulsory treatment of drug abuse: Research and clinical practice*, ed. C. G. Leukefeld and F. M. Tims, 209–35. Research Monograph Series, No 86. Rockville, Md.: National Institute on Drug Abuse.

Hayashida, M., A. I. Alterman, A. T. McLellan, C. P. O'Brien, J. J. Purtill, J. R. Volpicelli, A. H. Raphaelson, and C. P. Hall. 1989. Comparative effectiveness and costs of inpatient and outpatient detoxification of patients with mild-to-moderate alcohol withdrawal syndrome. *New England Journal of Medicine* 320: 358–65.

Horney, J., D. W. Osgood, and I. H. Marshall. 1995. Criminal careers in the short term: Intra-variability in crime and its relation to local life circumstances. *American Sociological Review* 60: 655–73.

Hubbard, R. L., and M. T. French. 1991. New perspectives on the benefit-cost and cost-effectiveness of drug abuse treatment. In *Economic costs, cost-effectiveness, financing, and community-based drug treatment*, ed. W. S. Cartwright and J. M. Kaple, 94–113. Research Monograph Series, No. 113. Rockville, Md.: National Institute on Drug Abuse.

Hubbard, R. L., M. E. Marsden, J. V. Rachal, H. J. Harwood, E. R. Cavanaugh, and H. M. Ginzburg. 1989. *Drug abuse treatment: A national study of effectiveness.* Chapel Hill: University of North Carolina Press.

Kleiman, M. R. 1997. Drug Free or unfree: To get heavy users to stay clean, link parole and probation to abstinence. *Washington Post* (Feb. 2): C3.

Langenbucher, J. W., B. S. McCrady, J. Brick, and R. Esterly. 1993. *Socioeconomic evaluations of addictions treatment: Prepared for the president's commission on model state drug laws*. Piscataway, N.J.: Rutgers University.

Leukefeld, C. G., and F. M. Tims. 1988. Compulsory treatment: A review of findings. In *Compulsory treatment of drug abuse: Research and clinical practice*, ed. C. G. Leukefeld and F. M. Tims, 236–51. Research Monograph Series, No. 86. Rockville, Md.: National Institute on Drug Abuse.

______. 1990. Compulsory treatment for drug abuse. *International Journal of the Addictions* 25: 621–40.

Lipsey, M. W. 1990. *Design sensitivity: Statistical power for experimental research.* Newbury Park, Calif.: Sage Publications.

Lipton, D. S. 1995. The effectiveness of treatment for drug abusers under criminal justice supervision. Presentation at the Conference on Criminal Justice Research and Evaluation. Washington, D.C.: National Institute of Justice.

MacKenzie, D. L. 1997. Criminal Justice and Crime Prevention. In *Preventing crime: What works, what doesn't, what's promising,* by L. W. Sherman, D. C. Gottfredson, D. L. MacKenzie, J. Eck, P. Reuter, and S. D. Bushway. Washington, D.C.: U.S. Department of Justice, National Institute of Justice.

MacKenzie, D. L., and C. Souryal. 1994. *Multi-site evaluation of shock incarceration.* Washington, D.C.: National Institute of Justice.

Martin, S. S., and J. A. Inciardi. 1996. Case Management outcomes for drug involved offenders. Presentation at the American Society of Criminology Meeting in Chicago.

Martin, S. S., J. A. Inciardi, F. R. Scarpitti, and A. L. Nielsen. In press. Case management for drug involved parolees: A hard act to follow. In *The effectiveness of innovative approaches to drug abuse treatment*, ed. J. A. Inciardi, F. M. Tims, and B. W. Fletcher. Westport, Conn.: Greenwood Press.

Martinson, R. 1974. What works? Questions and Answers about prison reform. *Public Interest* 35: 22–54.

McLellan, A. T., and A. I. Alterman. 1991. Patient treatment matching: A conceptual and methodological review with suggestions for future research. In *Improving drug abuse treatment*, ed. R. W. Pickens, C. G. Leukefeld, and C. R. Schuster, 114–35. Research Monograph Series, No. 106. Rockville, Md.: National Institute on Drug Abuse.

McClellan, A. T., G. E. Woody, L. Luborsky, C. P. O'Brien, and K. A. Druley. 1983. Increased effectiveness of substance abuse treatment: A prospective study of patient-treatment "matching." *Journal of Nervous and Mental Disease* 171: 597–605.

Metja, C., P. J. Bokos, J. H. Mickenberg, and E. M. Maslar. 1994. Case management with intravenous drug users: Implementation issues and strategies. In *Drug abuse treatment: The implementation of innovative approaches*, ed. B. W. Fletcher, J. A. Inciardi, and A. M. Horton, 97–113. Westport, Conn.: Greenwood Press.

Moore, S. T. 1990. A social work practice model of case management: The case management grid. *Social Work* 35: 444–48.

______. 1992. Case management and the integration of services: How service delivery systems shape case management. *Social Work* 37: 418–23.

Nurco, D. N., T. W. Kinlock, T. E. Hanlon, and J. C. Ball. 1988. Non-narcotic drug use over an addiction career: A study of heroin addicts in Baltimore and New York City. *Comprehensive Psychiatry* 29: 450–59.

Palmer, T. 1992. *Re-emergence of correctional intervention*. Newbury Park, Calif.: Sage Publications.

______. 1995. Programmatic and nonprogrammatic aspects of successful intervention: New directions for research. *Crime and Delinquency* 41: 100–131.

Parent, D., J. Byrne, V. Tsarfaty, L. Valade, and J. Esselman. 1995. *Day reporting centers*. Washington, D.C.: National Institute of Justice.

Pendergast, M. L., M. D. Anglin, and J. Wellisch. 1994. Community-Based treatment for substance-abusing offenders: Principles and practices of effective service delivery. Paper presented at "This Works! Community Sanctions and Services for Special Offenders: A Research Conference." International Association of Residential and Community Alternatives.

Peters, R. H. 1993. Drug treatment in jails and detention settings. In *Drug treatment and criminal justice*, ed. J. A. Inciardi, 44–80. Newbury Park, Calif.: Sage Publications.

Peters, R. H., and R. L. May. 1992. Drug Treatment services in jails. In *Drug abuse treatment in prisons and jails*, ed. C. G. Leukefeld and F. M. Tims, 38–50. Research Monograph Series, No. 118. Rockville, Md.: National Institute on Drug Abuse.

Peters, R. H., W. D. Kearns, M. R. Murrin, and A. S. Dolente. 1992. Effectiveness of in-jail substance abuse treatment: Evaluation results from a national demonstration program. *American Jails* 6: 98–104.

Petersilia, J. 1999. A decade with experimenting with intermediate sanctions: What have we learned? *Perspectives* 23, no. 1: 39–44.

Petersilia, J., and S. Turner. 1993. *Evaluating intensive supervision probation/parole: Results of a nationwide experiment*. Washington, D.C.: National Institute of Justice.

Pocock, S. J., and S. W. Lagakos. 1982. Practical experience of randomization in cancer trials: An international survey. *British Journal of Cancer* 46: 368–75.

Rufener, B. L., J. V. Rachal, and A. M. Cruze. 1977. *Management effectiveness measures for NIDA drug abuse treatment programs*. Washington, D.C.: Government Printing Office.

Scarpitti, F. R., J. A. Inciardi, and S. S. Martin. 1994. Assertive community treatment: Obstacles to implementation. In *Drug abuse treatment: The implementation of innovative approaches*, ed. B. W. Fletcher, J. A. Inciardi, and A. M. Horton, 115–29. Westport, Conn.: Greenwood Press.

Schuster, J. 1991. Ensuring highest-quality care for the cost: Coping strategies for mental health providers. *Hospital and Community Psychiatry* 42: 774–76.

Shwartz, M., G. Baker, K. P. Mulvey, and A. Plough. 1997. Improving publicly funded substance abuse treatment: The value of case management. *American Journal of Public Health*, 87, no. 10: 1659–64.

Sherman, L. W., D. C. Gottfredson, D. L. MacKenzie, J. Eck, P. Reuter, and S. D. Bushway. 1997. *Preventing crime: What works, what doesn't, what's promising.* Washington, D.C.: U.S. Department of Justice, National Institute of Justice.

Sherman, L. W., and D. Weisburd. 1995. General deterrent effects of police patrol in crime "hot spots": A randomized, controlled trial. *Justice Quarterly* 12: 625–48.

Siegal, H. A., and P. A. Cole. 1993. Enhancing Criminal justice based treatment through the application of the intervention approach. *Journal of Drug Issues* 23: 131–42.

Siegert, F. A., and B. T. Yates. 1980. Cost-effectiveness of individual in-office, individual in-home, and group delivery systems for behavioral child-management. *Evaluation and the Health Professions* 3: 123–52.

Simpson, D. D., G. W. Joe, and B. S. Brown. 1997. Treatment retention and follow-up outcomes in the Drug Abuse Treatment Outcome Study (DATOS). *Psychology of Addictive Behaviors* 11: 294–307.

Sullivan, W. P., D. J. Hartmann, D. Dillon, and J. L. Wolk. 1994. Implementing case management in alcohol and drug treatment. *Families in Society* 75: 67–73.

Taxman, F. S. 1998. *Reducing recidivism through a seamless system of care: Components of effective treatment, supervision, and transition services in the community.* Washington, D.C.: Office of National Drug Control Policy, Treatment and Criminal Justice System Conference, March 1998.

Taxman, F. S., and J. M. Byrne. 1994. Locating absconders: Results from a randomized field experiment. *Federal Probation* 58: 13–23.

Taxman, F. S., B. Kubu, and C. DeFastano, 1999. *Treatment as crime control: Reducing recidivism through a continuum of care.* College Park: University of Maryland.

Taxman, F. S., and D. Lockwood. 1996. *Systematic case management practices.* College Park: University of Maryland.

Taxman, F. S., and S. Sherman. 1998. Seamless systems of care: Using automation to improve outcomes. In *Criminal justice technology in the 21st century*, ed. L. Moriarty and D. Carter, 167–93. Springfield, Ill.: Charles C. Thomas.

Taxman, F. S., D. Soule, and A. Gelb. 1999. Graduated sanctions: Stepping into accountable systems and offenders. *Prison Journal* 72, no. 2: 182–205.

Taxman, F. S., and D. L. Spinner. 1997. *Recidivism reduction: An evaluation of a jail based substance abuse treatment program.* Report submitted to the Montgomery County, Maryland, government.

Tonry, M., and R. Will. 1988. *Intermediate sanctions.* Final Report to the National Institute of Justice. Castine, Maine: Castine Research Corporation.

Visher, C. A. 1990. Incorporating drug treatment in criminal sanctions. *NIJ Reports* 221: 2–7.

Weisburd, D. 1993. Design sensitivity in criminal justice experiments. In *Crime and justice: A review of research volume 17*, ed. M. Tonry, 337–79. Chicago: University of Chicago Press.

Weisburd, D., and L. Green. 1995. Policing drug hot spots: The Jersey City drug market analysis experiment. *Justice Quarterly* 12: 711–35.

Wexler, H. K., D. S. Lipton, and B. D. Johnson. 1988. *A criminal justice system strategy for treating cocaine-heroin abusing offenders in custody.* Washington, D.C.: National Institute of Justice.

Whitehead, J. T., and S. P. Lab. 1989. A meta-analysis of juvenile correctional treatment. *Journal of Research in Crime and Delinquency* 26: 276–95.

Wish, E. D., and B. A. Gropper. 1990. Drug testing by the criminal justice system: Methods, research, and applications. In *Drugs and crime*, ed. M. Tonry and J. Q. Wilson, 321–90. Chicago: University of Chicago Press.

Yates, B. T. 1980. *Improving effectiveness and reducing costs in mental health.* Springfield, Ill.: Charles C. Thomas.

______. 1985. Cost-effectiveness analysis and cost-benefit analysis: An introduction. *Behavioral Assessment* 7: 207–34.

______. 1994. Toward the incorporation of costs, cost-effectiveness analysis, and cost-benefit analysis into clinical research. *Journal of Consulting and Clinical Psychology* 62: 729–36.

______. 1995. Cost-effectiveness analysis, cost-benefit analysis, and beyond: Evolving models for the scientist-manager-practitioner. *Clinical Psychology: Science and Practice* 2: 385–98.

______. 1996. *Analyzing costs, procedures, processes, and outcomes in human services.* Thousand Oaks, Calif.: Sage Publications.

______. 1997a. From psychotherapy research to cost-outcome research: What resources are necessary to implement which therapy procedures that change what processes to yield which outcomes? *Psychotherapy Research* 7: 345–64.

______. 1997b. Formative evaluation of costs, cost-effectiveness, and cost-benefit: Toward cost → procedure → process → outcome analysis. In *Handbook of applied social research methods,* ed. L. Bickman and D. Rog, 285–314. Thousand Oaks, Calif.: Sage Publications.

Yates, B. T., W. G. Haven, and C. E. Thoresen. 1979. Cost-effectiveness analysis at learning house: How much change for how much money? In *Progress in behavior therapy with delinquents*, ed. J. S. Stumphauzer, 186–222. Springfield, Ill.: Charles C. Thomas.

Zelen, M. 1975. Importance of prognostic factors in planning therapeutic trials. In *Cancer therapy: Prognostic factors and criteria of response,* ed. M. J. Stqaquet. New York: Raven Press.

Zimring, F. E., and G. Hawkins. 1995. *Incapacitation: Penal confinement and the restraint of crime.* New York: Oxford University Press.

PART THREE

Economic Analysis Findings

3

A Review of Research on the Monetary Value of Preventing Crime

BRANDON C. WELSH
DAVID P. FARRINGTON

This chapter reviews evidence on the economic efficiency or monetary value of crime prevention programs. Twenty-six crime prevention studies meeting our criteria (see below) were identified. To organize our discussion of the costs and benefits of crime prevention programs, we relied on the general crime prevention classification scheme proposed by Tonry and Farrington (1995), which specifies four principal strategies: developmental, community, situational, and criminal justice prevention. For criminal justice prevention, it was possible only to investigate correctional intervention, because of an almost complete absence of benefit-cost studies of law enforcement– and court-based interventions. For the fourth principal strategy—community crime prevention—only one study (Jones and Offord 1989) meeting the criteria for inclusion could be located.

Evaluation studies of crime prevention programs were included in the present review if they met three criteria. First, the program had a measure of personal crime, where the primary victim was a person or household. Second, the outcome evaluation was based on a "real-life" program. That is, program outcomes were neither assessed using statistical modeling techniques alone nor hypothesized on the basis of case study data, but rather employed research designs with the capacity to control for threats to internal and external validity, such as experimental and quasi-experimental designs. Third, a benefit-cost analysis was performed that had either calculated or permitted the calculation of a benefit-cost ratio for the purpose of assessing the program's economic efficiency. Studies that did not perform a benefit-cost analysis were included if they presented sufficient cost and benefit data to enable an assessment of economic efficiency.

The second criterion—the use of real-life programs—was important, because the "scientific methods scale" developed by Sherman et al. (1997) was used to assess the methodological quality of the studies. It is as follows, with level 1 being the lowest and level 5 the highest:[1]

1. Correlational evidence: Low offending correlates with the program at a single point in time.
2. No statistical control for selection bias, but some kind of comparison (e.g., program group compared with nonequivalent control group, program group measured before and after intervention, with no control group).
3. Moderate statistical design (e.g., program group compared with comparable control group, including pre-post and experimental-control comparisons).
4. Strong statistical control (e.g., program group compared with control group before and after, with control of extraneous influences on the outcome, by matching, prediction scores, or statistical controls).
5. Randomized experiment: units assigned at random to program and control groups prior to intervention.

This methodological rating scale is concerned with the overall internal validity of evaluations; external validity, or the "generalizability of internally valid results" (Sherman et al. 1998, 3), was not addressed as part of the scientific methods scale.[2] Ideally, studies included in this review should have been restricted to benefit-cost analyses of programs with high-quality evaluation designs (level 3 or higher), but the small number of existing analyses militated against this.

The third criterion—that a benefit-cost analysis was performed—was important, because our interest was in the economic costs *and* benefits of crime prevention programs. Of the two main techniques of economic analysis—benefit-cost and cost-effectiveness analysis—only benefit-cost analysis enables an assessment of both costs and benefits. (See the Introduction for a discussion of the differences between benefit-cost and cost-effectiveness analysis and the methodology of economic analysis.)

To measure the economic efficiency of programs, we have used the benefit-cost ratio rather than net value (benefits minus costs). This was done for three principal reasons: (1) the benefit-cost ratio controls for differences in national currencies; (2) it controls for the different time periods of programs (e.g., a benefit-cost ratio of a program that used 1989 U.S. dollars can reasonably be compared with the benefit-cost ratio of a program that used 1999 U.S. dollars); and (3) it provides a single measurement of the benefits of a program that are gained from a one-monetary unit (one-dollar) investment or expenditure. Arguments such as "for every dollar spent, seven dollars were saved in the long run" (Schweinhart, Barnes, and Weikart 1993) have proved very powerful. The decision to use the benefit-cost ratio is particularly important because, in many cases, it is a direct measurement of the value the taxpaying public receives for its investment. It could be argued that expressing the value of publicly funded programs in this understandable form is concordant with the movement by governments toward a greater degree of transparency and accountability. Also, in reporting on the benefit-cost findings of the reviewed studies, we have used, as far as possible, the perspective of the public (government/taxpayer and crime victim; see the Introduction for a discussion of the different perspectives used in economic analysis).

To locate studies meeting the above criteria, we employed four strategies. First, we searched the Social Sciences Citation Index (1981 to 1998) of the Institute for Scientific Information (ISI) database on the Internet-accessible Bibliographic Databases service. Second, we searched the most recent issues of major European and North American criminological journals to cover any time lag in the updating of the ISI database. Third, we examined the bibliographies of leading narrative and empirical (e.g., metanalytic) reviews of the literature on the effectiveness of crime prevention programs. Fourth, we contacted leading academics and researchers in the fields of crime prevention and welfare economics in an effort to identify unpublished or in-press studies.

This chapter reports on what is known about the costs and benefits and, ultimately, the economic efficiency of crime prevention programs. Our specific focus on economic efficiency is not meant to imply that crime prevention programs should be continued only if benefits outweigh costs. There are many important noneconomic criteria on which crime prevention programs should be judged. Furthermore, no attempt is made here to assess which of the studies is most economically efficient. This is because of the small number of studies identified and reviewed here and the varied methodological rigor of their outcome evaluations and benefit-cost analyses, as well as limited or missing information in the studies.

Costs and Benefits of Crime Prevention Programs

This section examines the monetary costs and benefits of crime prevention programs from three principal crime prevention strategies: developmental, situational, and criminal justice prevention. As noted above, for criminal justice prevention, it was possible to investigate only correctional intervention and, for community crime prevention, only one study meeting the criteria for inclusion could be located. We previously reviewed the existing benefit-cost evidence of community crime prevention alongside the other three principal crime prevention strategies (Welsh and Farrington 2000). For each of the three prevention strategies we summarize the key features of the studies and the main findings pertaining to monetary costs and benefits and review in detail a selected study. The three studies reviewed were selected because of their high-quality research designs and their rigorous benefit-cost analyses.

Developmental Crime Prevention

The developmental perspective postulates that criminal offending in adolescence and adulthood is influenced by "behavioral and attitudinal patterns that have been learned during an individual's development" (Tremblay and Craig 1995, 151). Developmental prevention is informed generally by motivational or human development theories on criminal behavior, and specifically by longitudinal studies that follow samples of young persons from their early childhood experiences to the peak of their involvement with crime in their teens and twenties. It aims to influence the scientifically identified risk factors or "root causes" of juvenile delinquency and later criminal offending. Some of the major risk factors include growing up in poverty, living in poor housing, inadequate parental supervision and harsh or inconsistent discipline, parental conflict and separation, low intelligence and poor school performance, and a high level of impulsiveness and hyperactivity (Farrington 1996).

Two well-known developmental prevention studies that have measured delinquency or childhood aggression and presented data on the monetary value of the programs—the Syracuse University Family Development Research Project (Lally, Mangione, and Honig 1988) and the Yale Child Welfare Research Program (Seitz, Rosenbaum, and Apfel 1985)—have not been included here, because the published data was insufficient to calculate benefit-cost ratios to assess the economic efficiency of the programs. A third study (Coopers and Lybrand 1994), the only one found in the United Kingdom, has also been excluded because it did not evaluate a real-life program. This study employed a case-study design to assess the program costs of a nonrepresentative sample of Youth Service schemes that had as an explicit aim the prevention of crime. The Youth Service is a network of organizations (statutory and voluntary sectors) that provides the majority of the youth work schemes across England and Wales. It is a nonschool program aimed principally at fostering the "planned and social education" of young people.

Summary of Benefit-Cost Findings

Six developmental crime prevention studies meeting the criteria for inclusion were identified. Table 3.1 summarizes key features of the six studies, which are listed in chronological order. All were conducted in the United States. At the start of the intervention, subjects ranged in age from prebirth to eighteen years, with half of the programs commencing prior to the formal school years. The studies manipulated a variety of different risk factors, including parenting, education, cognitive development, and behavioral problems. The duration of the intervention ranged from ten weeks to four years. Two of the studies (Schweinhart, Barnes, and Weikart 1993; Olds et al. 1997) had long follow-up periods to assess outcomes. The methodological rigor of the six studies was very high, with three (Schweinhart, Barnes, and Weikart 1993; Hahn 1994; Olds et al. 1997) employing random assignment to experimental and control conditions. All interventions were successful. Five of the six studies performed a benefit-cost analysis, whereas the one study that did not (Earle 1995) provided sufficient cost and benefit data to permit an estimation of its economic efficiency.

The benefits measured by the six developmental prevention studies were wide-ranging, including reduced crime victim expenses, criminal justice system costs, public health care, and social service use. Five of the six studies yielded a desirable benefit-cost ratio (greater than 1.0). For these five studies the economic return on a one-dollar investment ranged from a low of $1.06 to a high of $7.16. The one study that did not show a desirable benefit-cost ratio (Earle 1995) was the one for which we carried out a simple benefit-cost analysis. It is important to note that the Elmira Prenatal–Early Infancy Project of Olds et al. (1997), which provided nurse home visitation services (e.g., advice on pre- and postnatal care) to teenage mothers, reported a desirable benefit-cost ratio for the higher-risk sample and an undesirable benefit-cost ratio for the whole sample at two years' postintervention. A more recent benefit-cost analysis of the Elmira program by Karoly et al. (1998), which also measured program effects on children's delinquency at age fifteen, found a favorable benefit-cost ratio for the higher-risk families, but not for the lower-risk families.[3]

As shown in Table 3.1, a desirable benefit-cost ratio was found for each of the four studies in which the intervention commenced after birth, ranging from 1.40 to 7.16. By comparison, the two studies that began prenatally (Earle 1995; Olds et al. 1997) reported mixed results. The Hawaii Healthy Start and the lower-risk sample for Elmira (at the latest follow-up) showed undesirable ratios of 0.38 and 0.62, respectively, whereas the higher-risk sample for Elmira (at the latest follow-up) showed a desirable ratio of 4.06. In the case of Hawaii Healthy Start, limited measurement of program effects—only program effects on child abuse and neglect could

TABLE 3.1 Summary of Development Crime Prevention Studies

Authors, Project Name, Place	*Age at Intervention*	*Risk Factors Manipulated*	*Context of Intervention*	*Duration and Type of Intervention*	*Sample Size*	*Scientific Methods Score*	*Follow-up[a] and Results[b]*	*Benefits Measured*	*Benefit-Cost Ratio[c]*
Long, Mallar, and Thornton, (1981). Job Corps	18 years (average)	Education, employment	Residential-based center	n.a., vocational training, education, health care	5,100 youths: T=n.a., C=n.a.	4 (before-after, experimental-control, with matching)	18 months (average) police arrests+, substance abuse+, school achievement+, employment+, wages+	Crime victim expenses (direct), criminal justice system, employment earnings, social service use	1.45
Lipsey (1984). Los Angeles County Delinquency Prevention Program	<15 years (average)	Behavioral problems	Community-based center	10 weeks; family counseling, academic tutoring, employment training	7,637 youths (all in program): T=n.a., C=n.a.	2 (before-after) and 3 (before-after) experimental control	Immediate outcome: police arrests+[d]	Criminal justice system	1.40
Schweinhart, Barnes, and Weikart (1993). Perry Preschool, Ypsilanti, Mich.	3–4 years	Cognitive development	Preschool, home	1–2 years; preschool intellectual enrichment, parent education	123 children (72 boys, 51 girls): T=58, C=65	5 (randomized experiment-stratified assignment)	9–10 years: delinquency+, school achievement+, cognitive functioning 0; 22 years police arrests+, school	Crime victim expenses (direct and indirect), criminal justice system, educational output and public school	9–10 years follow-up: 2.48; 14 years follow-up: 3.00; 22 years follow-up: 7.16

							achievement+, social service use+, educational achievement+	expenses, employment earnings, social service use	
Hahn (1994). Quantum Opportunities Program	15 years (average)	Education	Community-based agency, home	4 years; education, skill	250 youths: T=125, C=125	5 (randomized experiment)	6 months: police arrests+, school achievement+, social services use+	Educational output, fewer children	3.68
Earle (1995). Hawaii Healthy Start	Prenatal and birth	Parenting, family planning	Home	4 years; parent education, parent support, family planning, community support	2,706 families T=1,353, C=1,353	3 (before-after, experimantal control)	Immediate outcome: child abuse and neglect+	Child protective services	0.38
Olds et al. (1997, 1998). Prenatal/Early Infancy Project, Elmira, N.Y.	Prenatal	Parenting, family planning	Home	2 years; T1=parent education, parent support, community support, family planning, T2=T1 minus postnatal home visits, C=2 conditions not receiving	400 mothers: T1=116, T2=100, C=184	5 (randomized experiment)	Immediate outcome (T1 vs. C): mothers: child abuse and neglect+, discipline+, children: developmental quotent+ 13 years (T1 vs. C):	Child protective services, employment earnings, public health care, social service use	2 years follow-up: higher-risk sample= 1.06, whole sample=0.51 13 years follow-up: higher-risk sample=4.06, lower-risk sample=0.62

(*continues*)

TABLE 3.1 *(continued)*

Authors, Project Name, Place	*Age at Intervention*	*Risk Factors Manipulated*	*Context of Intervention*	*Duration and Type of Intervention*	*Sample Size*	*Scientific Methods Score*	*Follow-up[a] and Results[b]*	*Benefits Measured*	*Benefit-Cost Ratio[c]*
				home visits (Screening services and free transportation to clinic)			mothers: child abuse and neglect+, higher-risk mothers: arrests and convictions+, social service use+ children (of higher-risk mothers): arrests+		

[a]The period of time in which the progran effects were evaluated after the intervention had ended.

[b]'0' = no intervention effects, '+' = desirable intervention effects.

[c]Expressed as a ratio of benefits to costs in monetary units (national currencies).

[d]Based on earlier studies that employed both before-after (no control group) and before-after,experimental-control designs.

NOTES: T = treatment group, C = control group, n.a. = not available.

be monetized—contributed to its poor economic showing. Offering largely postnatal home visitation services, Hawaii Healthy Start operates as a statewide program available to all new mothers. It aims to reduce family stress and improve family functioning, improve parenting skills, enhance child health and development, and prevent child abuse and neglect (Earle 1995, 3).

For three of the four studies in which the intervention began after birth (Long, Mallar, and Thornton 1981; Lipsey 1984; Schweinhart, Barnes, and Weikart 1993), savings from reduced delinquency and later offending, as measured by less involvement with the justice system and fewer victims of crime, accounted for a substantial proportion of the measured benefits. In the case of the Perry program that provided experimental children with daily preschool classes, backed up by weekly home visits, usually lasting two years (covering ages three to four), reduced offending at age twenty-seven accounted for four-fifths (79.6 percent) of the total economic benefits, or $5.70 of $7.16. For the U.S. Job Corps, an ongoing federal training program for disadvantaged, unemployed youths, reduced criminal activity accounted for one-quarter (28.8 percent) of the total benefits, or $0.42 of $1.45. Some of the other benefits produced by these programs included reduced reliance on welfare, increased economic output of the program participants that generated increased tax revenue for the government, and increased educational achievement that, in some cases, meant less use of remedial school services (see Table 3.1). Overall, developmental prevention appears to be a promising strategy in reducing monetary costs associated with delinquency and later criminal offending and improving the life-course development of at-risk children and their families.

Elmira Prenatal–Early Intervention Project

Elmira, a semirural community in upstate New York, was the setting for the Prenatal–Early Infancy Project (PEIP) which started in the late 1970s. PEIP was designed with three broad objectives: (1) to improve the outcomes of pregnancy; (2) to improve the quality of care that parents (mostly mothers) provide to their children (and their children's subsequent health and development); and (3) to improve the mother's own personal life-course development, by completing their educations, finding work, and planning future pregnancies (Olds et al. 1993, 158).

Research design and methodology. A randomized-experimental design was used to evaluate the effects of PEIP. The program enrolled four hundred women prior to their thirtieth week of pregnancy. Women were recruited if they had no previous live births and had at least one of the following high-risk characteristics prone to health and developmental problems in infancy (85 percent had at least one of the characteristics): under nineteen years of age (47 percent), unmarried (62 percent), or low socioeconomic status (SES) (61 percent).

The women were randomly assigned to one of four treatment conditions. In the first condition (N=90) no services were provided during pregnancy. Screening for sensory and developmental problems took place at ages one and two and was provided in all four treatment conditions. Women in the second condition (N=94) were provided with transportation vouchers to attend regular prenatal and child visits to physicians. Women in the third condition (N=100), in addition to the free transportation, received nurse home visits during pregnancy on average once every two weeks, and those in the fourth condition (N=116) received the same services as those in the third, but received continued nurse home visits until the children reached the age of two years. Three major activities were carried out during the home visits: "(1) parent education about influences on fetal and infant development; (2) the involvement of family members and friends in the pregnancy, birth, early care of the child, and in the support of the mother; and (3) the linkage of family members with other health and human services" (Olds et al. 1993, 158).

Interviews and infant assessments were carried out at six different intervals during the program: prior to the thirtieth week of pregnancy and at six, ten, twelve, twenty-two, and twenty-four months of the infant's life. Information sources included medical records of the infants, child abuse and neglect registries for fifteen states, social service records, interviews with the mothers, and various developmental tests. Postprogram assessments used for the benefit-cost analysis involved interviews with the women and annual reviews of the medical and social service records of the infants up to age four, two years after the intervention ended.

Analyses focused primarily on comparisons among combined treatment conditions one and two (control group) and treatment condition four (treatment group). Conditions one and two (not visited by a nurse during pregnancy or infancy) were grouped together because no differences between the two groups were observed in the use of the free transportation service for prenatal and child visits to physicians. Condition three was excluded as few lasting benefits were observed for nurse home visits during pregnancy relative to pregnancy plus infancy (condition 4). Analyses also focused on higher-risk mothers and the sample as a whole (higher- plus lower-risk mothers). Higher-risk mothers were both unmarried and from households of low SES at the time of program enrollment. Sample retention at thirteen years' postintervention was 81.0 percent (324 of 400). Analyses of lost cases showed no differences across the four treatment conditions. Forty-six nonwhite women were excluded from the statistical analyses due to the methodological limitations that a small sample size would present in cross-classifying race with other variables (Olds et al. 1986).

Program effects. Compared to the control group, the treatment group showed impressive results across a range of indicators. The most striking finding was a three-fourths (78.9 percent) reduction in state-verified cases of child abuse and neglect during the first two years of the child's life for the higher-risk mothers in the treatment group compared to their control counterparts (4 percent versus 19 percent) (Olds et al. 1986). Other key findings for the treatment group compared to the control group included: (1) 32 percent fewer emergency room visits for all children at immediate outcome (age two); (2) 80 percent greater participation in the workforce for higher-risk mothers at two years' postintervention; and (3) 43 percent fewer subsequent childbirths for higher-risk mothers at two years' postintervention (Olds et al. 1993).

Thirteen years after the completion of the program, fewer treatment mothers compared to control mothers for the sample as a whole were identified as perpetrators of child abuse and neglect (29 percent versus 54 percent), and, for the higher-risk sample, fewer treatment mothers in contrast to the controls had alcohol or substance abuse problems or were arrested (Olds et al. 1997). At the age of fifteen, children of the higher-risk mothers who received the program reported fewer arrests than their control counterparts (Olds et al. 1998).

Benefit-cost results. Study investigators carried out a rigorous benefit-cost analysis to assess the effects of nurse home visitation on government spending up to the time when the children were four years old. The same treatment conditions were compared as above. Three data sets (in 1980 U.S. dollars) were used: (1) governmental costs of the program; (2) other governmental costs that were in some way affected by the program through improved maternal and child health; and (3) tax revenues realized through women's participation in the workforce.

The average per-family cost of the two-year program was $3,246 for the sample as a whole ($4,067 for treatment group minus $821 for control group) and $3,133 for the higher-risk sample ($4,113 for treatment group minus $980 for control group). In other words, nurse-visited families (treatment condition 4) were allocated between 4.2 and 5.0 times more program spending as families receiving only screening and free transportation (treatment conditions 1 and 2 combined). Two years after the completion of the program, per-family benefits to governmental agencies reached $1,772 for the sample as a whole and $3,498 for the higher-risk sample. After adjusting for inflation and discounting, these figures were \$1,664 and \$3,313, respectively.

The benefit-cost ratio was a desirable 1.06 (\$3,313 ÷ \$3,133) for the higher-risk sample, meaning that for each dollar that was invested in the program, the public received \$1.06 in return. For the sample as a whole, the benefit-cost ratio was an unfavorable 0.51 (\$1,664 ÷ \$3,246), or a net loss of \$0.49 for each dollar invested.

Of government savings to the higher-risk sample (\$3,313 per family), the largest portion (56 percent) was attributed to reductions in Aid for Dependent Children (AFDC) payments. Reductions in Food Stamps accounted for 26 percent of the savings; Medicaid, 11 percent; and increases in tax revenue, 5 percent. Fewer cases of child abuse and neglect among the treatment group compared to the control group accounted for only 3 percent of the government savings (to Child Protective Services), or approximately \$100 per family.

An external benefit-cost study of the Elmira program by RAND (Karoly et al. 1998) at thirteen years' postintervention, which measured program effects on children's delinquency and mothers' life-course development, found a favorable benefit-cost ratio of 4.06 for the higher-risk families and an unfavorable ratio of 0.62 for the lower-risk families.

To test the generalizability of the findings of the Elmira study, currently two urban replications are under way: one in Memphis, Tennessee (Kitzman et al. 1997), and the other in Denver, Colorado. Benefit-cost analyses are planned for both studies.

Situational Crime Prevention

Situational crime prevention is defined as "a preventive approach that relies, not upon improving society or its institutions, but simply upon reducing opportunities for crime" (Clarke 1992, 3). Reducing opportunities for crime is achieved essentially through some modification or manipulation of the environment. The origins of situational prevention are based in the larger body of opportunity theory that sees the offender "as heavily influenced by environmental inducements and opportunities and as being highly adaptable to changes in the situation" (Clarke 1995a, 57). An elaboration of the theoretical bases and principles of situational prevention is beyond the scope of this chapter; however, excellent reviews of these topics are provided by Clarke (1995b, 1997) and Newman, Clarke, and Shoham (1997).

Clarke and Homel (1997) classified situational crime prevention into sixteen techniques divided into four main approaches: (1) increasing perceived effort (target hardening, access control, deflecting offenders, and controlling facilitators); (2) increasing perceived risks (entry/exit screening, formal surveillance, surveillance by employees, and natural surveillance); (3) reducing anticipated rewards (target removal, identifying property, reducing temptation, and denying benefits); and (4) inducing guilt or shame (rule setting, strengthening moral condemnation, controlling disinhibitors, and facilitating compliance).

For comparison with other types of prevention, we have limited our review of the monetary costs and benefits of situational prevention to those programs that have targeted violent or property crimes (e.g., robbery, burglary, vandalism). Excluded are programs that have targeted various forms of fraud, shoplifting, and employee theft. Some of these excluded programs are: business initiatives in the United Kingdom to reduce "bouncing checks," bank passbook fraud, check and credit card fraud, shoplifting, and employee theft (Burrows 1991); the London Underground's attempt to reduce fare evasion (Clarke 1993; Clarke, Cody, and Natarajan 1994); a shoplifting prevention experiment (DiLonardo 1996); and a U.S. prison's attempt to reduce the high costs of illicit telephone use (La Vigne 1994). These programs have been excluded because the primary victim, for the most part, was a business, not a person or a household. The inclusion of four of the thirteen studies where the context of the intervention was a shop or transport system (see Table 3.2) was justified because there was also a measure of personal crime. Three other situational crime prevention studies that assessed costs and benefits and focused on crimes relevant to this review have also been excluded because two (Field 1993; Hakim et al. 1995) were not real-life programs and the third (Bridgeman 1996) provided incomplete cost and benefit data.

Thirteen situational crime prevention studies meeting the criteria for inclusion were identified. Table 3.2 summarizes key features of these thirteen studies. In those cases where a program targeted more than one of the crimes of interest, it was classified under the crime(s) for which cost and benefit data were presented. The studies originated in four different countries: Australia, the Netherlands, the United Kingdom, and the United States. In nine of the thirteen studies, residential areas provided the context for the intervention, whereas the remaining four took place in commercial premises or in public facilities (e.g., transport systems). The observed length of the intervention (the changed circumstances during which measurements were taken) ranged from six months to eight years. The most common primary intervention technique of the reviewed studies was surveillance by employees (three studies), formal surveillance (three studies), and natural surveillance (three studies). In only two of the projects (Schnelle et al. 1979; Laycock 1991) was there follow-up (defined as the period of time in which program effects were evaluated after the intervention had ended). Usually, the changed circumstances of the intervention continued to apply during the "after" period; there was no "re-

TABLE 3.2 Summary of Situational Crime Prevention Studies

Authors, Project Name, Place	*Crimes Targeted*	*Context of Intervention*	*Duration and Primary Technique[a] of Intervention*	*Sample Size*	*Scientific Methods Score*	*Follow-up[b] and Results[c]*	*Benefits Measured*	*Benefit-Cost Ratio[d]*
Cirel et al. (1977). Seattle, WA	Burglary	Home	1 year; natural surveillance (block watch)	1,474 homes	3 (before-after, experimental-control)	Immediate outcome: burglary+	Crime victim expenses (person, direct)	0.40
Schnelle at al. (1979). Nashville, TN	Armed robbery	Store	6 and 11 months: formal surveillance (silent alarms)	48 stores	2 (before-after)	5 and 15 months: armed robbery0	Crime victim expenses (private sector, direct)	0.36
Laycock (1986, 1991), Caerphilly, Wales	Burglary	Home	1 year; indentifying property (property marking)	2,234 homes	2 (before-after)	1 year: burglary+	Criminal justice system (police)	0.78 (at immediate outcome)
Skilton (1998). South Kilburn Estate. London Borough of Brent, England	Vandalism	Public housing estate	1 year; employee surveillance (concierges)	305 homes (in 2 high rises)	3 (before-after, experimental-control)	Immediate outcome: vandalism+	Crime victim expenses (public sector, direct), public housing	1.44
van Andel (1989). Netherlands	Vandalism, toll fraud, assault	Public transport system	3 and 4 years, formal surveillance (special transport officials)	Metro, tram, and bus in 3 cities	2 (before-after)	Immediate outcome: vandalism+, toll fraud+, assault+	Crime victim expenses (public sector. direct), toll revenue	0.32

Clarke and McGrath (1990). Victoria, Australia	Robbery	Betting shop	1–8 years; target hardening (time-locks, cash limits)	429 betting shops (average)	2 (before-after, some control)	Immediate outcome: robbery+	Crime victim expenses (public sector, direct)	1.71
Forrester et al. (1990). Kirkholt Burglary Prevention Project. Rochdale, England	Burglary	Public housing estate	3 years; target removal (removal of coin meters)	2,280 homes	2 (before-after, some control)	Immediate outcome: burglary+	Crime victim expenses (person, direct), criminal justice system, public housing	5.04
Poyner (1992). North Shields, England	Vandalism	Public transport system	9 months; employee surveillance (CCTVs)	5 buses	2 (before-after)	Immediate outcome: vandalism+,	Crime victim expenses (public sector, direct)	2.35
Davidson and Farr (1994). Mitchellhill Estate. Glasgow, Scotland	Vandalism, burglary	Public housing estate	15 months; employee surveillance (CCTVs)	5 housing blocks	2 (before-after)	Immediate outcome: vandalism+, burglary+	Crime victim expenses (public sector, direct), rental income	0.47
Knight (1994). Possil Park Estate. Glasgow, Scotland	Vandalism, burglary	Public housing estate	1 year; formal surveillance (security guards)	1,767 homes	2 (before-after)	Immediate outcome: vandalism+ burglary+	Crime victim expenses (person and private sector, direct)	1.31

(continues)

TABLE 3.2 (continued)

Authors, Project Name, Place	*Crimes Targeted*	*Context of Intervention*	*Duration and Primary Technique[a] of Intervention*	*Sample Size*	*Scientific Methods Score*	*Follow-up[b] and Results[c]*	*Benefits Measured*	*Benefit-Cost Ratio[d]*
Ekblom, Law and Sutton (1996). Safer Cities Programme. England and Wales	Burglary	Home	1–2 years; target hardening (locks, alarms, entry systems)	7,500 households	4 (before-after, experimental-control, and statistical analysis)	Immediate outcome: burglary+	Crime victim expenses (person, direct), criminal justice system (police)	1.83
Painter and Farrington (1997). Dudley, England	Property and personal crime in general	Residential streets	1 year; natural surveillance (streetlighting)	1,200 homes	4 (before-after, experimental-control, and statistical analysis)	Immediate outcoome: burglary+, theft+, vandalism+, vehicle theft+, personal crime+	Crime victim expenses (person, direct), criminal justice system (police)	4.34
Painter and Farrington (1996b). Stoke-on-Trent, England	Property and personal crime in general	Residential streets and footpaths	1 year; natural surveillance (streetlighting)	756 homes	4 (before-after, experimental-control, and statistical analysis)	Immediate outcoome: burglary+, theft+, vandalism+, vehicle theft+, personal crime+	Crime victim expenses (person, direct), criminal justice system (police)	2.93

[a]Based on Clarke and Homel's (1997) classification.
[b]The period of time in which the program effects were evaluated after the intervention had ended.
[c]'0' = no intervention effects, '+' = desirable intervention effects.
[d]Expressed as a ratio of benefits to costs in monetary units (national currencies).

SOURCE:

versal" design. Three of the thirteen studies used a methodologically sophisticated quasi-experimental evaluation design, comparing experimental and control units before and after, with control of extraneous variables in a regression analysis, and each was assigned a score of four on the scientific methods scale. Twelve of the thirteen studies reported a successful crime-reducing effect of the intervention (all except Schnelle et al. 1979).

Although not included in Table 3.2, it is important to mention briefly two important issues of situational crime prevention: displacement and diffusion of benefits.[4] Displacement is often defined as the unintended increase in targeted crimes in other locations following the introduction of a crime reduction scheme (see Barr and Pease 1990, for a discussion of "benign" effects of displacement). Five different forms of displacement have been identified by Reppetto (1976): temporal (change in time), tactical (change in method), target (change in victim), territorial (change in place), and functional (change in type of crime). Diffusion of benefits is defined as the unintended decrease in nontargeted crimes following a crime reduction scheme, or the "complete reverse" of displacement (Clarke and Weisburd 1994). Eight of the studies rigorously investigated the possibility of displacement following the introduction of the prevention measures, and four studies (Forrester et al. 1990; Poyner 1992; Davidson and Farr 1994; Painter and Farrington 1999b) considered the possibility of diffusion of benefits.

Summary of Benefit-Cost Findings

Nine of the thirteen studies carried out some form of economic analysis, whereas the other four merely provided cost and benefit data. The benefits that were measured by the studies were largely confined to decreases in direct or tangible costs for crime victims[5] and, to a lesser extent, decreased criminal justice system costs (see Table 3.2). A desirable benefit-cost ratio was calculated in eight of the thirteen studies. In these eight studies the measured economic return on a one-monetary unit investment ranged from a low of 1.31 units to a high of 5.04 units. For the five projects that showed an undesirable benefit-cost ratio, the economic return on a one-unit investment ranged from a low of 0.32 units to a high of 0.78 units. Seven of the eight studies published in 1990 or later yielded a desirable benefit-cost ratio, compared with only one of the five earlier studies.

Comparisons of the studies' benefit-cost ratios with both the primary intervention technique employed and the primary crime targeted by the intervention revealed no consistent findings. The three primary intervention techniques used in the majority of studies (nine of thirteen)—employee surveillance, formal surveillance, and natural surveillance—produced a desirable benefit-cost ratio in five of the nine studies. The two studies that employed target hardening as the primary intervention technique (Clarke and McGrath 1990; Ekblom, Law, and Sutton 1996) produced desirable benefit-cost ratios. For the eleven studies that targeted a primary type of crime (the improved-streetlighting studies by Painter and Farrington 1997 and 1999a, targeted property and personal crimes in general), no clear relationship was found between type of crime and the studies' benefit-cost ratios. In the four projects that addressed burglary as the primary crime, there were an equal number of desirable and undesirable benefit-cost ratios. For vandalism, three out of the five studies (Skilton 1988; Poyner 1992; Knight 1994) that targeted this crime produced desirable benefit-cost ratios.

From the available evidence, it appears that situational prevention can be an economically efficient strategy for the reduction of crime, but it is difficult to draw any general, substantive conclusions about what works most cost-effectively to reduce crime. That is to say, it is not clear if a particular type of intervention works best with a particular type of crime or in a specific time and place. This is not surprising considering the highly specific nature of situational crime prevention and its wide-reaching targets. On the latter point, Clarke (1995a, 56) notes that "situational prevention is assumed to be applicable to every kind of crime, not just to 'opportunistic' or acquisitive property offenses, but also to more calculated or deeply-motivated offenses." The evaluation literature on situational prevention provides some support for this assertion (e.g., Eck 1997; Homel et al. 1997).

Crime-specific reviews of situational prevention provide some conclusive findings about what works most effectively, which is helpful in thinking about why a program did or did not produce a desirable economic result. For instance, the failure and undesirable benefit-cost ratio of the armed robbery intervention program reported by Schnelle et al. (1979), which involved the use of silent alarms transmitted to police, is not at all surprising. This is because the literature on commercial robbery prevention (see Hunter and Jeffery 1992) suggests that a multilevel combination of situational interventions (e.g., two store clerks and security cameras) is needed to have any effect on this category of crime. On their own, alarms are an ineffective situational measure in the prevention of commercial robberies.

Aside from the limitations that are also evident in reviews of the monetary costs and benefits of developmental prevention and correctional intervention, two limitations are specific to the situational prevention studies we reviewed. First, there is almost a complete absence of follow-up of program effects. Follow-up research is needed to establish how far the effects (and benefits) persist after the program ends. This is also important for assessing how the benefit-cost ratio varies over time (see Welsh and Farrington 1998). Second, there are a number of methodological problems associated with the research designs of the studies. Few used experimental-control, before-after designs, which are needed to eliminate threats to internal validity. Ideally, randomized experimental designs should be used by researchers to test the merits of situational crime prevention programs. It is important to note, however, that it is difficult to assess program effects using randomized designs where the units of interest are areas, as opposed to individuals (Farrington 1997).

Stoke-on-Trent Improved-Streetlighting Project

The city of Stoke-on-Trent, located in the North Midlands of England, was the site of an empirical study to test a number of theory-based issues linking "street lighting, the urban environment and resident dynamics with the incidence of crime" (Painter and Farrington 1999b, 6). Through a program of improved streetlighting, initiated in late 1992, it was hypothesized that crime would decrease in the experimental area, not only after dark but also during the daylight hours. This represents a replication of the earlier streetlighting project carried out in Dudley, England (Painter and Farrington 1997). The Stoke-on-Trent study examined the situational crime prevention technique of natural surveillance.

Research design and methodology. The study employed a quasi-experimental design, using before and after measures in three types of comparison areas: experimental, control, and adjacent. The adjacent area was not clearly distinct from the experimental area. In the experimental area streetlighting was improved, whereas in the control and adjacent areas the lighting remained unchanged. Victimization surveys were carried out in all three areas and measured the prevalence (percentage of households victimized in the last year) and incidence (average number of victimizations per hundred households) of crime during two identical time intervals: one year prior to the installation of the improved streetlighting and one year after. The unit of analysis was the household.

The lighting improvement scheme in the experimental area involved the following components: Preexisting streetlighting was upgraded to the medium standard as defined by British Standard (preexisting lighting failed to meet the minimum standard), and lighting was installed in previously unlit detached footpaths. The experimental area was chosen for the relighting scheme by the city council based on its perceived need.

Unlike the experimental and adjacent areas, the experimental and control areas were physically separate, thereby limiting the possibility of any program contamination effects in the control area. The sociodemographic profile of the three different areas (experimental, control, and adjacent) showed a nonsignificant variation. Differences did exist between the experimental and control areas on reported prevalence of victimization in the previous year; no differences were evident on the same measure between the experimental and adjacent areas.

Program effects. A number of substantial crime reduction benefits were achieved after one year of the improved-streetlighting scheme. The experimental area showed statistically significant reductions in the prevalence of all crime categories,[6] with the exception of burglary. One-quarter (25.8 percent) fewer households in the experimental area were victimized of any crime from the before to after periods (57.7 percent to 42.8 percent), whereas in the adjacent area, one-fifth (21.2 percent) fewer households were victimized of any crime (55.6 percent to 43.8 percent). The same comparison for the control area showed a 12.3 percent increase in victimization (34.1 percent to 38.3 percent).

Changes in the incidence of crime from before to after the introduction of the prevention scheme were also found to be highly desirable in the experimental and adjacent areas. Statistically significant decreases were shown in the incidence of property crime, personal crime, and all crime for both the experimental and the adjacent areas, with the largest change being a 68.0 percent reduction in personal crime in the experimental area (43.8 percent to 14.0 percent). The control area showed a slight decrease in the incidence of all crime (-2.0 percent) with a high decrease in the incidence of vehicle crime (-34.7 percent) and personal crime (-39.2 percent), and a high increase in outside theft and vandalism (+32.6 percent).

When differences in the pretest victimization rates (prevalence and incidence) in all three areas were controlled, it was found that crime decreased significantly in the experimental and adjacent areas compared to the control area. No evidence of displacement was found in the adjacent area, but there was strong evidence that the improvements in streetlighting produced a substantial diffusion of benefits to this area.

Benefit-cost results. A benefit-cost analysis was carried out on the program's effects on the four categories of crimes in the experimental and adjacent areas and reported in 1993 British pounds. Total costs of the program were estimated at £8,952 per year. This was derived by adding together the increased maintenance (£157) and electrical energy (£945) costs of the lighting scheme to the annual debt payment on the capital expenditure (£7,850). The total capital cost of the scheme was £77,071. The annual debt payment was calculated on the basis of a fixed interest rate of eight percent over a period of twenty years, which was considered a reasonable life expectancy of the scheme.

Total benefits from crimes prevented in the experimental and adjacent areas were estimated at £228,747. In the experimental area, 266 prevented crimes translated into a tangible savings of £103,495, or 45.2 percent of the total monetary benefits produced by the scheme. In the adjacent area, 428.8 prevented crimes translated into a tangible savings of £125,252, or the remaining 54.8 percent of the total benefits.

Benefits from crimes prevented were calculated in two stages. First, U.K. estimates on the cost of property loss to crime victims, drawn from the 1993 *Criminal Statistics* (Home Office 1994), were calculated for the property crimes prevented in the experimental area. Second, in the absence of U.K. data on the full tangible costs of property crimes and the costs of personal crimes altogether, U.S. estimates[7] were used to scale-up property loss figures, as well as provide for the costs of personal crimes prevented in the experimental area. Also, the number of crimes prevented in the experimental area was scaled-up to the total number of occupied homes in the area.

Just considering the benefits produced in the experimental area, where it is more likely that the effects produced are attributable to the program, the improved-lighting scheme managed to recover the full annual costs, not to mention the capital costs, in the first year. Adding the benefits accrued from the effects of improved lighting in the adjacent area increased substantially the total recovered (total benefits minus total costs). It is more conservative to include the full capital cost of the scheme in an assessment of program efficiency, and this was £78,173 in the first year (£77,071 + £945 + £157). Dividing total benefits (£228,747) by total costs (£78,173) produced a desirable benefit-cost ratio of 2.93. This means that for each pound invested in the improved-lighting scheme, £2.93 was saved to the local council and victims of crime.

Correctional Intervention

Correctional intervention attempts to modify offender behavior through some combination of treatment and external controls (Palmer 1992). Treatment, according to Palmer, attempts to "affect the individual's future behavior, attitudes toward self, and interactions with others by focusing on such factors and conditions as the individual's adjustment techniques, interests, skills, personal limitations, and/or life circumstances" (1992, 3). In this chapter, correctional intervention is mainly concerned with offender treatment.

Offender treatment programs serve many purposes, and, as a result, their effectiveness can be measured using many different outcomes. Three main outcomes can be delineated: (1) to decrease offending behavior in the community; (2) to increase the offender's psychological and social adjustment within the institution (e.g., to reduce suicide and self-harm) (Skett 1995, 20); and (3) to improve other life-course outcomes, such as education, employment, health, relationships, and social service use.

Unlike the two other crime prevention strategies covered in this chapter, a great deal has been published on the application of economic evaluation techniques to correctional intervention. However, the overwhelming majority of these studies have consisted of statistical modeling exercises and analyses of hypothetical examples of correctional practices (e.g., Hofler and Witte 1979; Greenwood et al. 1994), and cost and cost-effectiveness analyses. The former have not been included here because they are not real-life programs, whereas the latter have been excluded because they do not provide an assessment of economic benefits, only of costs.

Seven correctional intervention studies meeting the criteria for inclusion were identified. Table 3.3 summarizes key features of the seven studies. The studies were published between 1974 and 1994, and all were carried out in the United States. Interventions were provided to a wide age range of subjects. Targeted offending behaviors included burglary, child molestation, and substance abuse. In six of the seven studies, the community was the setting for treatment; however, in three of these six (Pearson 1988; Gray and Olson 1989; Gerstein et al. 1994), treatment was also administered in institutional or residential settings. The sample size at the start of treatment ranged from 112 to 3,055 subjects.

Across the studies, there were few similarities in the type of primary treatment employed. As shown in Table 3.3, some of the different types of interventions included pretrial diversion, employment, and intensive supervision. Two of the studies (Austin 1986; Gerstein et al. 1994) did not evaluate correctional treatment per se. In the study by Austin (1986), the decision to release offenders from prison prior to the expiration of the prison sentence may not be a correctional intervention, but it does represent an alternative to incarceration that has received some consideration. In the study by Gerstein et al. (1994), which evaluated alcohol and drug abuse prevention services throughout California, not all of the participating subjects were under the authority of the Department of Corrections at the time of treatment. We decided to include these two studies partly because of the paucity of benefit-cost research on correctional intervention. Few similarities were also shown in the duration of treatment, which ranged from 2.8 months to 5.1 years, for the five studies that reported this information.

Five of the seven studies used an experimental evaluation design to evaluate program effects, although one of these five (Prentky and Burgess 1990) used a nonequivalent (retrospectively selected) control group. The study by Friedman (1977), which was aimed at reintegrating former offenders and drug addicts into the community through the provision of paid employment and aftercare (e.g., methadone maintenance for ex-addicts), employed random assignment to experimental and control conditions. Across the seven studies, the mean score on the scientific methods scale was 2.86, with three studies (Gray and Olson 1989; Prentky and Burgess 1990; Gerstein et al. 1994) having a score of 2.

Gray and Olson (1989) did not present before-after changes in offending, nor did other published papers on this study (Haynes and Larsen 1984; Gray et al. 1991; Gray 1994). Each of the other six studies that reported treatment effects assessed recidivism, and, in each case, the first rearrest or reconviction was the measure of recidivism used. The length of follow-up ranged from twelve months to twenty-five years, with two studies (Pearson 1988; Gray and Olson 1989) not reporting this information. Overall, treatment effects on recidivism were desirable. For example, Project Crossroads (Holahan 1974), which provided first-time property offenders with a range of short-term (three months) supportive services (e.g., counseling, job training, remedial education) in lieu of traditional criminal justice processing, achieved a 28.6 percent reduction in the rate of recidivism twelve months posttreatment (26.0 percent for the treatment group versus 36.4 percent for the control group), and New Jersey's Intensive Supervision Program (Pearson 1988; Pearson and Harper 1990) produced lower conviction rates for the treatment compared to the control group (12 percent versus 23 percent) after an unspecified period of time. As illustrated in Table 3.3, desirable program effects were also found for other outcomes, such as employment, health, and social service use, but two studies (Friedman 1977; Gerstein et al. 1994) reported undesirable program effects in some of these areas.

Summary of Benefit-Cost Findings

Six of the studies carried out a benefit-cost analysis. The seventh study (Pearson 1988) carried out a cost analysis, but published data that enabled us to calculate benefits and hence a benefit-cost ratio. Benefits realized by the correctional intervention programs included costs avoided by the criminal justice system and crime victims, increased employment

TABLE 3.3 Summary of Correctional Intervention Studies

Authors, Project Name, Place	*Age at Intervention*	*Targeted Offending Behavior*	*Context of Intervention*	*Duration and Primary Type of Intervention*	*Sample Size*	*Scientific Methods Score*	*Follow-up[a] and Results[b]*	*Benefits Measured*	*Benefit-Cost Ratio[c]*
Holahan (1974). Project Crossroads, Washington, D.C.	18–15 years	Property offending in general	Community	3 months; pretrial diversion with counseling, job training, and remedial education	307 adults; T=200 C=107	3 (before-after, experimental-control)	12 months: police arrests+,	Crime victim expenses (direct), criminal justice system, employment earnings	2.36
Friedman (1977). Supported Work Social Experiment, New York, N.Y.	32 years (average; T only)	n.a.	Community	8 months; (average); empolyment	229 adults; T=120, C=109[d]	5 (randomized experiment)	16 months (average): police arrests+ social service use+, employment+, health–, education–	Crime victim expenses, criminal justice system, employment earnings, social service use, public goods and services	1.40
Austin (1986). Early Release Program, Ill.	19–40 years (87.9% of sample)	Criminal offending in general	Community	Not applicable; early release	1,557 adults and youths; T=1,202 C=355	3 (before-after, experimental-control)	2.5 years: police arrests+	Criminal justice system	2.82

Pearson (1988). New Jersey Intensive Supervision Program	n.a.	Nonviolent offending in general	Community, institution	18 months (average); employment, intensive supervision, incapacitation	686 adults; T=554, C=132	3 (before-after, experimental-control)	n.a.: convictions+, institution time+	Criminal justice system, community service work, employment earnings	1.48
Gray and Olson (1989). Ariz.	18–44 years (median= 23 years)	Burglary	Community, institution	n.a.; multiple services, deterrence, incapitation, rehabilitation	112 adults	2 (before-after)	n.a.	n.a.	Probation 1.70 Prison=0.24 Jail=0.17
Pentky and Burgess (1990). Mass.	n.a.	Child molestation	Institution (maximum security)	5.1 years (median); rehabilitation[e]	182 individuals; T=129 (adults), C=53	2 (before-after, experimental-control, retrospectively chosen C)	5 and 25 years: victim-involved sexual offenses (15 charges)+	Crime victim expenses (direct), criminal justice system	1.16
Gerstein et al. (1994). California Drug and Alcohol Treatment Assessment	33.3 years (mean)	Criminal offending and substance abuse in general	Community, residential	2.8 months (mean); substance abuse (4 modalities)	3,055 adults	2 (before-after)	15 months (average): criminal activity+, substance abuse+, health+, social service use+, employment-	Crime victim expenses (direct), criminal justice system, employment earnings, public health care	7.14

[a]The period of time in which the progran effects were evaluated after the intervention had ended.

[b]'0' = no intervention effects, '+' = desirable intervention effects.

[c]Expressed as a ratio of benefits to costs in monetary units (national currencies).

[d]This comprises the remaining sample after two years from the start of the program; no information was provided on the sample at the onset of intervention.

[e]No Information was provided on the type of rehabilitation used.

NOTES: T = treatment group, C = control group, n.a. = not available.

earnings, and savings to public health care and welfare. All seven studies showed a desirable benefit-cost ratio. One of these seven (Gray and Olson 1989) calculated benefit-cost ratios for each of the three treatments being compared (one desirable and two undesirable; see Table 3.3). For the purposes of this discussion, only the desirable ratio for probation is considered, because probation more closely fits our concern with correctional (rehabilitative) intervention than does prison or jail (the other two treatments). For the seven studies, the benefit-cost ratios ranged from a low of 1.13 to a high of 7.14, meaning that for each dollar spent on the programs, the public (government/taxpayer and crime victim) received in return $1.13 to $7.14 in various savings.

No significant patterns emerge from a comparison among key features of the seven studies and their benefit-cost ratios. Some findings are, however, noteworthy. The two studies with the largest sample sizes (Austin 1986; Gerstein et al. 1994) produced the highest benefit-cost ratios: 2.82 and 7.14, respectively. However, the study with the largest sample size (Gerstein et al. 1994) used a comparatively weak evaluation design, relying on before-after measures with no control group. Also, a reduced sample size of unknown magnitude was used to estimate economic benefits. For the study by Austin (1986), which used an experimental-control design, the benefit-cost analysis was based on the treatment group only. This had the dual effect of reducing the sample size (from 1,557 to 1,202) and reducing confidence one can place in the program's reported benefit-cost findings.

A notable feature of all studies is the omission of indirect or intangible costs to victims of crime (e.g., pain, suffering, lost quality of life, fear of future victimization) in the benefit-cost calculations. In five of the seven studies,[8] the monetary costs to crime victims were limited to out-of-pocket expenses, such as property loss and damage and medical expenses. To be fair to the authors, the majority acknowledged the difficulties involved in assessing and quantifying in monetary terms intangible costs to crime victims. These difficulties include the lack of existing estimates of the intangible costs to victims of crime, which first appeared in the published literature in Cohen (1988), and the doubts of many researchers about the validity of these costs or the underlying theory used in their calculation or both (Zimring and Hawkins 1995, 138).

The importance of assessing and quantifying intangible costs to crime victims in benefit-cost analyses was illustrated in Cohen's (1988) reanalysis of Austin's (1986) benefit-cost calculations. For example, Cohen estimated that the average rape cost $51,058 (in 1985 dollars), made up of three main components: direct losses, $4,617; pain, suffering, and fear of injury, $43,561; and risk of death, $2,880. Adding the pain and suffering cost component to Austin's (1986) estimates of the direct losses incurred by crime victims, while maintaining the other costs, increased the total costs of the early-release program[9] to approximately $110 million (Cohen 1988, 550), a sixfold increase. This resulted in a reversal of the benefit-cost findings, from producing a dividend on public expenditure (a benefit-cost ratio of 2.82) to a loss or an undesirable benefit-cost ratio of 0.45 ($49 million divided by $110 million). Austin's findings have been presented in Table 3.3, because in most of the studies insufficient data were provided to allow for any recalculation of costs or benefits.

It is noteworthy that four of the seven studies (Holahan 1974; Friedman 1977; Pearson 1988; Gerstein et al. 1994) assessed and quantified in monetary terms outcomes other than recidivism. Education, employment, health, social service use, and illicit substance use were the different kinds of outcomes monetized in these studies. In two of these four studies (Friedman 1977; Pearson 1988), benefits from improvements in these outcomes exceeded benefits from reduced recidivism. Although far from conclusive, this is an important finding because it suggests that correctional intervention programs have the potential to influence other important areas of an offender's life and produce, in some cases, substantial economic returns for publicly funded services such as health and welfare.

New York City Supported Work Social Experiment

First started in 1972 in New York City and then expanded to other U.S. cities, the Supported Work social experiment was aimed at reintegrating former offenders and drug addicts into the community through the provision of paid employment and aftercare (e.g., methadone maintenance for ex-addicts). A "reasonable wage, working with peers, and flexible length of time in the program [were] intended to create a low-stress, rehabilitative environment" (Friedman 1977, 148). The main goals of the program were to deliver public services (e.g., work in libraries, painting, newspaper recycling), to reduce crime, to improve the health and well-being of clients, to reduce social service use, and to increase unsupported employment (non-wage-controlled jobs in the public and private sectors) after the program.

Research design and methodology. A randomized experiment was used to test the effectiveness of the Supported Work program. Eligible candidates were randomly assigned either to the treatment group who received the program (the approximately three hundred employment positions filled in the program's first year) or to the control group who did not. The exact number of individuals in the treatment and control groups at the start of the study was not reported by the author. The criteria for ex-addict admission to the program included: enrollment in a drug treatment program for a minimum of three months, eligibility to receive federal Supplemental Security Income benefits, and unemployment for at least twelve months in the previous two years.

Characteristics of the treatment and control groups prior to the start of the program were not provided. Instead, some characteristics were aggregated to give an overall picture of the two groups together. For example, their average numbers of prior arrests and criminal convictions were 8.2 and 4.5, respectively. The following are some of the characteristics of the treatment group prior to the start of the program: 92 percent were male, half were single, the average age was thirty-two, three-fourths had not completed high school, and 80 percent had not been employed in the previous six months. The program lasted an average of eight months, and follow-up data were available for an average of sixteen months from the time the program ended. Although the author claimed that a sample retention rate of approximately 90 percent was achieved two years after the start of the program (Friedman 1977, 159), information on program effects and economic efficiency was based on only 120 treatment- and 109 control-group members. Data sources used to evaluate the program included extensive annual and quarterly supplemental interviews with the experimental and control groups, and official documentation, such as police and welfare records.

Program effects. The Supported Work program was assessed on six criteria: criminal activity, education, employment, health, participation in drug treatment programs, and social service use. Observed differences between the treatment and control groups were found on all of the outcome variables with the exception of participation in drug treatment programs. At sixteen months' follow-up, program effects on the outcomes of criminal activity, employment, and social service use favored the treatment over the control group, whereas the control group fared better on the outcomes of health and education. For criminal activity, the average treatment-group member was arrested 0.05 fewer times per year than the average control-group member, an insignificant difference. More substantial, desirable differences were evident for social service use ($1,797 less) and employment earnings ($3,289 more) over the course of a year for the average experimental compared to the average control. For education, the average control was enrolled longer per year in vocational programs than the average experimental (1.97 versus 0.25 weeks). The number of weeks of enrollment per year in college and high school equivalency courses was higher for experimentals than controls, but only marginally.

Benefit-cost results. A rigorous benefit-cost analysis was carried out. Costs and benefits (in 1974 U.S. dollars) were estimated only for the (average) eight months of the program. Four benefit-cost calculations were presented, each concerned with different recipients of benefits and costs of the Supported Work program. The four perspectives and their central interests were as follows:

1. society: Is society as a whole more efficient with or without the program?
2. taxpayer or nonprogram participant: How much do taxpayers have to pay to operate the program, and how much do they receive from it?
3. welfare department (a principal funding agency of the program): How much would have been paid out in welfare funds without the program? and
4. participant: What do participants have to give up to enter the program, and what do they get in return? (Friedman 1977, 163–64).

To maintain consistency in the reporting of benefit-cost findings, only the perspective of the taxpayer (including victims) is discussed here. The taxpayer perspective includes the welfare department perspective, by virtue of the welfare department being a publicly funded institution.

The Supported Work program produced a dividend for the taxpaying public. For each dollar the public invested in the program it received $1.13 in return—a desirable benefit-cost ratio of 1.13. Total program costs and benefits, expressed as per treated person per year, were estimated at $6,131 and $6,920, respectively. Total program benefits were derived from: savings in public goods and services, $4,519; reduction in social service or welfare use, $1,797; increased income tax, $311; and reduced crime, $293 ($86 in savings to the criminal justice system and $207 in savings to crime victims). Disappointingly, no information was provided about how the benefits from reduced crime were calculated.

Discussion and Conclusion

This chapter reviewed research on the monetary costs and benefits of three principal crime prevention strategies: developmental prevention, situational prevention, and correctional intervention. It was not possible to determine which of the strategies produced the greatest economic return on investment. This was because of the small number of studies identified (and reviewed here), the varied methodological rigor of the program evaluations and benefit-cost analyses, and limited or missing information in the studies.

This review also has a number of other important limitations. Benefits tended to be estimated conservatively, whereas costs were often taken into account in full. And different perspectives (e.g., public, society) were used in the benefit-cost analyses so that the parties who were the recipients of the monetary benefits or losses were not always comparable. For many of the studies it was not possible to disaggregate the benefit-cost findings to provide a consistent perspective across the studies. As far as possible, we used the public perspective.

These problems aside, there are, nevertheless, a number of important points worth drawing attention to with respect to the independent and comparative economic efficiency of the three crime prevention approaches. First, each of the three strategies demonstrates value for money. Lower offending rates, fewer victims of crime, and improvements in such areas as education, health, and employment were some of the benefits produced by the programs under these strategies. Second, for situational prevention and correctional intervention programs it appears more likely that benefits will exceed costs in the short-term, whereas for (early-childhood) developmental prevention programs there is a greater chance that benefits will not begin to surpass costs until the medium- to long-term. In this sense, the different strategies seem to complement one another. Third, developmental prevention and, to a lesser extent, correctional intervention provide important monetary benefits beyond reduced crime. These monetary benefits can take the form of, for example, increased tax revenues from higher earnings, savings from reduced usage of social services, and savings from less health care utilization. The benefits of situational prevention, on the other hand, appear to be largely confined to reduced crime. However, this may be because only crime was measured in situational evaluations.

An emphasis on high-quality testing coupled with rigorous and comprehensive benefit-cost analyses of crime prevention programs will contribute greatly to the state of knowledge on the monetary value of preventing crime—helping to inform important research and policy questions.

Notes

1. Sherman et al. (1997) did not take account of differences between individual- and area-level studies. As noted in Chapter 1, it is very difficult to randomly assign areas to experimental and control conditions and analyze them as such. It could be argued that the "gold standard" for area evaluation designs should be level 4.

2. In the study by Sherman et al. (1997), external validity played a role in the final determination of what worked, what did not work, and what was promising. For example, in order for a type of crime prevention program, such as juvenile boot camps, to be classified as working, one of the criteria was that there had to be at least two level 3 evaluations with statistical significance tests showing effectiveness (Sherman and Gottfredson 1997, A–4).

3. Karoly et al. (1998) report on analyses of higher- (unmarried and low SES) and lower- (two-parent or higher SES) risk families, whereas Olds et al. (1993) report on analyses of higher-risk families and the sample as a whole (higher- plus lower-risk families).

4. These issues are not unique to situational crime prevention, but also apply to, at least, community crime prevention and law-enforcement prevention (e.g., tough drug-law enforcement in a city may shift drug dealing to the surrounding county). They are discussed here because of their prominence in the situational crime prevention literature.

5. In Table 3.2, we distinguish between the crime victim as a person/household, private sector (e.g., business), or public sector (e.g., government department).

6. Four categories of crime were delineated: "(1) burglary (including attempts); (2) theft outside the home, vandalism of the home or bicycle theft; (3) theft of or from vehicles or damage to vehicles; and (4) personal crime: robbery, snatch theft, assault, threatening behavior, sexual assault or sexual pestering" (Painter and Farrington 1997, 219).

7. Tangible costs of crime were taken from Miller, Cohen, and Wiersema (1996) and included: "property loss and damage, medical and mental health costs, police and fire services (but not other criminal justice) costs, social and victim services costs and lost productivity" (Painter and Farrington 1999b, 32).

8. One study (Friedman 1977) did not explain the type of victim costs quantified, whereas the other (Pearson 1988) did not assess or quantify victim costs.

9. Costs of the program were made up of criminal justice reprocessing of recidivists (e.g., arrest, prosecution), parole supervision of early releasees, and direct costs to crime victims (caused by early releasees).

References

Austin, J. 1986. Using early release to relieve prison crowding: A dilemma in public policy. *Crime and Delinquency* 32: 404–502.

Barr, R., and Pease, K. 1990. Crime placement, displacement, and deflection. In M. Tonry and N. Morris, eds., *Crime and justice: A review of research: Vol. 12*, 277–318. Chicago: University of Chicago Press.

Bridgeman, C. 1996. *Crime risk management: Making it work*. London: Home Office.

Burrows, J. 1991. *Making crime prevention pay: Initiatives from business*. London: Home Office.

Cirel, P., Evans, P., McGillis, D., and Whitcomb, D. 1977. *An exemplary project: Community crime prevention*. Washington, D.C.: National Criminal Justice Reference Service.

Clarke, R. V. 1992. Introduction to R. V. Clarke, ed., *Situational crime prevention: Successful case studies,* 3–36. Albany, N.Y.: Harrow and Heston.

______. 1993. Fare evasion and automatic ticket collection on the London Underground. In R. V. Clarke, ed., *Crime prevention studies: Vol. 1,* 135–46. Monsey, N.Y.: Criminal Justice Press.

______. 1995a. Opportunity-reducing crime prevention strategies and the role of motivation. In P.-O. H. Wikström, R. V. Clarke, and J. McCord, eds., *Integrating crime prevention strategies: Propensity and opportunity,* 55–67. Stockholm: National Council for Crime Prevention.

______. 1995b. Situational crime prevention. In M. Tonry and D. P. Farrington, eds., *Building a safer society: Strategic approaches to crime prevention.* Vol. 19 of *Crime and justice: A review of research,* 91–150. Chicago: University of Chicago Press.

______, ed. 1997. *Situational crime prevention: Successful case studies.* 2d ed. Guilderland, N.Y.: Harrow and Heston.

Clarke, R. V., and Homel, R. 1997. A revised classification of situational crime prevention techniques. In S. P. Lab, ed., *Crime prevention at a crossroads,* 17–27. Cincinnati: Anderson.

Clarke, R. V., and McGrath, G. 1990. Cash reduction and robbery prevention in Australian betting shops. *Security Journal* 1: 160–63.

Clarke, R. V., and Weisburd, D. 1994. Diffusion of crime control benefits: Observations on the reverse of displacement. In R. V. Clarke, ed., *Crime prevention studies: Vol. 2,* 165–83. Monsey, N.Y.: Criminal Justice Press.

Clarke, R. V., Cody, R. P., and Natarajan, M. 1994. Subway slugs: Tracking displacement on the London Underground. *British Journal of Criminology* 34: 122–38.

Cohen, M. A. 1988. Pain, suffering, and jury awards: A study of the cost of crime to victims. *Law and Society Review* 22: 537–55.

Coopers and Lybrand. 1994. *Preventative strategy for young people in trouble.* London: ITV Telethon, The Prince's Trust.

Davidson, J., and Farr, J. 1994. Mitchellhill Estate: Estate based management (concierge) initiative. In S. Osborn, ed., *Housing safe communities: An evaluation of recent initiatives,* 22–33. London: Safe Neighbourhoods Unit.

DiLonardo, R. L. 1996. Defining and measuring the economic benefit of electronic article surveillance. *Security Journal* 7: 3–9.

Earle, R. B. 1995. Helping to prevent child abuse—and future consequences: Hawaii Healthy Start. *Program Focus,* October. Washington, D.C.: National Institute of Justice, U.S. Department of Justice.

Eck, J. E. 1997. Preventing crime at places. In L. W. Sherman, D. C. Gottfredson, D. L. MacKenzie, J. E. Eck, P. Reuter, and S. D. Bushway. *Preventing crime: What works, what doesn't, what's promising,* chap. 7, pp. 1–62. Washington, D.C.: National Institute of Justice, U.S. Department of Justice.

Ekblom, P., Law, H., and Sutton, M. 1996. *Safer cities and domestic burglary.* London: Home Office.

Farrington, D. P. 1996. The explanation and prevention of youthful offending. In J. D. Hawkins, ed., *Delinquency and crime: Current theories,* 68–148. New York: Cambridge University Press.

______. 1997. Evaluating a community crime prevention program. *Evaluation* 3: 157–73.

Field, S. 1993. Crime prevention and the costs of auto theft: An economic analysis. In R. V. Clarke, ed., *Crime prevention studies, Vol. 1*: 69–91. Monsey, N.Y.: Criminal Justice Press.

Forrester, D., Frenz, S., O'Connell, M., and Pease, K. 1990. *The Kirkholt burglary prevention project: Phase II*. London: Home Office.

Friedman, L. S. 1977. An interim evaluation of the Supported Work experiment. *Policy Analysis* 3: 147–70.

Gerstein, D. R., Johnson, R. A., Harwood, H. J., Fountain, D., Suter, N., and Malloy, K. 1994. *Evaluating recovery services: The California Drug and Alcohol Treatment Assessment (CALDATA)*. Sacramento: Department of Alcohol and Drug Programs.

Gray, T. 1994. Research note: Using cost-benefit analysis to measure rehabilitation and special deterrence. *Journal of Criminal Justice* 22: 569–75.

Gray, T., and Olson, K. W. 1989. A cost-benefit analysis of the sentencing decision for burglars. *Social Science Quarterly* 70, 708–22.

Gray, T., Larsen, C. R., Haynes, P., and Olson, K. W. 1991. Using cost-benefit analysis to evaluate correctional sentences. *Evaluation Review* 15: 471–81.

Greenwood, P. W., Rydell, C. P., Abrahamse, A. F., Caulkins, J. P., Chiesa, J., Model, K. E., and Klein, S. P. 1994. *Three strikes and you're out: Estimated benefits and costs of California's new mandatory-sentencing law*. Santa Monica, Calif.: RAND.

Hahn, A. 1994. *Evaluation of the Quantum Opportunities Program (QOP): Did the program work?* Waltham, Mass.: Heller Graduate School, Center for Human Resources, Brandeis University.

Hakim, S., Gaffney, M. A., Rengert, G., and Shachmurove, J. 1995. Costs and benefits of alarms to the community: Burglary patterns and security measures in Tredyffrin Township, Pennsylvania. *Security Journal* 6, 197–204.

Haynes, P., and Larsen, C. R. 1984. Financial consequences of incarceration and alternatives: Burglary. *Crime and Delinquency* 30, 529–50.

Hofler, R. A., and Witte, A. D. 1979. Benefit-cost analysis of the sentencing decision: The case of homicide. In C. M. Gray, ed., *The costs of crime*, 165–86. Beverly Hills, Calif.: Sage Publications.

Holahan, J. 1974. Measuring benefits from prison reform. In R. H. Haveman, A. C. Harberger, L. E. Lynn, W. A. Niskanen, R. Turvey, and R. Zeckhauser, eds., *Benefit-cost and policy analysis 1973: An Aldine annual on forecasting, decision-making, and evaluation*, 491–516. Chicago: Aldine.

Homel, R., Hauritz, M., McIlwain, G., Wortley, R., and Carvolth, R. 1997. Preventing drunkenness and violence around nightclubs in a tourist resort. In R. V. Clarke, ed., *Situational crime prevention: Successful case studies*, 263–82. 2d ed. Guilderland, N.Y.: Harrow and Heston.

Home Office. 1994. *Criminal statistics, England and Wales, 1993*. London: Her Majesty's Stationery Office.

Hunter, R. D., and Jeffery, C. R. 1992. Preventing convenience store robbery through environmental design. In R. V. Clarke, ed., *Situational crime prevention: Successful case studies*, 194–204. Albany, N.Y.: Harrow and Heston.

Jones, M. B., and Offord, D. R. 1989. Reduction of antisocial behaviour in poor children by nonschool skill development. *Journal of Child Psychology and Psychiatry* 30, 737–50.

Karoly, L. A., Greenwood, P. W., Everingham, S. S., Houbé, J., Kilburn, M. R., Rydell, C. P., Sanders, M., and Chiesa, J. 1998. *Investing in our children: What we know and don't know about the costs and benefits of early childhood interventions.* Santa Monica, Calif.: RAND.

Kitzman, H., Olds, D. L., Henderson, C. R., Hanks, C., Cole, R., Tatelbaum, R., McConnochie, K. M., Sidora, K., Luckey, D. W., Shaver, D., Engelhardt, K., James, D., and Barnard, K. 1997. Effect of prenatal and infancy home visitation by nurses on pregnancy outcomes, childhood injuries, and repeated childbearing: A randomized controlled trial. *Journal of the American Medical Association* 278, 644–52.

Knight, B. 1994. Possil Park estate: Security scheme. In S. Osborn, ed., *Housing safe communities: An evaluation of recent initiatives,* 88–95. London: Safe Neighbourhoods Unit.

Lally, J. R., Mangione, P. L., and Honig, A. S. 1988. The Syracuse University family development research program: Long-range impact of an early intervention with low-income children and their families. In D. Powell, ed., *Parent education as early childhood intervention: Emerging directions in theory, research, and practice,* 79–104. Norwood, N.J.: Ablex.

La Vigne, N. G. 1994. Rational choice and inmate disputes over phone use on Rikers Island. In R. V. Clarke, ed., *Crime prevention studies,* 3: 109–25. Monsey, N.Y.: Criminal Justice Press.

Laycock, G. K. 1986. Property marking as a deterrent to domestic burglary. In K. Heal and G. Laycock, eds., *Situational crime prevention: From theory into practice,* 55–71. London: Her Majesty's Stationery Office.

______. 1991. Operation identification, or the power of publicity? *Security Journal* 2: 67–72.

Lipsey, M. W. 1984. Is delinquency prevention a cost-effective strategy? A California perspective. *Journal of Research in Crime and Delinquency* 21: 279–302.

Long, D. A., Mallar, C. D., and Thornton, C. V. D. 1981. Evaluating the benefits and costs of the Job Corps. *Journal of Policy Analysis and Management* 1: 55–76.

Miller, T. R., Cohen, M. A., and Wiersema, B. 1996. *Victim costs and consequences: A new look.* Washington, D.C.: National Institute of Justice, U.S. Department of Justice.

Newman, G., Clarke, R. V., and Shoham, S., eds. 1997. *Rational choice and situational crime prevention: Theoretical foundations.* Aldershot, England: Ashgate.

Olds, D. L., Eckenrode, J., Henderson, C. R., Kitzman, H., Powers, J., Cole, R., Sidora, K., Morris, P., Pettitt, L. M., and Luckey, D. 1997. Long-term effects of home visitation on maternal life course and child abuse and neglect: Fifteen-year follow-up of a randomized trial. *Journal of the American Medical Association* 278, 637–43.

Olds, D. L., Henderson, C. R, Chamberlin, R., and Tatelbaum, R. 1986. Preventing child abuse and neglect: A randomized trial of nurse home visitation. *Pediatrics* 78: 65–78.

Olds, D. L., Henderson, C. R., Cole, R., Eckenrode, J., Kitzman, H., Luckey, D., Pettitt, L. M., Sidora, K., Morris, P., and Powers, J. 1998. Long-term effects of home visitation on children's criminal and antisocial behavior: 15-year follow-up of a randomized controlled trial. *Journal of the American Medical Association* 280: 1238–44.

Olds, D. L., Henderson, C. R., Phelps, C., Kitzman, H., and Hanks, C. 1993. Effects of prenatal and infancy nurse home visitation on government spending. *Medical Care* 31: 155–74.

Painter, K. A., and Farrington, D. P. 1997. The crime reducing effect of improved street lighting: The Dudley project. In R. V. Clarke, ed., *Situational crime prevention: Successful case studies,* 209–26. 2d ed. Guilderland, N.Y.: Harrow and Heston.

______. 1999a. Improved street lighting: Crime reducing effects and cost-benefit analyses. *Security Journal* 12: 17–32.

______. 1999b. Street lighting and crime: Diffusion of benefits in the Stoke-on-Trent project. In K. A. Painter and N. Tilley, eds., *Crime prevention studies,* 10: 77–122. Monsey, N.Y.: Criminal Justice Press.

Palmer, T. 1992. *The re-emergence of correctional intervention.* Newbury Park, Calif.: Sage Publications.

Pearson, F. S. 1988. Evaluation of New Jersey's intensive supervision program. *Crime and Delinquency* 34: 437–48.

Pearson, F. S., and Harper, A. G. 1990. Contingent intermediate sentences: New Jersey's intensive supervision program. *Crime and Delinquency* 36: 75–86.

Poyner, B. 1992. Video cameras and bus vandalism. In R. V. Clarke, ed., *Situational crime prevention: Successful case studies,* 185–93. Albany, N.Y.: Harrow and Heston.

Prentky, R., and Burgess, A. W. 1990. Rehabilitation of child molesters: A cost-benefit analysis. *American Journal of Orthopsychiatry* 60: 108–17.

Reppetto, T. A. 1976. Crime prevention and the displacement phenomenon. *Crime and Delinquency* 22: 166–77.

Schnelle, J. F., Kirchner, R. E., Galbaugh, F., Domash, M., Carr, A., and Larson, L. 1979. Program evaluation research: An experimental cost-effectiveness analysis of an armed robbery intervention program. *Journal of Applied Behavior Analysis* 12: 615–23.

Schweinhart, L. J., Barnes, H. V., and Weikart, D. P. 1993. *Significant benefits: The High/Scope Perry Preschool study through age 27.* Ypsilanti, Mich.: High/Scope Press.

Seitz, V., Rosenbaum, L. K., and Apfel, N. H. 1985. Effects of family support intervention: A ten-year follow-up. *Child Development* 56: 376–91.

Sherman, L. W., and Gottfredson, D. C. 1997. Research methods. In L. W. Sherman, D. C. Gottfredson, D. L. MacKenzie, J. E. Eck, P. Reuter, and S. D. Bushway, *Preventing crime: What works, what doesn't, what's promising,* app., pp. 1–8. Washington, D.C.: National Institute of Justice, U.S. Department of Justice.

Sherman, L. W., Gottfredson, D. C., MacKenzie, D. L., Eck, J. E., Reuter, P., and Bushway, S. D. 1997. *Preventing crime: What works, what doesn't, what's promising.* Washington, D.C.: National Institute of Justice, U.S. Department of Justice.

______. 1998. Preventing crime: What works, what doesn't, what's promising. *Research in Brief* (July). Washington, D.C.: National Institute of Justice, U.S. Department of Justice.

Skett, S. 1995. What works in the reduction of offending behaviour? *Forensic Update* 42: 20–27.

Skilton, M. 1988. *A better reception: The development of concierge schemes*. London: Estate Action and Department of the Environment.

Tonry, M., and Farrington, D. P. 1995. Strategic approaches to crime prevention. In M. Tonry and D. P. Farrington, eds., *Building a safer society: Strategic approaches to crime prevention*. Vol. 19 of *Crime and justice: A review of research*, 1–20. Chicago: University of Chicago Press.

Tremblay, R. E., and Craig, W. M. 1995. Developmental crime prevention. In M. Tonry and D. P. Farrington, eds., *Building a safer society: Strategic approaches to crime prevention*. Vol. 19 of *Crime and justice: A review of research*, 151–236. Chicago: University of Chicago Press.

van Andel, H. 1989. Crime prevention that works: The care of public transport in the Netherlands. *British Journal of Criminology* 29: 47–56.

Welsh, B. C., and Farrington, D. P. 1998. Assessing the effectiveness and economic benefits of an integrated developmental and situational crime prevention programme. *Psychology, Crime, and Law* 4: 281–308.

______. 2000. Monetary costs and benefits of crime prevention programs. In M. Tonry, ed., *Crime and justice: A review of research*, 27: 305–61. Chicago: University of Chicago Press.

Zimring, F. E., and Hawkins, G. 1995. *Incapacitation: Penal confinement and the restraint of crime*. New York: Oxford University Press.

4

Estimating the Costs and Benefits of Early Childhood Interventions

Nurse Home Visits and the Perry Preschool

PETER W. GREENWOOD
LYNN A. KAROLY
SUSAN S. EVERINGHAM
JILL HOUBÉ
M. REBECCA KILBURN
C. PETER RYDELL
MATTHEW SANDERS
JAMES CHIESA

In recent years several scholarly reviews of the prevention literature have concluded that there are a number of targeted intervention strategies that do produce consistent positive effects in reducing future delinquency (McGill, Mihalic, and Grotpeter 1997; Greenwood et al. 1996; Karoly et al. 1998; Bayley 1998). Not only do these programs reduce the amount of future crimes committed by high-risk youth, but they can also save government, as well as potential crime victims, substantial sums of money. Policymakers interested in maximizing the effectiveness of their investments in fighting crime need to consider the cost-effectiveness of appropriate early interventions compared to additional expenditures on police, courts, jails, and prisons. In this chapter we show how some publicly funded early interventions may actually yield monetary returns in excess of their costs.[1]

To begin, consider some of the benefits of early-intervention programs to individuals other than the child and his or her immediate family. For example, a program that reduces the amount of crime committed by a treated child also lessens the victimization experienced by other people. These other people enjoy decreased loss from crime, primarily in the form of decreased property losses and less pain and suffering. If a program reduces the incidence of unhealthy behaviors in later life, such as drinking in conjunction with driving, everyone's insurance premiums—in this case, for automobile and possibly health insurance—could go down. Benefits also accrue more subtly. For example, an entire classroom of schoolchildren is better off if those class members who are less cognitively able are brought up to the level of the others. These indirect benefits that accrue to other individuals must be included when one considers the total value of such programs.

Benefits can also accrue to society at large. A principal recipient of such benefits is the government.[2] If a program results in higher earnings for a program participant, the government collects greater tax revenue. If a program participant is less likely to use welfare, the government's welfare outlays are reduced. Regardless, taxpayers are better off, either by receiving a larger collective benefit per dollar paid or, potentially, by receiving the same benefit from a reduced tax burden.

If it were possible to include and monetize *all* the benefits of a program, one could generate a complete cost-benefit ratio. However, monetizing many of the benefits of early-childhood intervention is difficult or impossible. It is difficult, for example, to monetize the benefits of improved behavior or IQ, either for the child or for other members of the child's family or classroom. We cannot easily attach a monetary value to a mother's greater satisfaction with her relationship with her child. Neither can we easily determine at this time the monetary value to society of greater academic achievement on the part of children participating in early interventions. The same goes for many of the health benefits realized. Furthermore, benefits that can be easily monetized may result in future benefits that cannot. For example, if early intervention means that a child will be more economically successful as an adult (a monetizable benefit), that adult's children may not be exposed to the same stressors that he or she was (a benefit that is difficult to monetize).[3] In this chapter, we restrict ourselves to benefits that can be easily monetized. Since the government is likely to be the funder for large-scale early-childhood programs, it is interesting to ask whether public expenditures for such programs could be justified, at least in part, by the savings to government they generate. If the savings generated by such programs are greater than their costs, government fiscal support for such programs may be considered a worthwhile investment of public funds. Thus, we devote most of our attention to costs and savings to the government, since we can more comprehensively account for those than we can for the costs and benefits to society at large. In the discussion that follows, we refer to this analysis as *cost-savings analysis*, to differentiate it from more traditional *cost-benefit analysis*. (The latter takes into account the benefits that accrue to other members of society, both program participants and nonparticipants.)

This is not to say that programs for which the measured costs are greater than the measured savings should not be funded by the government. Early-childhood intervention programs might be deemed worthy even if their costs exceed their savings to government, because not all of their benefits can be easily monetized. Measured net savings to the government should not be the sole basis for deciding whether to fund a program or which of a set of competing programs to fund. However, positive net savings should help allay the concerns of those troubled by the potential budgetary burden of government-funded early intervention.

Our principal objective, then, is to determine if early-childhood intervention programs have the potential to save more money than they cost. We do this by analyzing two programs documented in the literature that are amenable to such a cost-savings analysis. Those two programs are the Elmira Prenatal–Early Infancy Project (PEIP) and the Perry Preschool project.[4] That we judge only two program evaluations amenable to cost-savings analysis is worth some emphasis. It reflects the lack of measured outcomes and the attrition problems.[5] It also suggests the need for more comprehensively and rigorously evaluated programs. That we have analyzed only two programs limits our ability to generalize from the results; finding that these two programs save more than they cost obviously does not necessarily imply the same conclusion for dissimilar programs. However, such a finding serves as proof of the principle that programs generating net savings do exist.

In this chapter, we first describe the criteria for selecting programs for this cost-savings analysis and show how the two programs meet the criteria (and how others do not). Then we compare program costs to the government with savings they generate in order to determine if public expenditure can be justified on the basis of net savings to the government. Finally, we additionally include some of the benefits to other individuals—those benefits that can be easily and incontrovertibly monetized. This leads us to a more comprehensive estimate of the monetary benefit to society of such programs than we can get from our estimate of the benefits to the government alone. Even this more comprehensive estimate is still incomplete, however, since we are not able to monetize all of the benefits of the programs.

Programs Selected for Analysis

Although numerous early-childhood intervention programs have been developed and tested, only a fraction have been evaluated in any fashion. Very few have been rigorously and thoroughly evaluated over long periods of time. Yet, such an evaluation of a program is necessary for a defensible cost-savings analysis. Specifically, to implement our cost-savings analysis, we require that five criteria be met.

First, the evaluation must have an experimental design. It must measure the characteristics and behaviors of not only the treatment group but also a control group, that is, a group comparable in all respects to the treatment group except that its members do not participate in the program. Should the groups then differ during or after the program in some measure of interest (e.g., time on welfare), that difference can be ascribed to the program. The ideal way to ensure an experimental design is to conduct a randomized trial in which subjects are assigned to the treatment group and the control group randomly. If the sample size is sufficiently large, this ensures the necessary similarity between the two groups.

There are other ways to evaluate program effectiveness. For example, one could measure the behavior of interest before the treatment and at some time thereafter. However, this type of evaluation is not applicable to an early-childhood intervention program in which the subjects are developing children for whom the "before" value of the variable—time on welfare, in special education, and so on—is zero. One could also use a quasi-experimental design with retrospectively chosen control groups, although the inability to control for both observed and unobserved differences between treatment and control groups may bias such studies. Although various statistical techniques are available to try to minimize these potential biases, we are not aware of any evaluations in the literature that employ these techniques and also meet our other criteria.

Second, the sample size must be large enough for true differences between the treatment and control groups to be recognizable with statistical methods. The larger the sample, the more likely that a measured difference of a certain size between the treatment and control groups will be judged statistically significant, that is, the smaller the chance that the difference is a result of random variation. In practice, sample sizes are never large enough to totally eliminate the concern of sampling error, so we take the standard errors[6] of our savings estimates into account in drawing inferences from them.

Third, sample attrition over time must be small, for two reasons. First, attrition brings down the sample size. Second, differential attrition can skew the results. For example, if many of the families with the lowest socioeconomic status (SES) do not complete the treatment or are not available for later follow-up, the treatment and control groups will not be adequately comparable.

Fourth, the program outcomes or potential benefits (such as reduction in welfare usage) that lead to cost savings must be measured in the evaluation. For obvious logistical and budgetary reasons, the evaluator of a program can measure only a limited number of outcomes. In many of the program evaluations described in the literature, outcomes that imply direct cost savings have not been measured. Theoretically, the cost savings could be estimated on the basis of the outcomes that *have* been measured. But this can be done only if there is a well-understood relationship between the measured outcomes and the unmeasured cost-saving outcomes (e.g., between juvenile arrest record and time in prison as an adult). The selection of outcomes for inclusion in the evaluation is often based on the theory behind the program. For example, a program designed to improve cognition may measure the child's IQ. The program may also reduce welfare usage later in the child's life, but if that particular outcome is not measured, the cost savings associated with reduced welfare usage probably cannot be calculated (because of the lack of a clear relationship between IQ and welfare usage).

Finally, and most important, long-term follow-up of the subjects is required if savings are to be fully calculated. Most of the benefits that generate monetizable cost savings occur long after the intervention has been completed. Adequate time between the intervention and the measurement of outcomes must have elapsed for the benefits of interest to have occurred. An evaluation that follows subjects for only a few months or even years cannot be used to predict long-term benefits, and thus cost savings, with any confidence. In practice, evaluation periods have not been long enough to capture all the lifetime benefits to program participants, partly because early-intervention experiments were not conducted before the 1960s. For a cost-savings analysis, either the unobserved future benefits must be estimated from outcomes that have been observed or some long-term benefits must be omitted from the calculation, leading to an underestimate of the savings associated with the program.

Of the programs we identified in the published literature, only two meet all these criteria. They are the Elmira PEIP and the Perry Preschool program. There are several programs that meet the first three criteria (design, sample size, and attrition), but very few meet the remaining two criteria. For example, only the Early Training Project, Chicago Child-Parent Center (CPC), Carolina Abecedarian, and Syracuse Family Development Research Program (FDRP) have follow-ups that are as long as that of the Elmira PEIP (through age fourteen, fifteen, or nineteen), and no other program matches the age-twenty-seven follow-up available for Perry Preschool participants. At the same time, with the exception of measures of crime and delinquency in the CPC and FDRP programs, these programs largely did not assess measures of other outcomes for the child or mother that can be readily monetized (e.g., employment, welfare utilization). Though these types of benefits may be measured in future follow-ups, any estimates of savings based on current information would be incomplete. Thus, we have chosen not to undertake cost-savings analyses for programs where estimates of savings would be highly uncertain or clearly underestimated. However, as we note below, for the two programs we do analyze, concerns about the precision and comprehensiveness of our estimates of savings still remain, although to a lesser degree than would be the case for the programs we did not consider.

Elmira PEIP

The Elmira PEIP home-visits program helped infants and their mothers by providing parent education, social support for the mother, and referrals to social services starting in the prenatal period and continuing until the child was two years old. The program services were delivered through home visits to first-time mothers by trained nurses. The program cost about $6,000 (in 1996 dollars) per child. This paid for the average of thirty-two home visits that occurred during pregnancy and the first two years after birth.

The evaluation of the Elmira PEIP home-visits program was based on an experimental design, with mothers randomly assigned to treatment and control groups. Subjects in the program have been followed to age fifteen. Attrition over that period has been of the order of 20 percent for the children, and less for the mothers.

For the purposes of analyzing the long-term follow-up results of the Elmira PEIP (Olds et al. 1997), we report results for the full experimental group, as well as for a higher-risk sample. This latter group consists of women who, at the time of enrollment in the study, were unmarried and had low SES. In the results we present below, we separately evaluate savings for this higher-risk sample, as well as for the remaining experimental sample, which we call lower risk.[7] The lower-risk group thus consists of two-parent families or higher-SES families. At the time of the age-fifteen follow-up, there were 100 families in the higher-risk group (i.e., treatment plus control) and 145 families in the lower-risk group. These represent adequate sample sizes. However, they are small enough that we still have to be concerned with the uncertainty surrounding the estimates of effectiveness and thus of cost savings.

A follow-up through age fifteen is long enough to capture many of the cost savings generated by the program. Table 4.1 lists the outcomes measured by the Elmira PEIP evaluation and those we monetize. However, fifteen years is not long enough to derive estimates of the child's lifetime employment or welfare utilization. For instance, since fifteen year olds have little employment history, there are no good early indicators on

TABLE 4.1 Outcomes Measured in Elmira PEIP

Domain	*Mother/Child*	*Outcome Description*
Child development	Child	IQ at age 3
		IQ at age 4
Parent development	Mother	Home environment at age 4
		Reports of child abuse and neglect through age 15
Education	Mother	Years of education at age 4
Employment	Mother	*Months employed through age 15*
Welfare	Mother	*Months on AFDC through age 15*
		Months on Food Stamps through age 15
		Months on Medicaid through age 15
Crime	Mother	*Arrests through age 15*
		Convictions through age 15
		Jail days through age 15
	Child	*Arrests through age 15*
		Convictions through age 15
Health	Mother	Subsequent pregnancies and births through age 15
		Months between 1st and 2nd birth through age 15
		Substance abuse impairments through age 15
	Child	*ER visits, ages 25–50 months*
		Hospital days, ages 25–50 months

NOTES: Age references are to the age of the focal child. Italics indicates benefits we monetized.

which to base predictions of lifetime employment performance. In contrast, criminal careers can be predicted for the children on the basis of arrest records of fifteen year olds.

Our cost-savings analysis builds upon an earlier assessment of the Elmira PEIP, conducted with data measured for children and their mothers when the children were four (Olds et al. 1993). Two years after the program ended, the cost-savings analysis showed government savings that just exceeded program costs for low-income families (a net savings of $180 per child in 1980 dollars). For the sample as a whole, government savings did not exceed costs; rather, savings to government provided only a partial offset to program costs. In both cases, the bulk of government savings resulted from reductions in the use of Aid for Dependent Children (AFDC) and other social welfare programs by the mother. The data available for our analysis of the children through age fifteen permit an even more comprehensive assessment of longer-term savings generated by the program for both children and their mothers.

Perry Preschool Program

The Perry Preschool program provided preschool classes to a sample of children in Ypsilanti, Michigan, when they were three and four years old. The program cost, measured in 1996 dollars and discounted to the birth of the participating child, was about $12,000 per child.[8] Program costs were associated with time spent in preschool (two and one-half hours a day, five days a week, for three-quarters of the year), as well as weekly (one and one-half-hour) home visits by the child's preschool teacher.

The evaluation is based on an experimental design with random assignment to treatment and control groups. The sample (treatment plus control) includes 123 children from 100 families. Subjects of the evaluation have been followed through age twenty-seven, with an attrition rate of about 9 percent. Again, the sample size is adequate to make estimates but not to eliminate substantial uncertainty surrounding the outcomes and the cost savings.

Evaluations of the Perry Preschool program provide estimates of the program results for participating children versus the control group in terms of education, employment and income, welfare, and crime; see Table 4.2 for the outcomes measured and those previously monetized by Barnett (1993) that are incorporated in our analysis. The long follow-up period, longer than that in the Elmira PEIP evaluation, permits estimates of welfare costs and taxes from increased employment that are generated during adulthood by children who participated in the program. In addition, Barnett (1993) provides estimates of projected savings, beyond age twenty-seven, as a result of higher taxes from employment, lower welfare utilization, and reduced crime.

Data from the Perry Preschool age-twenty-seven follow-up have been previously used by Barnett (1993) to conduct a cost-benefit analysis. Barnett's estimates, consistent with early cost-benefit assessments of the program, indicate that the savings to government exceed program costs by a factor of more than seven to one. The largest component of savings is from reductions in crime, a large fraction of which is the estimated reductions in the intangible losses to victims of crime over the lifetime of the program participants. Other large savings components include taxes recovered over participants' lifetimes because of higher earnings and reduced K–12 education costs.

In the analysis we report below, we have used Barnett's results to calculate savings, generated by the Perry Preschool program, from higher

TABLE 4.2 Outcomes Measured in Perry Preschool

Domain	*Mother/Child*	*Outcome Description*
Child development	Child	IQ at age 5
		IQ at age 7
		IQ at age 8
		IQ at age 14
Education	Child	Achievement test score at age 9
		Achievement test score at age 14
		High school GPA at age 19
		Time in special education through age 19
		Years in educable mentally impaired programs through age 27
		Years retained in grade through age 27
		High school graduation rate by age 27
		Postsecondary education credits by age 27
Employment	Child	*Employment rate at age 19*
		Employment rate at age 27
		Monthly earnings at age 27
Welfare	Child	*Received public assistance at age 27*
		Received public assistance in last 10 years at age 27
Crime	Child	*Ever arrested by age 27*
		Lifetime arrests through age 27
Health	Child	Teen pregnancies per 100 females through age 19

NOTES: Age references are to the age of the focal child. Italics indicates benefits monetized by Barnett (1993) that we adjusted to 1996 dollars and rediscounted.

employment and reductions in the utilization of welfare, the criminal justice system, and special education.[9] For comparability with our analysis of the Elmira PEIP, Barnett's figures have been adjusted to 1996 dollars and rediscounted. On balance, these changes decrease estimates of both costs and savings. More important, our figures also differ from those reported by Barnett because we have elected, as discussed more fully below, not to monetize the reduction in pain and suffering for victims of crime. Thus, our estimates of the benefits to the rest of society are a more conservative figure than those reported by Barnett.

Comparing Program Costs to Government Savings the Programs Generate

Early-childhood intervention programs generate at least four types of significant savings to government:

Increased tax revenues. These result from increased employment and earnings by program participants, including income tax at the federal and state levels, Social Security contributions by both the employer and the employee, and state and local sales taxes. The Perry Preschool program measured the increased employment and income for the children in the evaluation through age twenty-seven, and Barnett (1993) projected future earnings and income through age sixty-five. The employment and earnings measures in the Elmira PEIP are limited to gains experienced by the mother through age fifteen of the child.

Decreased welfare outlays. This includes Medicaid, Food Stamps, AFDC, and general assistance (typically funded by counties). The savings to government include not only the reduced payments to recipients but also the reduced administrative expenses. The Perry Preschool evaluation took account of all of these factors, measuring welfare utilization for the children through age twenty-seven and projecting future savings through age sixty-five based on Barnett's (1993) calculations. The Elmira PEIP measured changes in months spent on welfare by the mother (and child) through the child's age fifteen.

Reduced expenditures for education, health, and other services. (For example, special education, emergency room visits, and stays in homeless shelters.) The Elmira PEIP evaluation measured emergency room visits when the child was between the ages of twenty-five and fifty months. The Perry Preschool evaluation measured net education savings through when the child was in high school (i.e., savings due to lower special education expenditures and less grade-repetition net of increased schooling costs due to greater educational attainment). To the extent that the programs reduce the need for other special services that were not measured in the evaluations, the savings figure is an underestimate of the true savings to government.

Lower criminal justice system costs. (Including arrest, adjudication, and incarceration expenses.) On the basis of the measured outcomes, we can predict criminal activity and thus criminal justice expenditures for the lifetime of the subject; therefore, the estimate of criminal justice savings covers the entire lifetime of the children in the Elmira PEIP and Perry Preschool interventions. In addition, the criminal justice system savings for mothers in the Elmira PEIP are included based on treatment-versus control-group differences in arrests and jail days through when the focal child was fifteen.

Estimates of government savings in each of these categories can be derived from the outcome data collected in the evaluations of the two pro-

TABLE 4.3 Costs and Savings: Elmira PEIP, Higher-Risk Families

	Dollars per Child			
	Due to Mother	*Due to Child*	*Total*	*SE*
Program cost			$6,083	
Savings to government	$20,384	$4,310	$24,694	$6,420
Reduction in health services	*	115	115	56
Taxes from increased employment	5,683	*	5,683	3,681
Reduction in welfare cost	14,067	*	14,067	4,905
Reduction in criminal justice cost	634	4,195	4,828	1,900
Net savings			18,611	

NOTE: *=not measured. All amounts are in 1996 dollars and are the net present value of amounts over time where future values are discounted to the birth of the participating child, using a 4 percent annual real discount rate. The standard error (SE) of individual line items in this table was estimated by multiplying the SE of the item's cost driver times the cost factor that converts the cost driver into estimated cost. For example, for welfare the cost driver is months on welfare, and the factor is the cost per month. The SE of the cost driver is estimated as one-fourth of the 95 percent confidence interval estimate of the difference between the treatment- and control-group outcomes. The SEs of the totals were approximated by the square root of the sum of squared SEs of the components. These estimates of the SEs are very rough, but they are sufficiently accurate to convey the level of uncertainty in the estimated program caused by the small sample size.

grams included in this analysis. (Note that some of the outcomes listed in Tables 4.1 and 4.2, e.g., increased IQ, may result in savings or costs to the government, but these are not easily quantified and are not included here.) In the results that follow, all dollar amounts are expressed in 1996 dollars. Net present values are estimated at the time of the birth of the child using a 4 percent discount rate.[10] The sensitivity of our results to the choice of the discount rate is addressed at the end of the chapter.

Elmira PEIP, Higher-Risk Families

Table 4.3 summarizes the costs and savings to government of the Elmira PEIP home-visit program for higher-risk families. These savings are estimated from benefits reported by Olds et al. (1994, 1997) and Olds (1996). The difference between the total savings ($24,694)[11] and the cost ($6,083) is the net savings to government ($18,611). The overall amount of savings is more than four times the cost of the program. Thus, this program clearly pays for itself through the reductions in future spending on existing government programs.

FIGURE 4.1 Sources of Savings to Government: Elmira PEIP, Higher-Risk Families

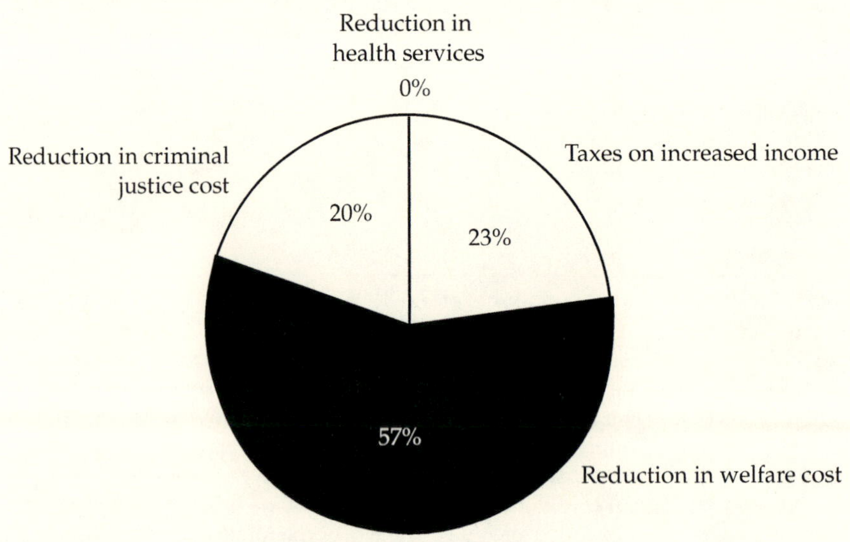

NOTES: Table 4.3 and authors'calculations.

More than 80 percent ($20,384) of the savings we can estimate is due to differences between the treated group and the control group with respect to behavior of the mother during the first fifteen years of the child's life. In particular, mothers in the treated group were employed more and used welfare less. The rest of the savings are from differences in the child's behavior ($4,310), primarily due to less crime over his or her lifetime.[12]

The behavior of both the mother and the child has been observed for only fifteen years. We have made no attempt to estimate the increases in the child's future income (and thus increases in tax revenue) or decreases in the child's use of welfare that may result from the child's participation in the program. Likewise, we have not attempted to guess at the possible increases in employment (and thus income and tax revenue) nor decreases in welfare usage by the mother after the child is fifteen years old. We have also not monetized other beneficial effects of the program through age fifteen of the child, such as those from reduced child abuse and neglect. Thus, the calculated net savings ($18,611) is likely an underestimate of the true savings to government that can be credited to this program.

FIGURE 4.2 Cumulative Costs and Benefits: Elmira PEIP, Higher-Risk Families

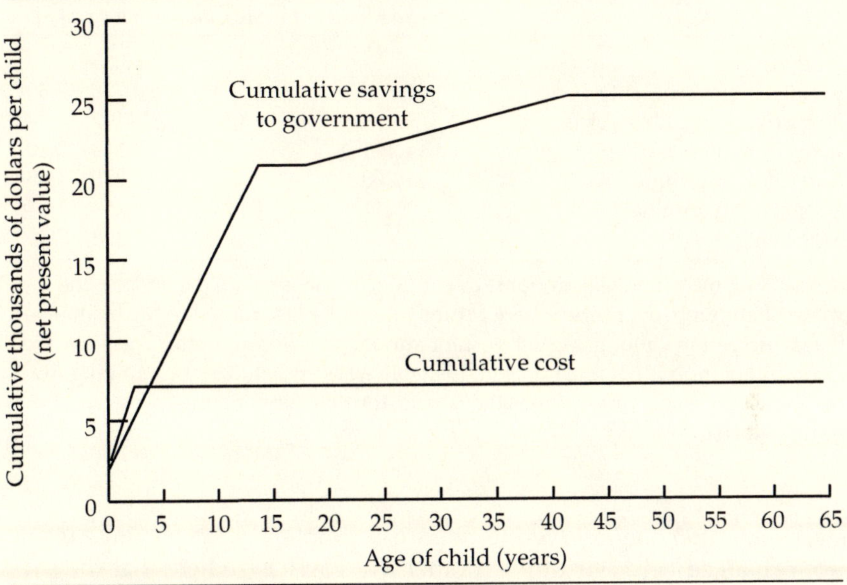

SOURCE: Authors'calculations.

Figure 4.1 depicts the sources of government savings for the Elmira PEIP home-visit program for higher-risk families. More than half the savings to government result from reductions in welfare costs. The remainder is split evenly between increased tax revenues and decreased criminal justice costs.

The program cost occurs at the time of the intervention, whereas the savings to government stretch out into the future. (In Table 4.3, the savings figure is a cumulative sum of those future savings, appropriately discounted.) In Figure 4.2 we show how those savings accumulate over time. The curves in the figure represent cumulative costs and savings through different years since the intervention, measured by the age of the child. Each point on a curve is the net present value (using a 4 percent discount rate) of the annual amounts up to that time. The home visits provided by the program stop after the child is two years old, so the cumulative cost curve levels off at two years.

In contrast, the savings continue to accumulate long after the intervention is complete. We see that cumulative savings exceed cumulative program costs after only three years. Many of the savings from this program

TABLE 4.4 Costs and Savings: Elmira PEIP, Lower-Risk Families

	Dollars per Child			
	Due to Mother	*Due to Child*	*Total*	*SE*
Program cost			$6,083	
Savings to government	$2,525	$1,250	$3,775	$5,591
Reduction in health services	*	107	107	47
Taxes from increased employment	1,144	*	1,144	3,101
Reduction in welfare cost	1,270	*	1,270	4,483
Reduction in criminal justice cost	111	1,143	1,254	1,246
Net savings			-2,308	

NOTE: *=not measured. All amounts are in 1996 dollars and are the net present value of amounts over time where future values are discounted to the birth of the participating child, using a 4 percent annual real discount rate. The standard error (SE) of individual line items in this table was estimated by multiplying the SE of the item's cost driver times the cost factor that converts the cost driver into estimated cost.

start soon after the intervention because so many of the savings result from changed behavior of the mother. We emphasize here that the savings occur early because we will see that this is not true in the case of the Perry Preschool program.

Elmira PEIP, Lower-Risk Families

Table 4.4 summarizes costs and savings to the government of the Elmira PEIP home-visits program for lower-risk families. Again, these savings are estimated from benefits reported by Olds et al. (1994, 1997) and Olds (1996).

We see that when this home-visits program serves families from the lower-risk group, there are no net savings to the government. The total savings to the government do not exceed the program costs. Although mothers from families participating in the program have more employment (resulting in increased tax revenues) and less use of welfare than mothers from the control group, the differences are not large enough to generate sizable savings. Likewise, children receiving the intervention were less involved in criminal activity than those in the control groups, resulting in a savings to the government in criminal justice costs. However, those savings ($1,143) are much less than they are for the higher-risk families ($4,195).

It is important to keep in mind, however, that the program may generate future savings to the government as the participants continue to

TABLE 4.5 Different Baselines May Explain Different Improvements

Recipients	*No Program*	*Home-Visits Program*
Higher-risk families	90	60
Lower-risk families	30	28

SOURCE: Olds et al. (1997) and unpublished tabulations provided by David Olds.

age. As with the higher-risk families, any difference between treatment and control groups in terms of the future earnings and welfare utilization for children is not observed and therefore not included in the savings estimates.

Since we do observe net savings when the program was offered to higher-risk families, we cannot blame the program design for the lack of savings for lower-risk families. Rather, it results from the choice of subjects. This is illustrated in Table 4.5, which considers just one category of savings: welfare usage by the mothers. Without the services of the home-visits program, the mother's usage of welfare over the first fifteen years of the child's life is considerably less for those from the lower-risk group than for those from the higher-risk group (thirty and ninety months, respectively). As might be expected from Table 4.5, the home-visits program reduces welfare usage by mothers in the lower-risk families only slightly below the already (relatively) low level in the controls. However, the program reduces welfare usage by mothers in the higher-risk families by 33 percent. One way to interpret these results is that lower-risk families need less assistance of the type offered by the program, so the program cannot accomplish as much. This underscores the need for matching the program to the population that needs its services. At least from the perspective of government savings, appropriate targeting is crucial.

Perry Preschool Program

Table 4.6 summarizes costs and savings to the government of the Perry Preschool program. Our calculations are based on those reported in Barnett (1993), although they are updated to 1996 dollars and rediscounted to present value at the time of the birth of the participating child, for comparability with other amounts reported here. As we note above, we have also omitted some of the factors included in the Barnett (1993) estimates. The savings to the government ($25,437) are more than twice as large as the program costs ($12,148), yielding net savings to the government of $13,289. Thus, like the Elmira PEIP home-visits program for higher-risk families, the Perry Preschool program pays for itself through future reductions in government expenditures.

TABLE 4.6 Costs and Savings: Perry Preschool

	Dollars per Child			
	Due to Mother	*Due to Child*	*Total*	*SE*
Program cost			$12,148	
Savings to government	*	$25,437	$25,437	$5,789
Reduction in health services	*	6,365	6,365	51
Taxes from increased employment	*	6,566	6,566	3,319
Reduction in welfare cost	*	2,310	2,310	4,422
Reduction in criminal justice cost	*	10,195	10,195	1,713
Net savings			13,289	

NOTE: *=not measured. All amounts are in 1996 dollars and are the net present value of amounts over time where future values are discounted to the birth of the participating child, using a 4 percent annual real discount rate. The standard error (SE) of individual line items in this table was estimated by multiplying the SE of the corresponding line item in Table 4.3 by the square root of the inverse ratio of sample sizes. The assumption is that the population variability for each item in the Perry Preschool sample is the same as in the Elmira PEIP higher-risk sample, so only sample size makes the standard errors of mean values differ. This assumption makes the estimated standard errors in this table even rougher than those in Table 4.3. However, they are still sufficiently accurate to convey the uncertainty of estimated program benefits.

The entries in the "mother" column of Table 4.6 are all unmeasured. It is not surprising that only the economic benefits to the child have been measured in the evaluation of this program, since it is a preschool program designed to improve child outcomes. Nonetheless, preschool is a form of child care, so conceivably some of the program mothers may have been able to increase their employment over what it would have been without the program (thus increasing income and tax contributions and decreasing welfare consumption). To the extent that the program enables mothers to work more, the calculated net savings is an underestimate of the true savings to the government that can be credited to this program.

Figure 4.3 shows how the savings to the government are distributed among the four savings categories. Forty percent of the savings to the government are from reductions in criminal justice system costs, because treated children commit less crime as they transition through adolescence to adulthood. Greater tax revenues as a result of greater employment and income over the lifetime of the child accounts for 26 percent of the savings. Lower use of education services—such as special education participation—accounts for another 25 percent of the savings. Reduction in the child's lifetime usage of welfare accounts for the remaining 9 percent of the savings to the government.

FIGURE 4.3 Sources of Savings to Government: Perry Preschool

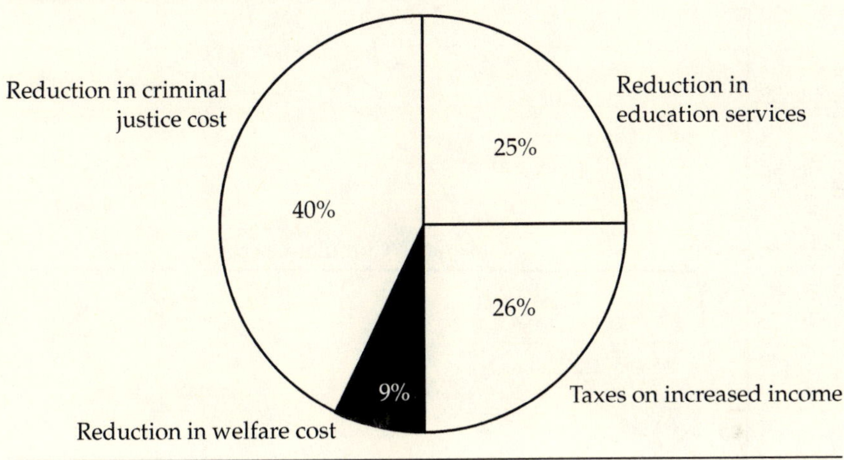

NOTES: Table 4.6 and authors'calculations.

In Figure 4.4 we show how the costs and government savings of the Perry Preschool program accumulate over time. As in Figure 4.2, the curves in this figure represent cumulative costs and savings through different years since the intervention, measured by the age of the child. The preschooling provided by the program occurs when the child is three and four years old, so the cumulative cost curve is zero until three years and levels off at four years. As was true with the Elmira PEIP home-visits program, the savings continue to accumulate long after the intervention is complete, but in the case of the Perry Preschool program the cumulative savings do not exceed program costs until age twenty-one. There are two reasons for this. First, the cost per participant in the Perry Preschool program is higher than the cost per family in the Elmira PEIP home-visits program (roughly, $12,000 versus $6,000). Second, in contrast to the Elmira PEIP, all the measured benefits of the Perry Preschool program accrue to the child, and most of the government savings arising from those benefits to the child do not occur until the child transitions through adolescence to adulthood.

Summary

Figure 4.5 summarizes the results of our cost-savings analysis. The black bars represent the program costs. The white bars represent the total savings to the government. The difference between the bars is the net savings. As we have already seen, both the Elmira PEIP home-visits pro-

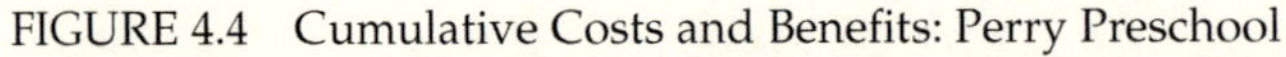

FIGURE 4.4 Cumulative Costs and Benefits: Perry Preschool

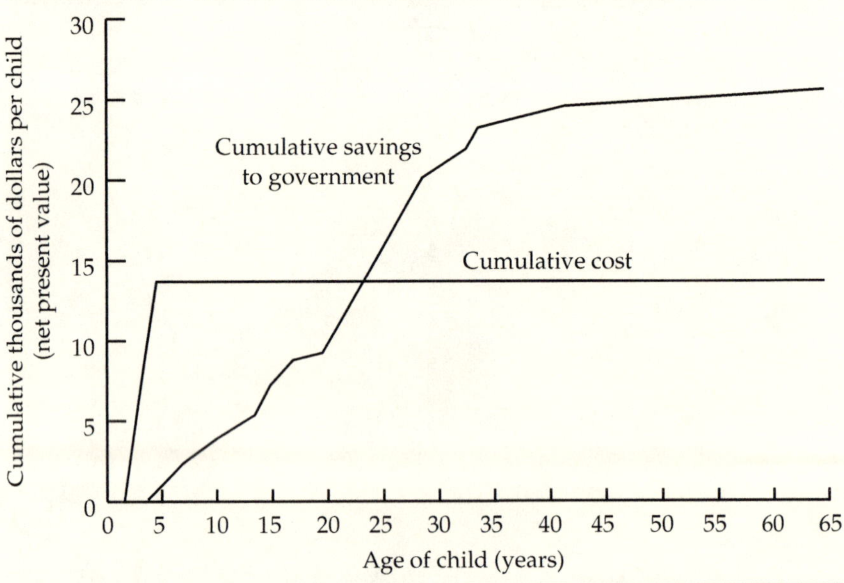

SOURCE: Authors'calculations.

gram for higher-risk families and the Perry Preschool program generate more than enough savings to offset program costs. However, when the participants of the Elmira PEIP home-visits program are from lower-risk families, the savings do not offset the costs.

Note that the uncertainty caused by the small sample sizes must be considered. The error bars on the savings estimates represent 66 percent confidence intervals, meaning that the true value of the savings has a two-thirds chance of being in the interval, a one-sixth chance of being above the interval, and a one-sixth chance of being below the interval. Doubling the size of these intervals would give a 95 percent confidence interval. These error bars are very wide and suggest caution in ascribing a particular savings number to these programs. We can be much more confident, as far as statistical uncertainty goes, in asserting that the savings associated with the Elmira PEIP when offered to higher-risk families are greater than the costs of that program.

The same goes for the savings and costs associated with the Perry Preschool program. However, in the case of the savings associated with the Elmira PEIP when offered to lower-risk families, the confidence interval dwarfs our "best estimate" of small possible savings. Thus, these savings may well be positive, but if so they are small and in all likelihood do not compensate for the program's costs.

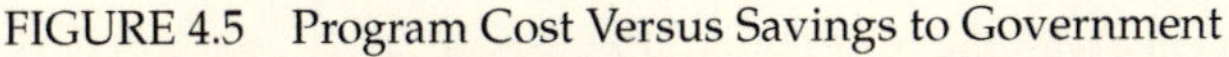

FIGURE 4.5 Program Cost Versus Savings to Government

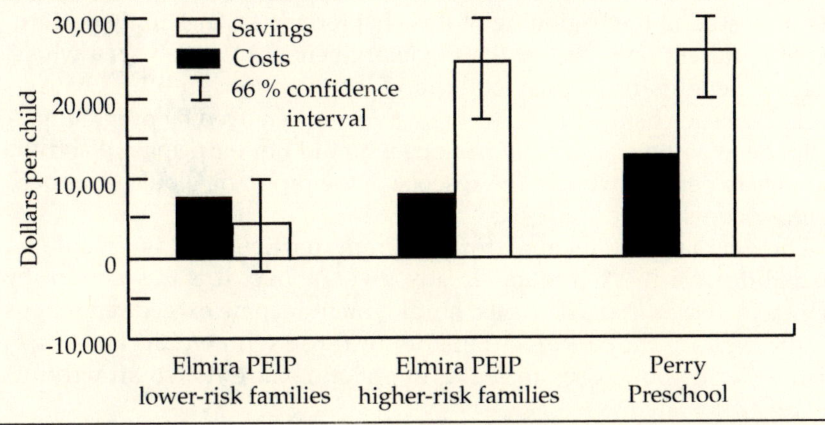

SOURCE: Tables 4.3, 4.4, and 4.6.
NOTES: All amounts are in 1996 dollars and are the net present value of amounts over time where future values are discounted to the birth of the participating child, using a 4 percent annual real discount rate.

The error bars in Figure 4.5, however, capture only statistical uncertainty—that associated with possible divergence from "true" values (those obtained with very large populations) when the number of subjects is not very large. Recall that the estimates of net savings to the government are also subject to uncertainty because some of the benefits to project participants have not been included in the cost-savings analysis. Most important, employment and welfare benefits to the child as well as long-term employment and welfare benefits (i.e., those beyond fifteen years) to the mother are not included in the Elmira PEIP analyses; no employment and welfare benefits to the mother (regardless of timing) are included in the Perry Preschool analysis. Moreover, additional benefits to the programs may have been experienced by program participants but not measured by the evaluations of those programs.

Another source of uncertainty limits the inferences that can be drawn from these results. For various reasons, scaling up these small demonstrations into broadly implemented programs could result in changes in benefits (probably reductions) and costs. The magnitude of these changes is unpredictable.

Although Figure 4.5 implies different net savings for the Elmira PEIP and Perry Preschool program, it is not appropriate to compare the two savings figures to decide which of the two programs is better. This is because the outcomes measured by the program evaluations—and thus the types of savings included in our analysis—differ between the two programs.

Additional Monetary Benefits to the Rest of Society

As discussed at the beginning of this chapter, the savings to the government represent only part of the monetary benefit to society as a whole. Society benefits from early-childhood interventions in other ways as well. Two such benefits are: The greater income enjoyed by program participants than by comparable persons who did not participate,[13] and the savings to persons who, in the absence of the program, would have been crime victims.[14]

The increase in income for program participants is calculated straightforwardly from data already given above. It is the amount by which increases in participants' employment income exceed reductions in the welfare they receive. Benefits to those who would have been crime victims, or losses to real crime victims, are not so straightforwardly calculated.

Crime victim losses can be divided into two categories: tangible and intangible losses. Tangible losses to the victim include property loss, medical expenses, and the income lost while injured. Intangible losses refer to pain and suffering. Tangible losses are relatively easy to estimate because the estimates can be based upon empirical evidence. On the other hand, experts disagree about how to count intangible losses. One way is to assume that the average jury award to a crime victim in compensation for pain and suffering represents the value of those intangible losses. Another way is to assume that what people are willing to pay to avert those losses represents their value. What they are willing to pay could be measured by what they pay for crime protection devices such as burglar alarms, for example, or by what they say they would pay when they respond to carefully constructed surveys.

These two different ways of monetizing the intangible crime losses lead to very different figures. In our analysis, we avoid this controversy by omitting the intangible losses from our calculations.[15] To the extent that the value of the intangible losses is great, our estimate of savings to persons who would have been crime victims is conservative.

Table 4.7 shows the results of adding these two sources of savings to the savings given in the preceding tables. In all three cases, more fully accounting for societal benefits naturally makes the programs look even better. In the case of the higher-risk families in the Elmira PEIP home-visits program, the more complete estimate of monetary benefit to society exceeds the estimate of savings to government alone by about 25 percent. Most of the additional benefit to society comes from the savings to crime victims. The gain in participant income is small because the gain in employment income is largely (although not completely) offset by the loss of welfare income. In the case of the Perry Preschool program, including

TABLE 4.7 Benefits to Society from Analyzed Early-Intervention Programs (Dollars per Child)

	Elmira PEIP		
	Lower-Risk	*Higher-Risk*	*Perry Preschool*
Savings to government	$3,775	$24,694	$25,437
Additional monetary benefits	2,938	6,072	24,535
Increase in mother's income net of welfare loss	1,622	1,010	NA
Increase in child's income net of welfare loss	NA	NA	13,846
Reduction in tangible losses to crime victims	1,315	5,062	10,690
Savings plus additional monetary benefits	6,713	30,766	49,972

NOTE: NA=not applicable. All amounts are in 1996 dollars and are the net present value of amounts over time where future values are discounted to the birth of the participating child, using a 4 percent annual real discount rate.

these additional monetary benefits nearly doubles our previous estimate. In the case of the lower-risk families in the Elmira PEIP home-visits program, the positive savings to crime victims and additional participant income add to the small savings to the government associated with this program. The savings to the government and additional monetary benefits just exceed program costs. It is important to note that these crime-related and participant income benefits are not the only other monetary benefits to society generated by early-childhood intervention programs. Thus, the totals in Table 4.7 are not a full estimate of the monetary benefits to society.

Sensitivity of Results to Discount Rate

All monetary figures in this analysis are given as the sum of the dollar amounts over all future years, but discounted to present value (at the time of the birth of the participating child). This takes into account the assumption common to much economic analysis that future dollars are worth less to people than today's dollars, quite apart from the effects of inflation. The choice of the discount rate is the subject of considerable debate among economists. The 4 percent used here falls within the range of rates commonly used in public-policy analysis and is consistent with previous RAND cost-effectiveness analyses.[16]

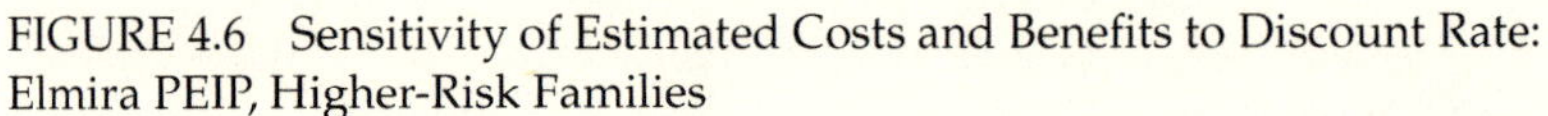

FIGURE 4.6 Sensitivity of Estimated Costs and Benefits to Discount Rate: Elmira PEIP, Higher-Risk Families

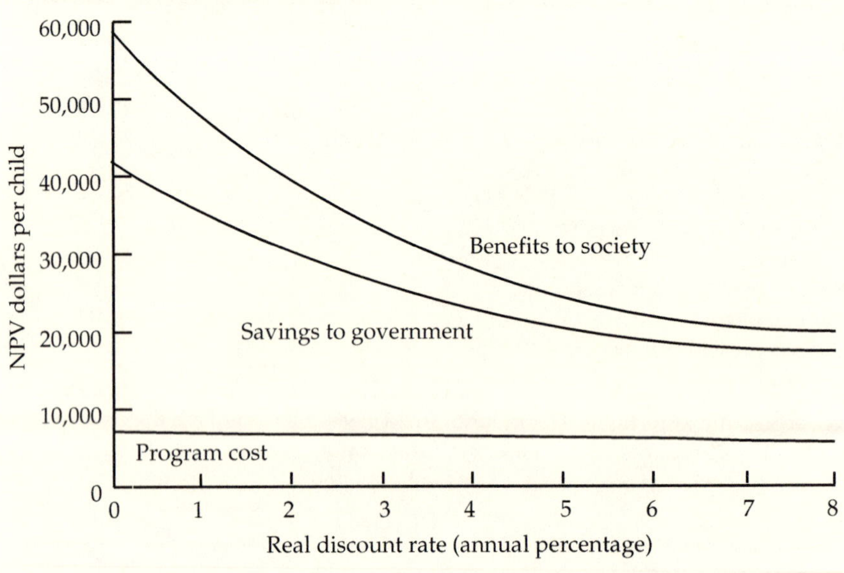

SOURCE: Authors'calculations.

Because the benefits are spread over so many years after the intervention, the estimated net present value of the benefits is very sensitive to the choice of discount rate. Even small variations (say, one percentage point above or below our base-case rate) affect the estimates appreciably. Figures 4.6 and 4.7 show how the choice of discount rate affects our estimates of government savings and monetary benefit to society for the Elmira PEIP higher-risk sample and the Perry Preschool sample, respectively. Despite the sensitivity to the discount rate, both the Elmira PEIP for the higher-risk sample and the Perry Preschool program generate positive savings to government and to society as a whole for a reasonable range of rates.

Findings from Cost-Savings and Cost-Benefit Analyses

In our cost-savings analysis, we analyzed two early-childhood intervention programs—one that involves home visits from before birth to when the child is two and focuses upon the mother, and one that involves preschool for children who are three and four years old. We have seen that these two very different programs can generate significant savings to

FIGURE 4.7 Sensitivity of Estimated Costs and Benefits to Discount Rate: Perry Preschool

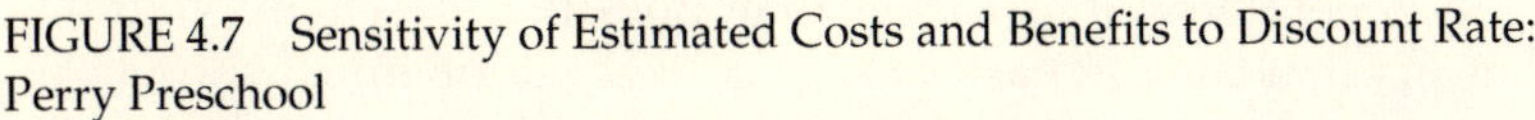

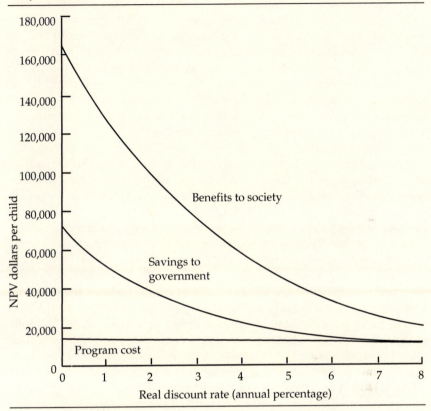

SOURCE: Authors'calculations.

the government that exceed their costs. This supports the argument that public funding of such programs may be justified.[17] Other programs like these two, or other types of programs, may also generate savings to the government, but none has the evaluation characteristics needed to estimate long-term cost savings with any accuracy. Although the two programs we have evaluated vary in their net savings, we cannot conclude that one type of program is better than the other, because the cost-savings numbers are not directly comparable (as a result of differences in the outcomes monetized).

Our analysis shows that although costs accrue at the time of program participation, the savings to the government take a considerable amount of time, at least a few decades, to accumulate. The home-visits program appears to generate savings earlier than does the preschool program, which means that the payback period is likely to be much shorter. In other words, one program might be considered a shorter-term investment than the other. This may, however, be an artifact of the Perry Preschool evaluation not attempting to measure any benefits for parents. Among the benefits we monetize in our analysis, those attributable to changes in parents' behavior generate savings sooner than benefits attributable to the child, most of which do not pay off until the child is grown. In any event, because the purpose of these programs is to promote child development, not to earn quick savings for the government, the payback period should not be used to decide between programs that offer different benefits to the child.

We see from comparing the net savings from the Elmira PEIP offered to higher-risk families (which were substantial) to those from the same program offered to lower-risk families (which were negative) that targeting matters. In other words, if program participation is not limited to the neediest families, net savings to the government may not be generated.

Finally, we see that the monetary benefit to society—even the partial estimate provided here—is even larger than the savings to the government alone. This is because there are persons who, in the absence of the program, would have been victimized by crime and who, if the program is implemented, are not. These persons experience a significant monetary benefit in forgone medical expenses and property losses. Also, children in the Perry Preschool program, by age twenty-seven, experience a monetary benefit related to the increase in their income. Likewise, mothers participating in the Elmira PEIP demonstrated an increase in their earned income. However, in the case of the Elmira PEIP home-visits program, the net income gains to the mother are small because the increase in employment income is largely offset by a decrease in welfare income. In addition, in considering any income-related findings from the Elmira PEIP, it must be kept in mind that participating children have not aged sufficiently to determine any income effects for them.

Notes

1. The cost-savings analysis reported in this chapter draws on previous assessments for both the Perry Preschool program (Barnett 1993) and the Elmira Prenatal–Early Infancy Project (Olds et al. 1993). Our contribution beyond these earlier analyses is highlighted in the discussion that follows.

2. The *government* is sometimes used as a term separate from, even set in opposition to, the *people.* We do not intend that here. Throughout this chapter, the *government* should be understood as the agent spending the taxpayers' money on their behalf, or simply as the public accounts of the people.

3. In some cases, benefits that cannot be easily monetized themselves (e.g., IQ gains) may be linked to other benefits that, when measured, can be monetized (e.g., higher earnings in adulthood).

4. In the Perry Preschool case, our analysis is limited to adaptation of Barnett's previous cost-savings analysis (Barnett 1993) for comparability with our Elmira PEIP estimates.

5. This observation and similar assertions in this chapter should not be taken as criticisms of those designing and carrying out programs we judged not amenable to cost-savings analysis. Designers and implementers of such programs may have had priorities other than scientifically sound cost-benefit evaluation or may have, in any case, done the best job possible considering available resources and other constraints.

6. The standard error, or standard deviation, is a measure of the degree to which a set of numbers varies from its mean.

7. At the time of the age-fifteen follow-up, the significant differences were primarily for the higher-risk families. We are grateful for the separate unpublished results for those in the lower-risk sample that were provided by David Olds.

8. This is a weighted average that accounts for the fact that about 20 percent of participants attended only one year of the two-year program (Barnett 1993).

9. Barnett (1993) also includes savings to government from reduced use of adult education and the increased costs to government from greater participation in college. These two factors are small and nearly cancel each other out.

10. By net present value, we mean the sum of the dollar amounts over all future years, discounted at a constant rate per year to take into account the fact that future dollars are worth less than today's dollars.

11. We show all numbers to the nearest dollar, so that readers can follow our calculations without the impediment of rounding errors. Obviously, the level of precision shown is much greater than the data can support. Our conclusions do not depend on it.

12. For convenience, we use average savings per child. For example, we do not mean to suggest that a typical child enrolled in the Elmira PEIP program would have cost the criminal justice system another $4,195 without the program. Many of these children incurred no criminal justice costs during their lifetimes. But some incurred very large expenses, resulting in the average $4,195 figure when those amounts are spread out over everyone.

13. We began this chapter by searching for benefits from early interventions beyond the families they were intended to serve. Although increased income to participants is not in direct terms such a benefit, these persons *are* part of society at large, and increased production benefits everyone indirectly. The amount of the benefit may not be equal to the income. In fact, a program participant, rather than occupying a new job slot, may be displacing someone else from an existing slot, so there may be no change in economic activity (and there may also be none of the new taxes counted above as benefits). However, full credit is typically taken for such increases in personal income in social-welfare analyses, and we follow suit here.

14. The reasoning here is that, as shown above, early interventions discourage criminal careers. Implementing such programs thus reduces the losses to society from crime.

15. Note that our approach differs from Barnett (1993) who includes intangible losses from crime in his estimates of the benefits of the Perry Preschool program.

16. This is a real discount rate, that is, one that ignores inflation or, to put it another way, one that applies after the effects of inflation have been taken into account.

17. Before it can be said that funding any given program is justified on the basis of a cost-savings (or cost-benefit) analysis, other uses of the money with potentially more favorable cost-savings ratios must be taken into account, along with other public priorities and budgetary constraints.

References

Barnett, W. S. 1993. Benefit-cost analysis of pre-school education: Findings from a 25-year follow-up. *American Journal of Orthopsychiatry* 63, no. 4: 500–508.

Bayley, D. H., ed. 1998. *What works in policing*. New York: Oxford University Press.

Greenwood, P. W., Model, K. E., Rydell, C. P., and Chiesa, J. 1996. *Diverting children from a life of crime: Measuring costs and benefits*. Santa Monica, Calif.: RAND.

Karoly, L. A., Greenwood, P. W., Everingham, S. S., Houbé, J., Kilburn, R. M., Rydell, C. P., Sanders, M., and Chiesa, J. 1998. *Investing in our children: What we know and don't know about the costs and benefits of early childhood interventions.* Santa Monica, Calif.: RAND.

McGill, D. E., Mihalic, S. F., and Grotpeter, J. K. 1997. *Blueprints for violence prevention: Big Brothers Big Sisters of America, book two*. Delbert S. Elliott, series ed. Boulder, Colo.: Institute of Behavioral Sciences, Regents of the University of Colorado.

Olds, D. L. 1996. *Reducing risks for childhood-onset conduct disorder with prenatal and early childhood home visitation*. Paper presented at the American Public Health Association Pre-Conference Workshop: Prevention Science and Families: Mental Health Research and Public Health Policy Implications, New York, Nov.

Olds, D. L., Eckenrode, J., Henderson, C. R., Kitzman, H., Powers, J., Cole, R., Sidora, K., Morris, P., Pettitt, L. M., and Luckey, D. 1997. Long-term effects of home visitation on maternal life course and child abuse and neglect: Fifteen-year follow-up of a randomized trial. *Journal of the American Medical Association* 278, no. 8: 637–43.

Olds, D. L., Henderson, C. R., and Kitzman, H. 1994. Does prenatal and infancy nurse home visitation have enduring effects on qualities of parental caregiving and child health at 25 to 50 months of life? *Pediatrics* 93, no. 1: 89–98.

Olds, D. L., Henderson, C. R., Phelps, C., Kitzman, H., and Hanks, C. 1993. Effects of prenatal and infancy nurse home visitation on government spending. *Medical Care* 31, no. 2: 155–74.

5

The Comparative Costs and Benefits of Programs to Reduce Crime

A Review of Research Findings with Implications for Washington State

STEVE AOS
POLLY PHIPPS
ROBERT BARNOSKI
ROXANNE LIEB

This chapter describes estimates of the costs and benefits of programs intended to reduce criminal behavior.[1] The analysis was carried out by the Washington State Institute for Public Policy (hereafter referred to as the "Institute") for the Washington State Legislature. The primary purpose of the estimates presented here is to assist public-sector decisionmakers in allocating prevention and criminal justice resources. For a wide range of programs—from prevention programs designed for young children to correctional programs for juvenile and adult offenders—the Institute examines whether a program's monetary benefits are likely to outweigh its monetary costs. The "bottom-line" findings are based on a common methodological approach, allowing an "apples-to-apples" comparison of the economics of programs aimed at very different age groups. This approach is similar to a financial analysis an investment adviser might undertake to study rates of return on mutual funds, bonds, real estate, or other diverse investments. The focus is on the *comparative* economic bottom line and identifying where an investor—in this case a taxpayer—is likely to get the most bang for his or her buck.

In recent years, researchers have increased their knowledge about "what works" and "what doesn't" in the criminal justice and crime prevention fields.[2] Although the number and quality of program evaluations are still well below the level researchers would prefer, the general state of knowledge about effective and ineffective programs has advanced. Despite these improvements, however, almost all criminal justice evaluations stop short of providing the type of financial information that can allow decisionmakers to allocate resources effectively. Either most evaluations do not perform an analysis of costs and benefits at all, or, if one is attempted, it is usually a brief, ancillary calculation at the end of the evaluation.[3] The premise underlying this chapter is that program economics need to be a central concern, not a sideshow curiosity. In particular, it is our view that in order to be useful for public policy making, the economic estimates for programs need to be calculated on a consistent basis so that one programmatic option can be compared directly to another.

To be useful for those who must decide how to fund and run criminal justice systems, more evaluation research is needed on the relative costs and benefits of different options. Like any investor considering modifications to his or her investment portfolio, criminal justice policymakers need bottom-line information in order to understand and compare the resource implications of their options and decisions. For example, is it worthwhile to spend $5,000 per juvenile offender on a treatment program if recidivism rates can be lowered by 50 percent? Is it worth it if recidivism rates can be reduced by only 5 percent? How about a 1 percent decrease? These are the practical economic questions that need to be answered if decisionmakers in the criminal justice field are to have the same type of financial information relied on in other areas. In a manufacturing business, for example, as important as it is to know if a piece of equipment works, it is even more important to know if the equipment can be profitable—that is, if its economic benefits are likely to exceed its costs. The results described in this chapter offer an attempt to supply that type of economic information for criminal justice and violence prevention programs.

This chapter is limited to a summary discussion of the results of the Institute's cost-benefit model. The model itself is not discussed. The technical modeling steps required to estimate costs and benefits on a consistent basis are described elsewhere (Aos et al. 1999). Additionally, the results presented here are current as of May 1999. Like any investment adviser, the Institute is continually updating and improving these estimates to provide the Washington State Legislature and executive agencies with the latest cost-benefit findings for this range of programs.[4]

The Institute's cost-benefit model analyzes program economics from two perspectives. First, the taxpayers' vantage point is considered. For every dollar of taxpayer money spent on a prevention or intervention program, can downstream criminal justice costs be avoided by at least that amount due to reduced criminal activity? In other words, by spending a taxpayer dollar now on a program, will more than one taxpayer dollar be saved in the years ahead? The results described in this chapter present taxpayer estimates for one political jurisdiction in the United States: state and local governments in the state of Washington.

In addition to the taxpayers' perspective, the model also uses information on the costs of crime to victims. If a program can reduce rates of future criminal offending, not only will taxpayers receive benefits through lower future criminal justice costs, but there will be fewer crime victims as well. Readers of this chapter should be aware that the Institute has been purposefully cautious in reporting the findings on victimization costs. For example, if an evaluation of a program indicates that it reduces officially reported crime statistics such as arrests or convictions, then some number of victimizations will also be avoided. Since few studies estimate effects on victimizations, however, it is difficult to estimate the number of victimizations avoided. The conservative approach—the one used in this chapter—is to assume that there is always one victimization associated with one officially reported criminal event. It is more likely, however, that if a program reduces officially reported criminal events, then more than one victimization will be avoided. This is borne out in research on offending rates in different offender populations.[5] The Institute's cost-benefit model is capable of being run with multiple victimization estimates, but we have chosen to be conservative in the results reported here. The net effect of this decision is to understate the crime reduction benefits associated with successful programs.

It is also important to note that this cost-benefit model concentrates on program economics in one outcome area: criminality. Many, if not most, programs have additional or alternative goals. For example, the primary goals of some prevention programs are to reduce teen pregnancy, substance abuse, or drop-out rates. The principal goal of some adult offender programs is to maintain in-prison control of inmates. Although society, program participants, and taxpayers can benefit from changes in these and other behaviors, our analysis measures only the costs and benefits of crime-related outcomes.

At present, this review does not include the full range of criminal justice topics. We omit, for example, research on policing practices and the effect of deterrence and incapacitation in sentencing policies. As more research is undertaken both in Washington State and elsewhere, our cost-benefit analysis can be extended to encompass these and other areas of interest to policymakers.

In its simplest form, the model computes costs and benefits by following a three-step procedure for each program reviewed:

1. The results of existing evaluations are standardized to gauge whether a particular program has been shown to be effective in lowering crime rates. The Institute uses standard "effect size" methods to record the results from program evaluations.[6] The Institute adjusts these program effects to account for the quality of the research design[7] and implementation; that is, the effect sizes from evaluations with weaker statistical designs are lowered systematically. The Institute also makes several other adjustments to the published results to account for the seriousness of the crimes averted; the length of the follow-up period; the transferability of experimental program results to a real-world setting; and the possibility that marginal criminal justice costs may not fall as fast as they rise in response to changes in crime. The interested reader can find more on these topics in Aos et al. (1999).
2. The cost-benefit model then estimates the value to Washington taxpayers of reducing crime (from the first step) in terms of avoided downstream state and local criminal justice costs. The value to crime victims is also estimated at this stage. Per-unit criminal victimization costs are taken from Miller, Cohen, and Wiersema (1996).
3. Finally, the model calculates an economic "bottom line" by subtracting the expected costs of a particular program from its projected benefits (from the second step).

With these three pieces of information, the cost-benefit model produces standard financial statistics (net present value, benefit-cost ratios, internal rates of return, break-even levels, and years to payback) on the net economic position of programs and policy alternatives. Some of these summary statistics are discussed in this chapter.

Findings About Specific Programs

We divide the research literature on "what works and what doesn't" into five broad areas:

- early-childhood programs,
- middle-childhood programs,

- adolescent (nonjuvenile offender) programs,
- juvenile offender programs, and
- adult offender programs

In this chapter, we summarize our findings for each area. The principal results of our economic analysis are displayed in Table 5.1. This table contains our comparative, "apples-to-apples," bottom-line findings. All dollar values are expressed in present-valued 1998 dollars. For each program, three key summary measures are reported in Table 5.1.

Cost of the Program, per Participant

The estimated program cost is shown in the first column of Table 5.1. These costs are estimates of the incremental costs of adding the program. The costs are expressed as *net* direct costs. That is, for certain programs, there may be a direct taxpayer cost avoided if the participants would otherwise be in a publicly funded alternative program. For example, a program for counseling a juvenile offender and his or her family may cost $5,000 per participant. Depending on how the program is administered, if the youth enters the program he or she may not participate in the usual services offered to juvenile offenders. If these usual services cost, say, $500 per participant, then the net "up front" direct cost of the program reported in column one of Table 5.1 would be $4,500.

Taxpayer Benefits

Columns two and three provide our estimates of the present value of crime-related benefits to Washington taxpayers that a program can produce. If a program reduces future crime, then these are the estimates of how many dollars taxpayers will save, in present value terms, by not having to pay for the reduced level of crime. Column two indicates the estimated *total* dollar amount of benefits—per program participant—a taxpayer is expected to receive in avoided downstream criminal justice costs. Column three divides the total taxpayer benefits (in column two) by the costs (in column one) to arrive at a benefit-to-cost ratio. Values in column three greater than $1.00 mean that, from a taxpayer's perspective, the crime-reducing benefits are greater than the costs.

Taxpayer and Crime Victim Benefits

Columns four and five provide our estimates of the taxpayer benefits (from column two) and the benefits to crime victims when a program lowers crime. Column four reports the *total* estimated taxpayer and vic-

TABLE 5.1 Summary of Key Economic Measures for Programs (All Dollar Values Are in 1998 Dollars)

	Estimated Program Cost per Participant	*Criminal Justice System Benefits (Taxpayer Cost Savings)*		*Criminal Justice System and Crime Victim Benefits*	
		Per Participant	*Benefits per Dollar of Cost*	*Per Participant*	*Benefits per Dollar of Cost*
	(1)	*(2)*	*(3)*	*(4)*	*(5)*
Early Childhood Programs					
Perry Preschool	$13,938	$9,237	$0.66	$20,954	$1.50
Syracuse Family Development Research Program	45,092	8,613	0.19	15,487	0.34
Nurse Home Visitation	7,403	6,155	0.83	11,369	1.54
Middle School Programs					
Seattle Social Development Project	$3,017	$2,704	$0.90	$5,399	$1.79
Adolescent (Nonjuvenile Offender) Programs					
Quantum Opportunities Program	$18,292	$1,582	$0.09	$2,290	$0.13
Big Brothers Big Sisters of America	1,009	1,313	1.30	2,143	2.12
Juvenile Offender Programs					
Community-Based Programs					
Multisystemic Therapy	$4,540	$38,047	$8.38	$61,068	$13.45
Functional Family Therapy	2,068	14,167	6.85	22,739	10.99
Aggression Replacement Training	404	7,896	19.57	12,674	31.40
Adolescent Diversion Project	1,509	11,508	7.62	20,547	13.61
Multidimensional Treatment Foster Care	1,934	27,202	14.07	43,661	22.58
Juvenile Intensive Supervision (Probation)	1,500	1,347	0.90	2,235	1.49
Juvenile Intensive Supervision (Parole)	n.a.	n.a.	n.a.	n.a.	n.a.
Institutional-Based Programs					
Juvenile Boot Camps	-1,964	(4,680)	0.42	(7,511)	0.26
Juvenile Institutional Treatment services	n.a.	n.a.	n.a.	n.a.	n.a.

Adult Offender Programs					
Community-Based Programs					
Job Counseling & Job Search for Inmates Leaving Prison	$539	$1,532	$2.84	$2,154	$4.00
Drug Courts	2,000	3,385	1.69	4,368	2.18
Short-term Financial Assistance for Inmates Leaving Prison	2,718	2,080	0.77	2,924	1.08
Subsidized Jobs for Inmates Leaving Prison	10,089	6,750	0.67	9,490	0.94
Adult Intensive Supervision Programs	3,345	1,298	0.39	1,730	0.52
Case Management Substance Abuse Programs	2,144	(329)	(0.15)	(456)	(0.21)
Work Release Programs	0	0	n.a.	0	n.a.
Community-Based Substance Abuse Treatment	n.a.	n.a.	n.a.	n.a.	n.a.
In-Prison Programs					
Moral Reconation Therapy	$285	$2,330	$8.17	$3,275	$11.48
Reasoning and Rehabilitation	296	750	2.54	1,039	3.51
In-Prison Vocational Education	1,876	4,316	2.30	6,068	3.23
Adult Basic Education	1,888	3,220	1.71	4,528	2.40
In-Prison Therapeutic Communities	5,500	4,202	0.76	5,908	1.07
Sex Offender Treatment Programs	6,435	1,591	0.25	1,681	0.26
Life Skills Programs	809	0	0.00	0	0.00
Correctional Industries	n.a.	1,725	n.a.	2,426	n.a.
In-Prison Nonresidential Substance Abuse treatment	n.a.	n.a.	n.a.	n.a.	n.a.
Other Cognitive Behavioral Therapy	n.a.	n.a.	n.a.	n.a.	n.a.

NOTE: n.a. means that the Institute was not able to develop estimates because of insufficient information.

tim benefits per program participant, whereas column five divides this sum by the program costs (from column one) to produce a benefit-to-cost ratio.

We will discuss, in summary terms, each program below. A fuller discussion of the research studies underlying these conclusions can be found in Aos et al. (1999). In particular, the citations for 141 individual research studies reviewed for this cost-benefit analysis are listed in Aos et al. (1999).

Early-Childhood Programs

The Institute found three programs designed for very young children that have been evaluated for crime-related outcomes. All three also found desirable effects for non-crime-related outcomes. For example, the nurse home-visitation program found significant effects on child abuse and neglect, subsequent pregnancies, welfare dependence, and behavior problems due to substance abuse, in addition to reduced criminal behavior by the mothers and their children. As mentioned above, however, our economic analysis measures only the benefits associated with the crime-related effects of these programs. Thus, the estimates in Table 5.1 understate—to a degree—the total benefits that taxpayers or society might be able to achieve with these programs.[8]

Perry Preschool. The Perry Preschool program provided early-childhood education to disadvantaged children to improve their later school and life performances. The goal was to overcome school failure associated with childhood poverty by promoting the intellectual, social, and physical development of young children. By increasing academic success, the program sought to improve employment opportunities and wages and decrease crime, teenage pregnancy, and welfare use. The program was aimed at low-socioeconomic families with children ages three and four. Perry Preschool was a two-year intervention that operated 2.5 hours per day, five days per week, seven months per year, and included weekly home visitations by teachers. The school operated in the 1960s in Ypsilanti, Michigan. Its most recent evaluation reported on the life outcomes of participants at age twenty-seven.

After reviewing the Perry Preschool evaluation results, the Institute found an effect size of about 0.26 for basic crime outcomes.[9] Overall, taxpayers gain approximately $9,237 in subsequent criminal justice costs for each program participant. In 1998 dollars, the program cost $13,938 per child. Therefore, taxpayers receive $0.66 in criminal justice system benefits for every $1.00 spent. Crime victims save an average of $11,717 in costs for each program participant, for a combined taxpayer and crime victim benefit of $1.50 for every $1.00 spent.

Syracuse Family Development Research Program. The Syracuse Family Development Research Program (FDRP) was a five-year program in the early 1970s for low-income, mostly single-parent families, providing prenatal care, weekly home visits, parent training, child care, and nutrition. FDRP sought to bolster child and family functioning and interpersonal relationships. The intervention targeted African American single-parent, low-income families to improve the children's cognitive and emotional functioning, foster children's positive outlooks, and decrease juvenile delinquency. The mothers were young (eighteen years on average), had little or no work history, and were in the last trimester of their first or second pregnancy.

After reviewing the evaluation of FDRP, the Institute found an effect size of about 0.54 for basic crime outcomes. Overall, taxpayers gain approximately $8,613 in subsequent criminal justice costs for each program participant. In 1998 dollars, the program cost $45,092 per child. Therefore, taxpayers receive $0.19 in criminal justice system benefits for every $1.00 spent. Crime victims save an average of $6,875 in costs for each program participant, for a combined taxpayer and crime victim benefit of $0.34 for every $1.00 spent.

Nurse home visitation. The nurse home-visitation program consists of intensive and comprehensive home visitation by nurses during a woman's pregnancy and the first two years after birth. The goal is to promote the child's physical, cognitive, and social-emotional development, and to provide general support and instructive parenting skills to the parents. The program is designed to serve low-income, at-risk pregnant women bearing their first child. The program helps women plan future pregnancies, educational achievement, and participation in the workforce. Typically, a nurse visitor is assigned to a family and works with that family through the duration of the program. Treatment begins during pregnancy, with an average of eight one-hour visits, and continues postpartum with visits diminishing in frequency.

The evaluation found successful outcomes when the program assisted unmarried, low-income, higher-risk women. Follow-up at fifteen years' postpartum showed significant effects on child abuse and neglect, subsequent pregnancies, welfare dependence, behavior problems due to substance abuse, and criminal behavior by the mothers and their children. The Institute's cost-benefit analysis, calculated for this higher-risk group, estimates the crime-related benefits from the program's effects on the nurse-visited mothers as well as their children. Overall, taxpayers gain approximately $6,155 in subsequent criminal justice costs for each program participant. The program is estimated to cost $7,403 (in 1998 dollars) per program participant. Therefore, taxpayers receive $0.83 in criminal justice system benefits for every $1.00 spent. Crime victims save an average of $5,215 in costs for each program participant, for a combined taxpayer and crime victim benefit of $1.54 for every $1.00 spent.

Middle-Childhood Programs

Seattle Social Development Project. The Seattle Social Development Project (SSDP) is a three-part intervention for teachers, parents, and students in grades 1 to 6. The focus is elementary schools in high-crime urban areas. The intervention trains teachers to manage classrooms to promote bonding to school. SSDP also offers training to parents to promote bonding to family and school. It provides training to children designed to affect attitudes toward school, behavior in school, and academic achievement.

After reviewing the evaluation of SSDP, the Institute found an effect size of about 0.23 for basic crime outcomes. Overall, taxpayers gain approximately $2,704 in subsequent criminal justice costs for each program participant. The program is estimated to cost $3,017 (in 1998 dollars) per program participant. Therefore, taxpayers receive $0.90 in criminal justice system benefits for every $1.00 spent. From a taxpayer's perspective, the program can "break even" if it achieves a 21.3 percent reduction in crime outcomes. Crime victims save an average of $2,695 in costs for each program participant, for a combined taxpayer and crime victim benefit of $1.79 for every $1.00 spent.

Adolescent (Nonoffender) Programs

Quantum Opportunities Program. The Quantum Opportunities Program (QOP) is designed to serve disadvantaged adolescents by providing education, service, and development activities, as well as financial incentives from ninth grade through high school graduation. QOP is designed for adolescents from families receiving public assistance. Each participant is eligible to receive annually 250 hours of education (participating in computer-assisted instruction, peer tutoring to enhance basic academic skills, and so on), 250 hours of development activities (participating in cultural enrichment and personal development, acquiring life and family skills, planning for college or advanced technical or vocational training, and job preparation), and 250 hours of service activities (participating in community service projects, helping with public events, and working as a volunteer in various agencies).

After reviewing the evaluation of QOP, the Institute found an effect size of about 0.42 for basic crime outcomes. Overall, taxpayers gain approximately $1,582 in subsequent criminal justice costs for each program participant. In 1998 dollars, the program cost $18,292 per youth for the four years, including both operating and administrative costs. Therefore, taxpayers receive $0.09 in criminal justice system benefits for every $1.00 spent. Crime victims save an average of $707 in costs for each program participant, for a combined taxpayer and crime victim benefit of $0.13 for every $1.00 spent.

Big Brothers/Big Sisters of America. Big Brothers/Big Sisters of America (BBBSA) is a mentoring program that links at-risk youths with volunteer adults. The mentors act as positive resources for youths who may otherwise lack such role models. Length of participation can vary from several months to several years. Contacts usually occur three times monthly, for four hours a visit. Adult mentors are trained to refer any ancillary needs (e.g., substance abuse treatment, mental or physical health concerns) to program personnel for follow-up.

The existing evaluation of BBBSA did not measure criminal outcomes directly (the question tested was the "number of times hit someone"). Therefore, the Institute lowered the estimated effect of BBBSA in its cost-benefit calculations (from an effect size of 0.11 to 0.05). Overall, taxpayers gain approximately $1,313 in subsequent criminal justice costs for each program participant. Based on the Institute's estimates, a typical average cost per BBBSA participant is $1,009 (in 1998 dollars). Therefore, taxpayers receive $1.30 in criminal justice system benefits for every $1.00 spent. From a taxpayer's perspective, the BBBSA program can "break even" if it achieves a 10.5 percent reduction in crime outcomes. Crime victims save an average of $830 in costs for each program participant, for a combined taxpayer and crime victim benefit of $2.12 for every $1.00 spent.

Juvenile Offender Programs

Multisystemic Therapy. Multisystemic Therapy (MST) is an intensive home-based intervention for chronic, violent, or substance abusing juvenile offenders, ages twelve to seventeen. Trained therapists work with the youth and his or her family. The MST intervention is based on several factors, including an emphasis on addressing the known causes of delinquency. The treatment services are delivered in the youth's home, school, and community settings, with a strong focus on treatment adherence and program fidelity. Service duration averages sixty hours of contact over four months. Each MST therapist works in a team of four therapists and carries a caseload of four to six families.

The Institute's review of national research found that MST has been well evaluated in several settings. After reviewing the evaluations, the Institute found an average effect size of about 0.68 for basic recidivism.

Overall, taxpayers gain approximately $38,047 in subsequent criminal justice costs for each program participant. Based on the Institute's estimates, a typical average cost per MST participant is about $4,540 (in 1998 dollars). Therefore, taxpayers receive $8.38 in criminal justice system benefits for every $1.00 spent. From a taxpayer's perspective, the MST program can "break even" if it achieves a 10.2 percent reduction in recidivism. Crime victims save an average of $23,021 in costs for each program participant, for a combined taxpayer and crime victim benefit of $13.45 for every $1.00 spent.

Functional Family Therapy. Functional Family Therapy (FFT) targets youths, ages eleven to eighteen, with problems of delinquency, violence, and substance use. FFT focuses on altering interactions among family members and seeks to improve the functioning of the family unit. FFT is provided by individual therapists, typically in the home setting, and focuses on increasing family problem-solving skills, enhancing emotional connection, and strengthening the parental ability to provide appropriate structure, guidance, and limits to their children. FFT generally requires eight to twelve hours of direct service to youths and their families, and generally no more than twenty-six hours for the most severe problem situations.

The Institute's review of national research found that FFT has been evaluated in several trials. After reviewing the evaluations, and giving greater weight to the better studies, the Institute found an average effect size of about 0.34 for basic recidivism. Overall, taxpayers gain approximately $14,167 in subsequent criminal justice costs for each program participant. Based on the Institute's estimates, a typical average cost per FFT participant is $2,068 (in 1998 dollars). Therefore, taxpayers receive $6.85 in criminal justice system benefits for every $1.00 spent. From a taxpayer's perspective, the FFT program can "break even" if it achieves a 7.3 percent reduction in recidivism. Crime victims save an average of $8,572 in costs for each program participant, for a combined taxpayer and crime victim benefit of $10.99 for every $1.00 spent.

Aggression-Replacement Training. Aggression Replacement Training (ART) is a cognitive-behavioral intervention that attempts to reduce the antisocial behavior, and increase the prosocial behavior, of juvenile offenders. ART has three components. In the anger-control component, participants learn what triggers their anger and how to control their reactions. The "skill-streaming" behavioral component teaches a series of prosocial skills through modeling, role playing, and performance feedback. In the moral-reasoning component, participants work through cognitive conflict in "dilemma" discussion groups. The program is run in groups of eight to ten juvenile offenders.

The Institute's review of ART research found a few evaluations of these programs. Using the Institute's weighting scheme to combine the study results, the evaluations have an average effect size of 0.26 for basic recidivism. Overall, taxpayers gain approximately $7,896 in subsequent criminal justice costs for each program participant. Based on the Institute's estimates, in 1998 dollars, the program costs $404 per participant. Therefore, taxpayers receive $19.57 in criminal justice system benefits for every $1.00 spent. From a taxpayer's perspective, the ART program can "break even" if it achieves a 1.4 percent reduction in recidivism. Crime victims save an average of $4,778 in costs for each program participant, for a combined taxpayer and crime victim benefit of $31.40 for every $1.00 spent.

Adolescent Diversion Project. The Adolescent Diversion Project (ADP) serves 125 adolescent offenders per year diverted from the Ingham County Juvenile Court in Lansing, Michigan. The program stems from researched experiments conducted in the 1970s and 1980s. ADP diverts youths from the juvenile court to prevent them from being labeled as "delinquent." ADP "change agents" (usually college students) work with youths in their environment to provide community resources and initiate behavioral change. Change agents are trained in a behavioral model (contracting with rewards written into actual contracts between youth and significant other person in youth's environment) and to become advocates for community resources. Youths and change agents are matched, whenever possible, on race and gender. The evaluation results are for males only.

After reviewing the ADP evaluations, the Institute found an average effect size of about 0.57 for basic recidivism. Overall, taxpayers gain approximately $11,508 in subsequent criminal justice costs for each program participant. Based on the Institute's estimates, in 1998 dollars, the program costs $1,509 per participant. Therefore, taxpayers receive $7.62 in benefits for every $1.00 spent. From a taxpayer's perspective, the ADP program can "break even" if it achieves a 10.1 percent reduction in recidivism. Crime victims save an average of $9,039 in costs for each program participant, for a combined taxpayer and crime victim benefit of $13.61 for every $1.00 spent.

Multidimensional Treatment Foster Care. Multidimensional Treatment Foster Care (MTFC) is an alternative to group residential placement for high-risk and chronic juvenile offenders. The youth is placed with two trained and supervised foster parents for six to twelve months, and the youth's parents participate in family therapy. Near the end of the child's stay, the youth and his or her parents participate in family therapy together. The intervention is intensive, with at most two, and usually one, youths placed in the foster family. Community families are recruited, trained, and closely supervised. MTFC-placed adolescents are given treatment and intensive supervision at home, in school, and in the community; clear and consistent limits with follow-through on consequences; positive reinforcement for appropriate behavior; a relationship with a mentoring adult; and separation from delinquent peers. MTFC training for community families emphasizes behavior management methods to provide the youth with a structured and therapeutic living environment.

After reviewing the evaluation of MTFC, the Institute found an effect size of about 0.63 for basic recidivism. Overall, taxpayers gain approximately $27,202 in subsequent criminal justice costs for each program participant. A typical cost per MTFC participant (MTFC cost compared to regular group home cost) is $1,934, in 1998 dollars. Therefore, taxpayers receive $14.07 in criminal justice system benefits for every $1.00 spent. From a taxpayer's perspective, the MTFC program can "break even" if it achieves a 4.3 percent reduction in recidivism. Crime victims save an average of $16,459 in costs for each program participant, for a combined taxpayer and crime victim benefit of $22.58 for every $1.00 spent.

Juvenile Intensive Supervision Programs. Juvenile Intensive Supervision Programs (ISP) are designed for juvenile offenders serving a local sentence. The programs are characterized by more intense levels of supervision and surveillance than are exercised in routine juvenile court probation. The program features differ substantially across jurisdictions and in the type and risk levels of offenders participating in the programs. The Institute's review of the national research found several evaluations of ISPs for juvenile court populations. This research indicates only a slight effect in reducing recidivism.

After reviewing the evaluations and giving greater weight to the better studies, the Institute found an average effect size of about 0.03 for basic recidivism. Overall, taxpayers gain approximately $1,347 in subsequent criminal justice costs for each program participant. The Institute estimates that lowering a juvenile court probation counselor's caseload from fifty to twenty adds a cost of about $1,500 per offender (in 1998 dollars) to regular court probation costs. Therefore, taxpayers receive $0.90 in criminal justice system benefits for every $1.00 spent. From a taxpayer's perspective, the programs can "break even" if they achieve a 4.0 percent reduction in recidivism. Crime victims save an average of $889 in costs for each program participant, for a combined taxpayer and crime victim benefit of $1.49 for every $1.00 spent.

The Institute has not completed its literature review of intensive supervision programs for juvenile offenders on parole from institutional settings. Therefore, a cost-benefit analysis has not been undertaken.

Boot camps. The Office of Juvenile Justice and Delinquency Prevention (OJJDP) funded demonstration programs at three sites to develop prototypical camps and aftercare programs for male juveniles: Cleveland, Denver, and Mobile. According to OJJDP, the programs were intended to serve as a cost-effective alternative to institutionalization; promote discipline through physical conditioning and teamwork; instill moral values and a work ethic; promote literacy and increase academic achievement; reduce drug and alcohol abuse; encourage participants to become productive, law-abiding citizens; and ensure that offenders are held accountable for their actions. The three OJJDP studies, together with an evaluation of a California juvenile boot camp, found an average increase in the recidivism rates of boot camp participants compared to regular case processing.

After reviewing the boot camp evaluations, the Institute found an average effect size of about –0.11 for basic recidivism. Overall, taxpayers lose approximately $4,680 in subsequent criminal justice costs for each program participant. The boot camps cost about $1,964 less than regular juvenile case processing, in 1998 dollars, but this lower cost is more than offset by future criminal justice system costs associated with the increased recidivism rates. Therefore, taxpayers receive $0.42 in criminal justice system benefits for every $1.00 spent. From a taxpayer's perspective, boot camps can "break even" if they achieve a 5.2 percent reduction in recidivism. Crime victims lose an average of $2,831 in costs for each program participant, for a combined taxpayer and crime victim benefit of $0.26 for every $1.00 spent.

The Institute has not completed its literature review of treatment programs for juvenile offenders in institutional settings. Therefore, a cost-benefit analysis has not been undertaken.

Adult Offender Programs

Job counseling and job search for inmates leaving prison. Efforts to improve the labor market performance of ex-offenders are based on the theory that employed ex-offenders will be less likely to commit new crimes. One class of programs focuses on job search and employment counseling. In general, these programs attempt to link offenders with certain marketable skills to specific employers. The Institute found evaluations of five programs where a primary component was job search and counseling.

Overall, using the Institute's weighting scheme, the five evaluations have an average effect size of about 0.04 for basic recidivism. Taxpayers gain approximately $1,532 in subsequent criminal justice costs for each program participant. Based on the Institute's estimates, a typical average cost per participant is $539 (in 1998 dollars). Therefore, taxpayers receive $2.84 in criminal justice system benefits for every $1.00 spent. From a taxpayer's perspective, job counseling and search programs can "break even" if they achieve a 1.4 percent reduction in recidivism. Crime victims save an average of $622 in costs for each program participant, for a combined taxpayer and crime victim benefit of $4.00 for every $1.00 spent.

Drug courts. First introduced in Dade County, Florida, in 1989, a typical drug court targets nonviolent offenders whose current involvement with the criminal justice system stems primarily from substance addiction. Defendants eligible for a drug court are identified soon after arrest and, if accepted, are referred to a treatment program. The court usually requires several contacts per week (often daily) with a treatment provider. Frequent urinalysis tests and regular status hearings with the drug court judge are key elements. Many drug courts require participants to maintain employment and honor financial obligations, including court fees and child support, as well as perform community service.

Most evaluations to date have relatively weak research designs, making it difficult to determine program effectiveness in reducing recidivism. After reviewing the evaluations, and giving greater weight to the better studies, the Institute found an average effect size of 0.15 for basic recidivism. Overall, taxpayers gain approximately $3,385 in subsequent criminal justice costs for each program participant. Based on the Institute's estimates, a typical average cost per participant is about $2,000 (in 1998 dollars). Therefore, taxpayers receive $1.69 in criminal justice system benefits for every $1.00 spent. From a taxpayer's perspective, drug court programs can "break even" if they achieve a 10.0 percent reduction in recidivism. Crime victims save an average of $983 in costs for each program participant for a combined taxpayer and crime victim benefit of $2.18 for every $1.00 spent.

Short-term financial assistance for inmates leaving prison. One type of employment-related program that operated in the late 1970s distributed income supplements (similar to unemployment insurance payments) to offenders after release from prison. The purpose was to lessen the need to commit crime for financial gain after release and prior to employment.

Two high-quality research studies found conflicting results: One study (Berk, Lenihan, and Rossi 1980) found no recidivism effect for the payments, whereas the other (Mallar and Thornton 1978) found a relatively small effect. The Institute found an average effect size of 0.07 for basic recidivism. Overall, taxpayers gain approximately $2,080 in subsequent criminal justice costs for each program participant. Based on the Institute's estimates, a typical average payment per offender is $2,718 (in 1998 dollars). Therefore, taxpayers receive $0.77 in criminal justice system benefits for every $1.00 spent. From a taxpayer's perspective, short-term financial assistance programs can "break even" if they achieve a 9.1 percent reduction in recidivism. Crime victims save an average of $844 in costs for each program participant, for a combined taxpayer and crime victim benefit of $1.08 for every $1.00 spent.

Subsidized jobs for inmates leaving prison. If an inmate is provided a subsidized job after leaving prison, will he or she be less likely to commit new crimes? One study examined data from the National Supported Work Demonstration Project (NSWDP), a large-scale federally funded project undertaken in the 1970s to answer this question. The research concluded that, overall, there was no effect on recidivism. The research then examined the separate effects on older and younger ex-offenders. The study found there was a significant effect on offenders older than twenty-seven, but no significant effect on younger adults.

The Institute found an average effect size of 0.24 for basic recidivism based on the NSWDP for older (than twenty-seven) adult offenders. Overall, taxpayers gain approximately $6,750 in subsequent criminal justice costs for each program participant. Based on the Institute's estimates, the cost of subsidized jobs per participant is $10,089 (in 1998 dollars). Therefore, taxpayers receive $0.67 in criminal justice system benefits for every $1.00 spent. From a taxpayer's perspective, short-term financial assistance programs can "break even" if they achieve a 34.0 percent reduction in recidivism. Crime victims save an average of $2,740 in costs for each program participant, for a combined taxpayer and crime victim benefit of $.94 for every $1.00 spent.

Adult Intensive Supervision Programs. Adult Intensive Supervision Programs provide criminal sanctions that are a middle ground between prison and community corrections and are characterized by more intense levels of supervision and surveillance than are found in routine probation and parole. The program features differ substantially across jurisdictions and in the type and risk levels of offenders participating in the programs. The Institute's review of the national research found a significant number of program evaluations. Many evaluations have strong research designs. These programs have demonstrated only a slight, or no, effect in reducing recidivism.

After reviewing the evaluations and giving greater weight to the better studies, the Institute found an average effect size of about 0.05 for basic recidivism. Overall, taxpayers gain approximately $1,298 in subsequent criminal justice costs for each program participant. Based on the data from fourteen programs, a typical average cost per ISP participant is

$3,345 (in 1998 dollars). Therefore, taxpayers receive $0.39 in criminal justice system benefits for every $1.00 spent. From a taxpayer's perspective, ISP programs can "break even" if they achieve a 14.1 percent reduction in recidivism. Crime victims save an average of $433 in costs for each program participant, for a combined taxpayer and crime victim benefit of $0.52 for every $1.00 spent.

Case management substance abuse programs. Offenders in the community are often referred to substance abuse treatment through a case management program, which provides a liaison between the criminal justice system and the treatment programs. These programs usually assess offender needs and either provide or refer offenders to services. Community-based treatment usually involves outpatient drug-free treatment and, to a lesser extent, residential treatment.

The Institute's review of national research found a number of evaluations of these programs, many with strong research designs. Using the Institute's weighting scheme to combine the study results, the evaluations have an average effect size of –0.01 for recidivism, essentially no effect. Overall, taxpayers lose approximately $329 in subsequent criminal justice costs for each program participant. Based on available data from four programs (including treatment costs), a typical average cost per participant is $2,144 (in 1998 dollars). Therefore, taxpayers lose $0.15 in criminal justice system benefits for every $1.00 spent. From a taxpayer's perspective, programs can "break even" if they achieve an 8.4 percent reduction in recidivism. Crime victims lose an average of $127 in costs for each program participant, for a combined taxpayer and crime victim loss of $0.21 for every $1.00 spent.

Work release programs. Work release programs permit selected prisoners nearing the end of their terms to work in the community, returning to prison or community residential facilities for the nonworking hours. The programs are designed to prepare inmates to return to the community in a relatively controlled environment. Work release also allows inmates to earn income, reimburse the state for part of their confinement, build up savings for their eventual release, and acquire more positive living habits.

The only study we found on work release evaluated Washington's program. The study found no significant difference in recidivism rates between a group of inmates that participated in work release and those that did not, after about a ten-month follow-up. Rearrest data were used to measure recidivism. The study also conducted a cost analysis and found no significant difference in program costs between the two groups.

Community-based substance abuse treatment. Community-based treatment for offenders usually involves outpatient drug-free treatment and, to a lesser extent, residential treatment, with a limited number of offenders participating in methadone maintenance programs. The Institute's review of the national research found few evaluations of community substance abuse treatment programs independent of case management programs. Given the scarcity of evaluations, the Institute has not attempted to estimate the cost and benefits for this program area.

Moral Reconation Therapy. Moral Reconation Therapy (MRT) is a cognitive-behavioral program designed for treatment-resistant populations. The program involves a step-by-step process designed to raise offenders from low to high levels of moral development in order to insulate them from criminal behavior. Since MRT is conducted by correctional staff in a group setting, the cost per participant is low.

The Institute's review of national research found that a few MRT programs have been evaluated; however, the existing evaluations have shortcomings. After reviewing the evaluations, and giving greater weight to the better studies, the Institute found an average effect size of about 0.08 for basic recidivism. Overall, taxpayers gain approximately $2,330 in subsequent criminal justice costs for each program participant. Based on the Institute's estimates, a typical average cost per MRT participant is $285 (in 1998 dollars). Therefore, taxpayers receive $8.17 in criminal justice system benefits for every $1.00 spent. From a taxpayer's perspective, MRT programs can "break even" if they achieve a 1.0 percent reduction in recidivism. Crime victims save an average of $946 in costs for each program participant, for a combined taxpayer and crime victim benefit of $11.48 for every $1.00 spent.

Reasoning and Rehabilitation. Reasoning and Rehabilitation (R&R) is a program designed to teach social-cognitive skills to offenders. It is based on the premise that offenders lack the cognitive skills and attitudes essential for social competence and that acquiring such skills will better enable them to achieve success in legitimate pursuits and withstand pressures toward criminal behavior. The central goals are to modify offenders' impulsive, rigid, and illogical thinking patterns in favor of thought before action and consideration of behavioral consequences. Since R&R is conducted by correctional staff in a group setting, the cost per participant is low.

The Institute's review of the national research found that a few R&R programs have been evaluated. The existing evaluations, however, have shortcomings. After reviewing the evaluations, the Institute found an average effect size of about 0.03 for basic recidivism. Overall, taxpayers gain approximately $750 in subsequent criminal justice costs for each program participant. Based on the Institute's estimates, a typical average cost per R&R participant is $296 (in 1998 dollars). Therefore, taxpayers receive $2.54 in criminal justice system benefits for every $1.00 spent. From a taxpayer's perspective, R&R programs can "break even" if they achieve a 1.2 percent reduction in recidivism. Crime victims save an average of $289 in costs for each program participant, for a combined taxpayer and crime victim benefit of $3.51 for every $1.00 spent.

In-prison vocational education. Many adult offenders in the criminal justice system have poor job market skills and records. Vocational education to inmates is intended to improve the odds of postprison employment and thereby decrease the chance of subsequent criminal activity. Vocational education can include, for example, improving work-related math skills for the automotive or construction trades. Some programs offer in-prison apprenticeships and an accreditation element that can make it easier for offenders to obtain trade licenses.

The Institute's review of the evaluation research found very few published studies that have measured the effect of this strategy on criminal recidivism. Moreover, most studies used fairly weak research designs, making it difficult to generalize the findings. Of the three evaluations that met minimum research quality standards, the Institute found a weighted-average effect size of about 0.12 for basic recidivism. Overall, taxpayers gain approximately $4,316 in subsequent criminal justice costs for each program participant. Based on the Institute's estimates, a typical average cost per participant for Washington's vocational education program is $1,876 (in 1998 dollars). Therefore, taxpayers receive $2.30 in criminal justice system benefits for every $1.00 spent. From a taxpayer's perspective, programs can "break even" if they achieve a 4.7 percent reduction in recidivism. Crime victims save an average of $1,752 in costs for each program participant, for a combined taxpayer and crime victim benefit of $3.23 for every $1.00 spent.

Adult Basic Education. A premise of Adult Basic Education (ABE) is that many inmates lack basic abilities in reading, writing, and mathematics, and if these skills can be increased, offenders may have a better chance of avoiding criminal behavior when released from prison.

The Institute's review of the national research found that this question has not been extensively or rigorously evaluated. Only a handful of studies have been published, and most employ fairly weak research designs. Of the three evaluations that met minimum research quality standards, the Institute found a weighted-average effect size of about –0.09 for basic recidivism. Overall, taxpayers gain approximately $3,220 in subsequent criminal justice costs for each program participant. Based on the Institute's estimates, the average cost per ABE participant in Washington's program is $1,888 (in 1998 dollars). Therefore, taxpayers receive $1.71 in benefits for every $1.00 spent. From a taxpayer's perspective, programs can "break even" if they achieve a 4.8 percent reduction in recidivism. Crime victims save an average of $1,307 in costs for each program participant, for a combined taxpayer and crime victim benefit of $2.40 for every $1.00 spent.

In-prison Therapeutic Communities. In-prison Therapeutic Community (TC) substance abuse programs are multifaceted residential programs coming out of a "self-help" tradition and involve a strong group orientation, with a focus on changing criminal thinking and behavior patterns in order to reduce future crime.

The Institute's review of the national research found that many in-prison TC programs have been evaluated, a number of which employed fairly strong research designs for at least some program components. Using the Institute's weighting scheme to combine the study results, the evaluations have an average effect size of 0.11 for basic recidivism. Overall, taxpayers gain approximately $4,202 in subsequent criminal justice costs for each program participant. Based on cost data from seven programs, the Institute estimates a typical average cost per TC participant of about $5,500 (in 1998 dollars). Therefore, taxpayers receive $0.76 in criminal justice system benefits for every $1.00 spent. From a taxpayer's perspective, TC programs can "break even" if they achieve a 13.9 percent reduction in recidivism. Crime victims save an average of $1,706 in costs for each program participant, for a combined taxpayer and crime victim benefit of $1.07 for every $1.00 spent.

Sex offender treatment programs. Treatment of sex offenders includes traditional psychotherapies, insight therapy, and cognitive behavioral therapy. The latter, an increasingly popular method, is targeted at reducing deviant arousal, increasing appropriate sexual desires, improving social skills, and modifying distorted thinking. The treatment occurs both in prison and in the community; this analysis involves in-prison programs only.

The Institute's review of the international research found that few sex offender programs have been evaluated, and fewer still have a strong research design. Using the Institute's weighting scheme to combine the three most robust in-prison studies, the evaluations have an average effect size of 0.04 for basic recidivism. Overall, taxpayers gain approximately $1,591 in subsequent criminal justice costs for each program participant. The cost of sex offender programs, based on estimates for Washington State's program, is $6,435 per offender (in 1998 dollars). Therefore, taxpayers receive $0.25 in criminal justice system benefits for every $1.00 spent. From a taxpayer's perspective, sex offender treatment programs can "break even" only if they achieve at least a 26 percent reduction in recidivism. Crime victims save an average of $91 in costs for each program participant, for a combined taxpayer and crime victim benefit of $0.26 for every $1.00 spent.

Life-skills programs. Life-skills programs teach offenders a variety of daily living skills. The topics covered include employment skills, money management, social skills, and personal health issues.

The Institute's review of the national research found that few life-skills programs had been evaluated, and the ones with stronger research designs indicated no significant effect on recidivism. Using the Institute's weighting scheme to combine the results of these studies, the evaluations have an average effect size of 0.00 for recidivism, that is, no effect. The cost of a life-skills program, based on available data from one program, is estimated at $809 per offender (in 1998 dollars). Since the programs are estimated to have no effect of recidivism, there are $0.00 dollars in criminal justice system or crime victim benefits per $1.00 of program cost.

Correctional industries. Few well-designed studies have examined the effect that correctional industry programs have on criminal recidivism. Of the two evaluations that met minimum research quality standards, the Institute found a weighted-average effect size of about 0.05 for basic recidivism. The Institute was unable to complete its cost-benefit analysis of correctional industries programs because it is not clear how much money, if any, correctional industry programs cost taxpayers. In order to estimate the bottom line, a detailed cost study of Washington's correctional industries program would need to be undertaken.

In-prison nonresidential substance abuse treatment. A diverse collection of treatment interventions for substance abusing offenders have operated in prisons, including drug education, group and individual therapy, and relapse prevention. The programs are usually nonresidential (that is, inmates receiving treatment are not housed in separate quarters), and the length of treatment ranges from several weeks to approximately six months.

The Institute's review of national research found that few of these programs have been evaluated, although they are probably the most common type of substance abuse treatment conducted in prison. Given the scarcity of evaluations, the Institute has not attempted to estimate the costs and benefits for this program area. An evaluation of Washington's in-prison substance abuse programs would help establish whether these programs cost-effectively reduce recidivism.

Other cognitive behavioral therapy. The Institute found few cognitive behavioral program evaluations in the national research literature other than Moral Reconation Therapy and Reasoning and Rehabilitation (see above). Two other programs were a residential program called "Cognitive Self-Change" and an anger management program. Given the scarcity of evaluations, the Institute did not attempt to estimate the cost and benefits for these program areas.

Conclusion

Some Prevention and Intervention Programs Lower Criminality; Some Do Not

- Our first finding is *not* that "prevention works" or that "intervention works." That is too general a statement since we found well-researched programs that failed to affect rates of criminality. Rather, the main lesson is that some prevention or intervention programs work with certain groups of people in certain settings. Selecting and successfully implementing the right programs for the right populations are the real challenges for policymakers and program administrators.
- In reviewing program evaluations, we found some successful interventions across the age spectrum. We found successful *prevention* programs for young children or youths, and we found successful *intervention* programs for juveniles and adults already in the criminal justice system.
- Programs with the most favorable outcomes often demonstrate success rates that many would consider modest. For example, we found that the most successful programs for adult offenders lower the chance of reoffending by 10 to 15 percent. An example can help put this number in perspective. In Washington State, about 50 percent of all adult offenders leaving prison are subsequently reconvicted for another felony offense within eight years from release.[10] A 10 to 15 percent reduction from a 50 percent starting point would result in a 43 to 45 percent recidivism rate—a significant but not ostensibly huge reduction in recidivism. Based on our economic analyses, however, we found that programs that can deliver—at a reasonable cost—even modest

reductions in future criminality are likely to have an attractive economic bottom line.

- In Washington, as in the rest of the United States, most programs designed to reduce crime have not been rigorously evaluated. Some programs may be working and could be expanded. Others may not be achieving their goals, yet continue to absorb scarce tax dollars that could be directed toward more effective programs. Although evaluations are not cost-free, making decisions without objective information on effectiveness can result in inefficient resource allocation. Evaluating the costs and benefits of programs and policies should be a key part of the overall strategy.

Some Programs Not Only Work but Also Save More Money Than They Cost

- The Institute applied a cost-benefit analysis to the program evaluations we reviewed. The cost of crime to taxpayers (who pay for the criminal justice system) and crime victims (who suffer personal and property losses) is high. We found that reasonably priced programs that achieve even modest reductions in future crime rates yield positive economic returns.
- We found the largest and most consistent economic returns are for programs designed for juvenile offenders. Several of these interventions produce benefit-to-cost ratios in the order of five to ten dollars of taxpayer benefits for each dollar of taxpayer cost. Three of these programs are now being implemented by the juvenile courts in Washington State as a result of recent legislative and administrative actions.
- We also found economically attractive prevention programs for young children and adolescents and, at the other end of the age spectrum, for adult offenders. A nurse home-visitation program, an antidrug and antiviolence curriculum for grade schools in high-risk neighborhoods, and a mentoring program for high-risk adolescents can produce positive economic returns. For adult offenders, we found a few employment, education, drug treatment, and counseling programs that produce favorable returns.
- Not all of the economic findings, however, are positive. We found some programs that do not lower criminality and, thus, have a negative economic bottom line. Resources spent on these programs would be better directed toward programs that yield positive returns.

- We also found programs that demonstrate some success in reducing the criminality of participants, but the cost of the programs is greater than any savings realized. The economics of crime prevention or intervention require not only program effectiveness but also that the services must be delivered economically. In this regard, crime prevention and intervention is like any business: In order to have a positive economic bottom line, a product not only needs to work and be successful, but also needs to be produced in a cost-efficient manner. In our review of the available options, not all programs passed these two tests.
- The crime-reduction benefits of some prevention programs take many years to be realized. Typically, prevention programs are designed for children or adolescents. Their benefits of reduced crime may not occur until the participants are teenagers or young adults. Therefore, research-proven prevention programs should be part of a *long-term* resource allocation strategy. Other intervention programs are designed for offenders already in their crime-prone years, and their benefits are achieved in the near term. An overall criminal justice plan should develop an allocation of resources among these long-term and near-term prevention and intervention approaches.
- Because the research base for "what works" is limited, a degree of uncertainty must be applied to the economic estimates in this report. We believe that it would be a mistake to allocate all prevention and intervention dollars into one program. That is, like any investor, criminal justice decisionmakers should avoid putting all of the eggs into one basket. We recommend that a "portfolio approach" be developed so that a reasonable balance is achieved between near-term and long-term resources, and between research-proven strategies and those that are promising but in need of research and development.

Notes

1. A more detailed presentation of this material, together with a technical discussion of the cost-benefit model, can be found in Aos et al. (1999).

2. See, for example, the summaries of research in the following publications: Belenko (1998); Cullen, Wright, and Applegate (1996); Lipsey and Wilson (1998); MacKenzie and Hickman (1998); and Sherman et al. (1997).

3. One notable exception to the general lack of economic analysis in the criminal justice field has been the work of the RAND Corporation. See, for example, the excellent studies by Karoly et al. (1998) and Greenwood et al. (1996).

4. Interested readers can obtain the Institute's latest publications on our home page at the following Internet address: http://www.wa.gov/wsippp.

5. See, for example, Canela-Cacho, Blumstein, and Cohen (1997); Levitt (1996); Marvell and Moody (1994); and Spelman (1994).

6. The Institute uses standard statistical methods to calculate the "effect sizes" of different programs; see Cohen (1988). These research-based effect sizes are calculated from the published results of program evaluations. When the Institute reviews an evaluation, we record four types of information on a program's effectiveness in reducing crime. Relative to a control or comparison group: (1) Did the program affect the percentage of the population that offended? (2) Of those unoffended, did the program change the average number of offenses? (3) Did the program affect the types (i.e., the seriousness) of offenses of those that offended? (4) Of those that offended, did the program change the timing of the offenses? Almost all of the evaluations we review analyze and record information on the first effect. Far fewer evaluations report information on the second effect. Still fewer evaluations report information on the third effect, and almost no evaluations study or report findings on the fourth effect.

7. The five-point scale developed by researchers at the University of Maryland is used to rate the research design (see Sherman et al. 1997).

8. The Perry Preschool evaluation estimated that the crime-related benefits accounted for about 65 percent of the total benefits (see Schweinhart, Barnes, and Weikart 1993, 166).

9. See note 6 for a discussion of effect sizes.

10. The 50 percent felony recidivism rate is based on longitudinal analyses conducted by the Institute.

References

Aos, S., Phipps, P., Barnoski, R., and Lieb, R. 1999. *The comparative costs and benefits of programs to reduce crime: A review of national research findings with implications for Washington State, version 3.0.* Olympia: Washington State Institute for Public Policy. This document is available on the website of the Washington State Institute for Public Policy at http://www.wa.gov/wsipp.

Belenko, S. 1998. *Research on drug courts: A critical review.* New York: Columbia University, National Center of Addiction and Substance Abuse.

Berk, R. A., Lenihan, K. J., and Rossi, P. H. 1980. Crime and poverty: Some experimental evidence from ex-offenders. *American Sociological Review* 45: 766–86.

Canela-Cacho, J. A., Blumstein, A., and Cohen, J. 1997. Relationship between the offending frequency λ of imprisoned and free offenders. *Criminology* 35: 133–75.

Cohen, J. 1988. *Statistical power analysis for the behavioral sciences, second edition.* Hillsdale, N.J.: Lawrence Erlbaum.

Cullen, F. T., Wright, J. P., and Applegate, B. K. 1996. Control in the community: The limits of reform? In A. T. Harland, ed., *Choosing correctional options that work: Defining the demand and evaluating the supply,* 69–116. Thousand Oaks, Calif.: Sage Publications.

Greenwood, P. W., Model, K. E., Rydell, C. P., and Chiesa, J. 1996. *Diverting children from a life of crime: Measuring costs and benefits.* Santa Monica, Calif.: RAND.

Karoly, L. A., Greenwood, P. W., Everingham, S. S., Houbé, J., Kilburn, M. R., Rydell, C. P., Sanders, M., and Chiesa, J. 1998. *Investing in our children: What we know and don't know about the costs and benefits of early childhood interventions,* Santa Monica, Calif.: RAND.

Levitt, S. D. 1996. The effect of prison population size on crime rates: Evidence from prison overcrowding litigation. *Quarterly Journal of Economics* 111: 319–51.

Lipsey, M. W., and Wilson, D. B. 1998. Effective intervention for serious juvenile offenders: A synthesis of research. In R. Loeber and D. P. Farrington, eds., *Serious and violent juvenile offenders: Risk factors and successful interventions,* 313–45. Thousand Oaks, Calif.: Sage Publications.

MacKenzie, D. L., and Hickman, L. J. 1998. *What works in corrections? An examination of the effectiveness of the type of rehabilitation programs offered by Washington State Department of Corrections.* Olympia: Joint Legislative Audit and Review Committee.

Mallar, C. D., and Thornton, C. 1978. Transitional aid for released prisoners: Evidence from the Life Experiment. *Journal of Human Resources* 13: 208–36.

Marvell, T. B., and Moody, C. E. 1994. Prison population growth and crime reduction. *Journal of Quantitative Criminology* 10: 109–40.

Miller, T. R., Cohen, M. A., and Wiersema, B. 1996. *Victim costs and consequences: A new look.* Washington, D.C.: U.S. Department of Justice, National Institute of Justice.

Schweinhart, L. J., Barnes, H. V., and Weikart, D. P. 1993. *Significant benefits: The High/Scope Perry Preschool study through age 27.* Ypsilanti, Mich.: High/Scope Press.

Sherman, L. W., Gottfredson, D. C., MacKenzie, D. L., Eck, J., Reuter, P., and Bushway, S. D. 1997. *Preventing crime: What works, what doesn't, what's promising.* Washington, D.C.: U.S. Department of Justice, National Institute of Justice.

Spelman, W. 1994. *Criminal incapacitation.* New York: Plenum.

PART FOUR

International Policy Perspectives

6

Evaluation of the United Kingdom's "Crime Reduction Programme"

Analysis of Costs and Benefits

SANJAY DHIRI
PETER GOLDBLATT
SAM BRAND
RICHARD PRICE

In 1998 the U.K. government launched the "Crime Reduction Programme." This program aims to reduce crime and disorder through an evidence-led strategy of what works. Central to the program is the need to evaluate the effectiveness and cost-effectiveness of initiatives. This chapter sets out the principles that underpin the evaluation and highlights the key issues that have arisen in designing a methodology for analyzing the costs and benefits of crime reduction interventions.

Background

In May 1997 the incoming British government launched a review of public expenditure covering all areas of government activity. The purpose of this Comprehensive Spending Review was to reshape the pattern of public expenditure to reflect their priorities and to examine how their objectives could be most effectively and cost-effectively met. The review was completed in July 1998.

As part of this process, a Cross-Departmental Review of the criminal justice system (CJS) was undertaken to review the objectives, performance, and management of the system and existing practices to reduce crime and disorder in England and Wales. A working group commissioned a review of the effectiveness of policies for tackling offending behavior, and it devised an evidence-led strategy for crime reduction.

Reviewing the Evidence

This review culminated in a study that assessed research evidence on different methods of reducing crime (Goldblatt and Lewis 1998). Drawing on the typology developed by Sherman et al. (1997), the report sought to identify where there was sufficient research evidence to be able to say with a degree of certainty that an approach worked or not. It concluded that there was clear evidence that certain approaches were more effective and more cost-effective than others in reducing crime. The report also identified approaches and techniques that were "promising" and warranted further development and testing but for which there was insufficient evidence to say for certain that they both worked and were cost-effective.

The report brought together evidence from a broad range of crime prevention techniques that sought to:

- promote a less criminal society by preventing the development of criminality among young people and investing in situational crime prevention to reduce the opportunities for crime;
- prevent crime in the community by acting on the social conditions that sustain crime in residential communities and by implementing effective police strategies for reducing crime; and
- improve criminal justice interventions through changes in sentencing policy or extending the use of effective interventions with offenders and drug users.

The report concluded that a program of initiatives built on these objectives would offer the real prospect of a sustained reduction in the long-term rise in crime but recognized in particular that:

- An effective crime reduction strategy is one in which an integrated package of best practice is developed and delivered consistently over time;
- Multiple interventions are generally more cost-effective than initiatives with a single focus. For example, prevention pro-

grams for young people should target risk factors affecting all aspects of a child's life;

- Many promising initiatives bring their main crime reduction benefits over a long period. However they have earlier, beneficial effects on other outcomes (education, employment, informal social control, and family cohesion), the absence of which are predictors of subsequent criminality.

- Evidence on effectiveness, and more particularly cost-effectiveness, is currently limited, cannot easily be extrapolated nationally from small-scale pilots, and is not collected in a way which allows for comparisons between initiatives (Goldblatt and Lewis 1998).

This highlighted the need to develop crime reduction initiatives by drawing on existing evidence and to generate more and improved evidence on a consistent basis to allow comparisons among initiatives in the future. Comparative information was found to be particularly limited for evidence on cost-effectiveness. Few examples existed of programs evaluated in such a way as to allow a cost-effectiveness or cost-benefit analysis to be undertaken. In spite of these limitations, the report suggested that substantial crime reduction could be achieved through a coherent evidence-led program of initiatives within an overarching crime reduction strategy.

"Crime Reduction Programme"

In July 1998 the government announced a new Crime Reduction Programme (CRP) based on this review. This cross-departmental program for England and Wales is based on concrete evidence of what has proved effective in reducing crime and tackling its causes, rather than just dealing with its effects.

The £250 million (US$400 million) over three years committed to the CRP[1] makes it the biggest single investment in an evidence-based approach to crime reduction to have ever taken place in any country. The CRP is intended to contribute to reversing the long-term growth rate in crime by ensuring that the greatest impact for the money spent is achieved and that this impact increases progressively. It will do so by promoting innovation, generating a significant improvement in knowledge about effectiveness and cost-effectiveness, and fostering progressive mainstreaming of emerging knowledge about good practice. Projects will be carefully selected to ensure that they contribute to achieving these objectives. All CRP-funded initiatives will be independently evaluated.

Five key themes were identified in the development of the program:

- Working with families, children, and schools to prevent young people from becoming the offenders of the future;
- Tackling crime in communities, particularly high-volume crime such as domestic burglary;
- Developing products and systems that are more resistant to crime;
- More effective sentencing practices; and
- Working with offenders to ensure that they do not reoffend.

In April 1999 the CRP was extended with the announcement of a further £153 million for closed circuit television (CCTV) initiatives and other interventions particularly aimed at tackling vehicle crime.

The evidence-led approach was also applied to related programs that received funding under the Comprehensive Spending Review, in particular, those to combat drug use and related crime (£211 million) and to provide constructive prison regimes (£226 million). Initiatives under these programs are to be evaluated to the same standard as initiatives funded under the CRP.

Through a rigorous selection process, a number of initiatives have already been identified for CRP funding. These include:

- Tackling domestic burglary in and around five hundred high burglary neighborhoods;
- Targeted policing to ensure that police take a problem-solving approach to identifying and tackling crime and disorder;
- Domestic violence and violence against women;
- Tackling school exclusions to improve school management of attendance, behavior, and bullying to reduce the risk of future offending;
- Improving fine enforcement; and

- Design against crime to influence industry and the design bodies to produce more crime resistant designs.

Evaluation Principles

Any initiative taken forward as part of the program must be suitable for evaluation, and an evaluation plan must be included in the proposed design. The purpose of these evaluations is not simply to confirm existing knowledge about the intervention. It is to build on the knowledge about a particular technique or policy by:

- indicating how generalizable it is to similar settings;
- demonstrating more comprehensively the contexts, mechanisms, and processes essential to its success;
- indicating the time scales and sustainability of benefits;
- quantifying its cost-effectiveness; and
- indicating the likely requirements for and consequences of larger-scale implementation.

The information provided by external evaluations at key stages in the life of the initiative needs to be sufficient for decisions to be made on whether or not to continue (or change the level of) funding. The evaluation plan for each intervention will ensure that adequate information is available at key decision points. This will not, of course, preclude the collection of long-term impact information, which is central to the accumulation of knowledge from the program. For example, many decisions will need to be taken on the basis of the effect on risk factors for criminality, well before reductions in offending can be measured.

In considering mainstreaming and wider replication of successful initiatives, evaluation evidence will be brought together on the mechanisms by which the initiative achieved its impact, the contexts in which these were most successfully achieved, the processes needed for implementation (e.g., targeting and tailoring to specific contexts), and the procedures needed to ensure the integrity of outputs.

An assessment of cost-effectiveness will reflect these considerations. Initiatives and their evaluations will be conducted to a sufficient standard to ensure that comparative cost-effectiveness information is sufficiently good to support strategic decisions.

Analysis of Costs and Benefits

Objective

Measuring cost-effectiveness is a central part of the evaluation strategy for the "Crime Reduction Programme" and the wider government focus on ensuring value for money of all criminal justice system programs. The Home Office is currently developing a framework for the systematic evaluation of the costs and benefits of different CRP initiatives to allow for more informed decisions on resource allocation among different policy options to be made and enable the following key questions to be answered:

- What was the true opportunity cost of an intervention?
- Did the outcome(s) achieved justify the investment of resources?
- Was this the most efficient way of realizing the desired outcome, or could the same outcome have been achieved at a lower cost through an alternative course of action? and
- How should limited resources be spent to achieve the biggest possible sustained reduction in crime?

The cost-effectiveness analysis will therefore inform decisions on how to allocate scarce resources both within and among initiatives, including mainstream programs outside the CRP. It will also make this decision process more transparent by organizing information on inputs, outputs, impacts, and outcomes in a single comparative framework. Of course, there are likely to be a host of reasons for allocating resources in a particular way that fall outside the analysis, but it will provide a useful tool for assessing the use of scarce resources and comparing the relative cost-effectiveness of different interventions on a common basis. The framework for the analysis is developmental, and the methodology will be extended and refined as more experience is gained through the evaluation process.

Methodological Principles

Few previous evaluations of crime reduction initiatives have included a detailed cost-effectiveness analysis (Goldblatt and Lewis 1998; Welsh and Farrington 1999). Where attempts have been made to assess the cost-effectiveness of initiatives, they have typically been hampered by incomplete data on the cost of inputs and the lack of clear specification of outputs and outcomes (Stockdale, Whitehead, and Gresham 1999). A failure to capture the full costs of intervention has partly been the result of a ten-

TABLE 6.1 Key Principles in the Analysis of Costs and Benefits of CRP Initiatives

Comparability: The analysis will be methodologically consistent across initiatives so as to enable comparisons to be made between the cost-effectiveness of different approaches and techniques to reduce crime. Given the breadth of coverage of the CRP, it will not be possible to evaluate interventions in exactly the same way, nor would it be appropriate to do so. However, consistent principles and minimum standards have been set that apply to all interventions (Dhiri and Brand 1999). These will ensure that cost-effectiveness comparisons can be made across groups of initiatives.

Additionality: The analysis will compare additional costs with additional outputs and outcomes. On the input side, only those resources that have been mobilized as a result of the CRP project will be included. On the output/outcome side only those that have clearly resulted from the CRP project will be included.

Fully costed initiatives: Resources used in implementation of a project will be valued at their opportunity, rather than financial, cost. All resources mobilized as a result of the interventions will be included, not just those directly funded under the CRP. In addition, the wider social consequences of CRP initiatives will be included, although the primary focus will be on the reduction of crime.

Ongoing collection of data: An evaluation plan is required before a project can receive CRP funding. Sources of cost, output, and outcome data are explored before, or early in, the implementation process and are collected on an ongoing basis. This will provide fuller and more accurate information than would be possible in a retrospective analysis.

Replicability: Much of the CRP is focused on development projects. The analysis of costs and benefits will provide information both on the value for money of a particular project and on the likelihood that, if replicated elsewhere, it would remain cost-effective and how this could be ensured.

dency to estimate the cost of inputs retrospectively (Schweinhart, Barnes, and Weikart 1993; Greenwood et al. 1996; Waller, Welsh, and Sansfaçon 1997), rather than by routinely collecting data during the implementation period. This has made it difficult to compare the cost-effectiveness of different interventions.

Learning from this experience, inputs, outputs, and expected outcomes will be identified at an early stage, and systematic and consistent methods of data collection, collation, and analysis will be established. Generating information on a common basis will enable a comparative analysis of costs and benefits to be undertaken. This will help to guide the decision to modify, mainstream, or terminate development projects. Table 6.1 summarizes key principles.

Economic evaluation will be undertaken at two levels:

- Independent evaluators will carry out a cost-effectiveness analysis of the projects that they are evaluating; and
- A central Home Office team will carry out a comparative cost-benefit analysis, which will draw on data generated by the external evaluations.

A large number of independent researchers will be involved in evaluating CRP initiatives. Since the application of economic evaluation to crime reduction initiatives has been limited in the past, a major part of the Home Office's task has been to encourage the academic criminological community to undertake economic analyses. In addition, economists and other researchers with experience in parallel fields, such as health or social services, have been encouraged to apply their skills in this field of research.

To facilitate this process and to help ensure consistency of methodology across the different evaluation teams, a generic guidance document has been distributed (Dhiri and Brand 1999). It is designed primarily to meet the needs of practitioners and nonspecialist evaluators and provides practical guidance to those involved in devising a methodology for analyzing costs and benefits. It includes the methodological principles, processes, and standards that underpin such an analysis and specifies the key tasks and responsibilities of evaluators. It focuses on the practical issues of how to gather and analyze information on the costs of intervention and to relate this to outputs and outcomes. The Home Office is also providing more detailed guidance notes to evaluators for specific categories of interventions.

One of the first tasks for the Home Office team was to begin to develop a common language among the many managers, practitioners, and evaluators involved in CRP initiatives and in their evaluations. A set of clear definitions was required (see Table 6.2).

Cost-Effectiveness Analysis and Cost-Benefit Analysis

The two main techniques that will be used for CRP interventions will be cost-effectiveness analysis (CEA) and cost-benefit analysis (CBA). CEA compares alternative cost streams to produce broadly similar outputs or outcomes (HM Treasury 1997). The least-cost alternative to produce a defined outcome (or set of outcomes) is the most desirable option, subject to account being taken of wider outcomes that cannot be incorporated in the analysis. For the purposes of the CRP, a CEA will estimate the costs of achieving defined outcomes, typically measured in terms of a reduction in crime or disorder.

TABLE 6.2 Key Definitions[1]

For the purposes of the "Crime Reduction Programme" evaluations:

Inputs are defined as any additional human, physical and financial resources that are used to undertake a project. For example, in an intervention that installs fences across paths at the backs of houses as a target-hardening measure to prevent domestic burglary, inputs would include the materials and labor used to install the fences.

Outputs are defined narrowly as the direct products of the process of implementation. They can arise only during the implementation period. Following the above example, the fences installed are outputs and the number of fences installed is an output measure.

Impacts on risk factors are defined as the effects of outputs that *disrupt the causes of criminal events.* Measuring such impacts is therefore a way of monitoring the process through which the intervention is expected to reduce crime. In our fence example, this could be a reduction in non-residents entering the path, thereby reducing the opportunity for burglary.

Outcomes are defined as the consequences of the intervention.[2] These can arise both during and after the implementation period. Key outcomes will relate to the stated objectives of the intervention. In our example, the reduction in burglaries attributable to the installation of fences is the primary outcome. But there are likely to be wider outcomes such as a change in the fear of crime or the reduction in other types of crime. These wider outcomes may or may not be measurable and can be negative as well as positive.

Costs are defined as the monetary value of inputs.

Benefits are defined as the value of outcomes to society that are attributed to the intervention (expressed in monetary terms). Negative outcomes attributed to the CRP intervention are referred to as *disbenefits.*

[1]These definitions have been adapted from Hough and Tilley (1998). They are, however, for the purpose of the CRP intervention and may not be identical to those used in other programs. They have been constructed to allow evidence to be gathered not only on the final consequences of an intervention, but also on the mechanism through which an intervention is assumed to achieve stated objectives.

[2]Previous evaluations have tended to concentrate on outputs rather than final outcomes. For example, many projects to change offending behavior have been measured on the basis of how many offenders had successfully completed the program or showed attitudinal changes. CRP initiatives, however, need to demonstrate a link to a reduction in crime or criminal behavior.

The cost-effectiveness of a project is expressed as the *input cost per unit of output or outcome* achieved. For example, we may want to know the cost per offender attending a literacy program (cost per output) or the cost per burglary prevented (cost per outcome). Outcomes, however defined, need to be *quantified* (i.e., measured numerically). In order to compare the cost-effectiveness of alternative interventions, those interventions must share common outputs or outcomes and be measured on a common basis. Examples include the number of (defined) crimes prevented, the unit reduction in probability of a crime occurring, or the change in the number of offenders reconvicted.

Cost-benefit analysis (CBA) takes cost-effectiveness analysis a stage further by attaching monetary values to the outcomes of an intervention. Once both the costs of inputs and the value of outcomes (benefits) are expressed in monetary terms, a direct comparison can be made. The decision rule for a given project is to maximize the benefit-cost ratio or the net economic benefit, or minimize the net economic cost, taking into account any outcomes that are not included in the calculation.

For many CRP interventions, outcomes will be quantified in terms of a reduction in crime. Since crime has costs to society, including costs to victims, potential victims, and the criminal justice system, the value of an intervention can be measured by the avoidance of costs (savings) to society of those crimes that *would otherwise have taken place.*

In contrast to CEA, to the extent that variables are expressed in common (monetary) terms, interventions with different outcome measures can be compared under CBA. In addition, multiple outcomes arising from an intervention will all be expressed in monetary terms, and their relative quality will be reflected in their valuation. In reality, however, CBA cannot capture all of the costs and benefits to society of an intervention, making it all the more desirable to base the CBA on common measures as far as is practicable.

Not all crimes have the same level or types of costs to society. The simple quantification of crimes prevented in a CEA ignores the difference in the quality of outcomes achieved. By attaching monetary values to different types of crime, CBA presents the opportunity to weight different outcomes by their social value. This will partly be done by estimating, as accurately and comprehensively as possible, the average cost to society of different types of crime. The total value of benefits as a result of the intervention can then be estimated by multiplying the number of crimes prevented by the average cost of a crime.

Key responsibilities. The primary task of the evaluators will be to identify and quantify inputs, outputs, impacts, and outcomes. Attaching monetary values to inputs, to enable a CEA to be undertaken, will be carried out by evaluators with guidance from the central Home Office team.

For most input costs, this will involve the straightforward monitoring of actual project expenditure, but for some inputs, centrally determined standard costs will be used to ensure consistency among evaluations.

As well as undertaking a CEA, evaluators will also report detailed information on inputs, outputs, impacts, and outcomes to a central cost database at the Home Office. The central Home Office team will be responsible for attaching monetary values to benefits and carrying out a comparative cost-benefit analysis.

As with any impact evaluation, we are interested in *additional* inputs, outputs, impacts, and outcomes. Separating out additional elements from those that would have occurred anyway (i.e., in the absence of the intervention) is rarely straightforward. This involves setting a baseline against which the intervention can be evaluated.

One of the key tasks of evaluators is to establish this baseline as early in the process and as accurately as possible. For inputs, this requires distinguishing between existing and planned resource use and demands for additional resources that have arisen as a result of the CRP intervention. For impacts and outcomes, it involves analyzing existing conditions and trends to determine what would have happened in the absence of the CRP intervention. This will allow evaluators to measure deviations from these conditions and trends that can then be attributed either to the CRP intervention or to other external influences.

Measuring Inputs and Costs

Identifying and Quantifying Inputs

Expected inputs need to be identified as early as possible, so that data on resource use can be collected on an ongoing basis rather than retrospectively. Evaluators will identify and quantify all physical, human, or financial resources used in implementing an intervention. The types of inputs required vary considerably among interventions but typically include staff costs, materials, the use of premises, management inputs, and both initial and ongoing training. In addition, voluntary inputs and "levered-in" resources from partner agencies, as well as those funded under the CRP, need to be recorded.

CRP-funded inputs will be separately recorded from other inputs. Most "levered-in" resources are likely to include inputs from public sector sources, such as additional activities by the police, prison, probation, or local government staff. Resources funded from outside the public sector are also included, so long as they have been mobilized to support the intervention and contribute to its objectives. These might include inputs by local community or voluntary groups, participants in neighborhood watch schemes, or supporting grants from local businesses.

Additionality of Costs

The evaluation is concerned with inputs that have been mobilized as a result of the CRP intervention. Resources that would have been mobilized anyway (in the absence of the intervention) will be excluded from the CEA. This is particularly important where the intervention uses an existing input more intensively rather than introducing an entirely new input.

Complementary initiatives, such as interventions by education or social services, that could be expected to have an impact on crime or disorder should be reported as part of the baseline as a description of the context within which the CRP intervention is taking place.

Valuing Inputs

Costs of CRP interventions will be fully determined. The opportunity (rather than financial) cost of inputs, defined as the value of their next most valuable alternative use, will be used in the analysis.

For many inputs their market value is assumed to reflect their opportunity cost. Even where no cash transaction takes place, resources will be valued accordingly. This is to ensure that the full resource implications are taken into account for purposes of replicability of the initiative, as the cost of the same input may vary substantially among different parts of England and Wales. For example, if office space in a police station is used to coordinate a crime reduction project, the nature and use of the space will be noted, even if its cost is covered under existing overheads that are not funded under the CRP. Should the initiative be replicated elsewhere in the country, this input may be essential for the successful implementation and should therefore be included in the analysis.

Public servant staff costs (e.g., administrators, police, and prison and parole officers) will be valued on a common basis. Centrally determined accounting conventions will be applied. The central Home Office team will provide evaluators with the accounting conventions to be used that are specific to the type of intervention that is being undertaken. Evaluators also need to take account of any additional overhead costs such as time off "in lieu," additional training, clothing and equipment, supervision costs, and pensions.

Costs are incurred by different groups and at different stages of the intervention process. There may be additional costs to various parts of the criminal justice system, health services, education services, or individuals. It is important to identify who bears the cost of intervention to direct future support to those groups whose participation is found to be crucial to the success of an intervention.

Attributing Costs to Project Objectives

Some interventions will have multiple crime prevention objectives. A division of inputs (and their costs) among objectives may be possible and desirable in exceptional cases, but in general the cost-effectiveness of an intervention will be measured against a *set* of defined outcomes. Where initiatives are run in parallel with, or even as part of, cross-departmental initiatives with much broader objectives than just crime reduction, evaluators will need to separate out the crime reduction element in order to attach a cost to that part of the initiative that targets crime.

Average and Marginal Costs

Both the average and the marginal costs of interventions are important to be able to assess the relative value for money of different interventions (average cost) and the level of investment in an intervention that yields the highest net benefit (marginal cost).

The average cost per output or outcome provides a measure of the overall return to an intervention, which can be used for comparing the cost-effectiveness of different interventions. The cost of an input can be measured in a number of ways. For instance, in the Safer Cities Programme (Ekblom, Law, and Sutton 1996) the measurement used was *action intensity,* defined as the total investment divided by the number of households targeted in the scheme to give a cost per targeted household. This concept of action intensity might be applied to other types of intervention (e.g., the cost per child treated in an early intervention).

Marginal cost refers to the extra spending required to achieve *one extra unit of output or outcome*. For example, the marginal cost of a burglary intervention would be the amount of extra spending that is required to prevent one more burglary. Only those inputs that are required to achieve that extra outcome are included. If the cost of a marginal increase in intervention spending results in a greater reduction in the cost of crime to society (in other words, the marginal return exceeds the marginal cost), it is, in principle, worth continuing to increase spending on the intervention. This has important implications for the future mainstreaming and expansion of projects that have proved cost-effective.

Collecting Cost Data

To avoid duplication and minimize the additional burden on practitioners, maximum use is being made of existing data sources that can yield the input information required or be modified to do so. In many cases, however, new cost monitoring systems will need to be established. These will be as consistent as possible with existing practices and should enable continued data collection after the end of the initial intervention period. Evaluators are required to make an early assessment of available data for each intervention, specify any limitations, and suggest alternative sources. They will then work with implementing partner agencies and the central Home Office team to devise the most efficient way of obtaining the data required for undertaking a sufficiently rigorous cost-effectiveness analysis. This may involve activity sampling exercises to measure additional time inputs required to implement an intervention.

There is, of course, a limit to the amount of information that can be gathered in the course of the cost-effectiveness analysis. Evaluators will have to balance the level of detail needed in determining the costs of an intervention against the time and cost burden on participants and on the evaluation process.

Measuring Outcomes and Benefits

Identifying and Quantifying Outcomes

The outcomes of CRP interventions need to be carefully defined, and a convincing causal link will need to be drawn between the inputs, outputs, impacts on risk factors, and outcomes. The robustness of this link will be tested by monitoring and measuring outputs and impacts, as well as outcomes. Crime reduction is the central aim of CRP interventions and the expected final outcome of the CRP as a whole. Outcomes will typically be measured in terms of an additional reduction in the number of specified crimes, such as the number of burglaries or car thefts, or of a reduction in the overall crime rate in a specified location that can be attributed to the intervention.

A key task of the evaluators will be to attribute observed reductions in crime to a CRP intervention rather than the multitude of other influencing factors that will impact on the control and targeted groups in different ways over the evaluation period. Since no two groups or areas are identical, replicating a successful intervention in other areas does not guarantee success. A central part of the exercise is to collect information on what works and in what context. In addition, information on the mechanisms through which an intervention works is also being collected. This will help determine the expected impact of mainstreaming or widening projects.

CRP interventions may specify a single outcome measure, but in most cases a range of outcomes will need to be measured. Where more than one outcome is defined (e.g., the deterrence of shop theft and street violence using CCTV cameras), some form of weighting will need to be applied to arrive at a single cost-effectiveness measure, which will depend on the stated objectives of an intervention.

The link with an observable reduction in crime may not, however, be so direct or immediate. Early interventions with children and families pose particular problems for the measurement of impacts and outcomes since their principal benefits are expected to occur in only the medium to long term. The full benefits of such a program may not be observable for many years, but its probability of success will need to be determined, and the decision to continue with the program will need to be made, in the interim period. Intermediate outcome measures should therefore be established that reflect final outcome measures and pick up any benefits that occur in the short term (Karoly et al. 1998). Examples of such intermediate outcome measures include a decline in a child's disruptive behavior or improved school attendance. An assessment of project effectiveness will therefore be based on these intermediate outcomes and a convincing causal link between intermediate outcomes and final impacts.

Displacement of crime. Evaluators will need to take into account the potential displacement of crime or disorder outside the target area or group (Barr and Pease 1990; Ekblom and Pease 1995). An intervention may reduce crime in one area but displace it to other areas, or criminals may abandon one type of crime in favor of another. A reduction in one type of (targeted) crime in an area does not, therefore, automatically mean a net reduction in crime. Similarly, the conviction and incarceration of an offender does not necessarily mean a reduction in crime. Gang members and drug dealers are often rapidly replaced. If such negative outcomes can be attributed to the existence of the CRP intervention, the effects should be set against positive outcomes in any cost-effectiveness calculation.

Diffusion of benefits. Benefits may be diffused into other areas or groups (Clarke and Weisburd 1994). These additional benefits will be added to direct outcomes in the cost-effectiveness calculations. This implies that evaluators will need to monitor a broader range of crimes, locations, and groups than just those specifically targeted by the intervention (e.g., crime rates in neighboring districts or the criminal behavior of close associates of offenders).

Wider outcomes. CRP interventions may have a range of wider outcomes that are not directly related to the objectives of the intervention. Local situational interventions could promote greater economic activity and inward commercial investment. Offender programs may promote employability. Improved household security may increase the value of local housing.

If there is evidence to show a plausible relationship with the CRP intervention, evaluators will record these wider outcomes. If they are likely to be significant, evaluators will try to quantify them. For example, an early intervention with young children may have a significant impact on a child's school attainment and eventually on their employment prospects (Schweinhart, Barnes, and Weikart 1993). Where it is not possible to quantify such outcomes, evaluators are expected to at least provide a broad indication of their magnitude.

These wider outcomes will, however, remain outside the cost-effectiveness framework. Their separation from the cost-effectiveness calculations does not preclude later restricted analysis incorporating the valuation of wider social benefits. But in the first instance we are interested in the efficiency of achieving the stated objectives of the intervention.

Onset, longevity, and decay of outcomes. The outcomes of an intervention may occur immediately or in the longer term and will, in most cases, occur in both. Some interventions, such as installing CCTVs, can be expected to have an immediate impact in deterring crime, but this impact may be short-lived (Brown 1995). Similarly, the effects of treatment programs for offenders may eventually wear off. Some early interventions with children and families, on the other hand, may not have any significant crime-reducing impact in the short term.

The expected and actual timing of outcomes are crucial aspects of the evaluation and have a significant bearing on the results of the cost-effectiveness analysis. As well as the nature and scale of attributable outcomes, evaluators need to record their timing. Evaluators should record the point in the intervention process at which beneficial outcomes begin, how long they last, at what rate they diminish, and at what point they disappear. This will allow a measurement of the payback period (i.e., the point at which benefits start exceeding costs) and an identification of the conditions that give rise to sustained benefits.

Standard measures for the longevity of impacts and outcomes, which will need to be applied for each type of intervention, will be built into the cost-effectiveness analysis until further evidence can be gathered from evaluations.[2]

Nonquantifiable outcomes. Outcomes that cannot be quantified will not be ignored in the CEA but will be identified and recorded in qualitative terms. For example, if a CRP intervention leads to a reduction in the fear of crime, this will be reported. A good example of where it will be difficult to quantify outcomes is a targeted policing project to tackle racially motivated crime in London. One of the key objectives of the scheme is to reduce the fear of victimization, which can be measured only through local surveys. Quantification of the impact on the fear of crime will inevitably be somewhat subjective.

Valuing Outcomes

Evaluators will collect information required for a cost-effectiveness analysis. However, attaching monetary values to outcomes as part of a comparative cost-benefit analysis is the responsibility of the central Home Office team.

As noted above, CRP interventions will be evaluated on the basis of a range of expected outcomes. Since the principal concern is a reduction in crime, a monetary value needs to be attached to this reduction, to measure the benefits of interventions and of the CRP as a whole. Benefits are therefore measured primarily in terms of the *costs of crimes prevented* by a CRP intervention. Two key pieces of information are required: the number of crimes prevented and the gain or saving from each (average) prevented crime. The former will be derived as part of the broader impact evaluation undertaken by evaluators. The latter will be drawn from an ongoing exercise on the costs of crime being carried out in the Home Office.

There are a great number of impacts of crime on different groups in society. An operationally useful way of categorizing the costs of crime is by the bearers of the costs. These include costs to victims, potential victims, the criminal justice system, and others.

- Victims: The victim of a crime bears the direct monetary costs of any property stolen, damaged or destroyed, and any pain and suffering resulting from a crime. Victims may also incur medical costs and unpaid time off work caused by injury or psychological damage (or both) resulting from violent crime.
- Potential victims: Part of the cost of crime falls on society as a whole, or more precisely on potential victims. Potential victims take preventative action (e.g., driving children to school or not going out after dark) or defensive measures (e.g., fitting burglar alarms) or both to reduce the risk of victimization. Crime will also impact on potential victims through increased fear of crime, distrust, loss of enjoyment in employment or leisure activities, reduced freedom of movement, and many other ways.
- Criminal justice system: Crime imposes costs on taxpayers, through the criminal justice system. This includes crime prevention activity, preconviction costs including all police investiga-

tion costs, offender processing through the court system, Crown Prosecution Service costs (trial costs), and postconviction costs for the prison and probation services, young offenders' institutions, and so on.

- Others: The costs of crime are also incurred to varying degrees by the exchequer through lost tax revenue, by the employers of victims through paid time off work for employees that have been victimized, by victim support services, and by health services.

Transfers. Many property crimes involve a transfer of property from the victim to the offender. When a property crime involves an illegal transfer of property that is *unwanted by one party* (i.e., the victim), the value of that property will be treated as lost to legal society, and therefore a cost of crime.

Insurance is another cost of crime that involves a transfer of resources. Potential victims who take out insurance policies in anticipation of crime pay insurance premiums. Insurance payments as reimbursements to victims represent a transfer of value from nonvictim policyholders to victims. However, unlike property that is transferred from victims to offenders, insurance has been entered into willingly by both parties, and thus represents a *transfer of resources* rather than a loss to society. The only resources involved that represent a cost of crime to society rather than a transfer are those used in insurance *administration*. These represent an opportunity cost to society, because in the absence of crime these resources could be employed in a productive way elsewhere in the economy.

Measuring benefits that are not easily valued. The emotional and physical impact on victims or the reduced quality of life of potential victims are difficult to value, since there is no obvious market "price." A variety of techniques for measuring nonmarketed goods and services have been developed. They focus on the amount people are willing to pay (WTP) to reduce the risk of defined, negative outcomes or their willingness to accept (WTA) such outcomes. WTP and WTA are estimated using either "revealed" or "stated" preference techniques.

Using revealed preference involves analyzing actual expenditure patterns to estimate the amount people are prepared to spend to reduce the risk of an undesired outcome. For example, an economic assessment of the cost of injury on public transport would assess how much more travelers would be prepared to pay in fares to reflect improvements in safety standards that reduce the risk of injury by a certain proportion. This provides an estimate of the value placed on avoiding the risk of injury and, by extension, the injury itself.

TABLE 6.3 Summary of Average Cost Estimates for Selected Crimes

	Average Cost to:						
Type of Crime	*Victim (£)*	*Potential Victim (£)*	*Criminal Justice System (£)*	*Other (£)*	*Average Cost per Offense (£)*	*Estimated No. of Offenses (000's)*[1]	*Total Cost 1996 Prices (£ Millions)*
Residential Burglary	1,000	800	500	30	2,300	1,639	3,800
Commercial Burglary	500	2,700	500	0	3,800	303	1,200
Car Crime	500	300	200	30	1,100	3,483	3,800

[1]1997 British Crime survey (Mirrlees-Black et al. 1998) estimates except for commercial burglary; 1993 estimate from 1994 Commercial Victimization Survey (Mirrlees-Black and Ross 1995).

Using stated preference involves the direct questioning of sample populations to discover how much they claim they would be prepared to pay to reduce the risk of an outcome by a given proportion. Such valuation techniques have been used extensively by government departments in the United Kingdom (Jones-Lee et al. 1993), and in the United States (Miller, Cohen, and Wiersema 1996).

There are many parallels between crime prevention and, for example, the valuation of the risk of injury or premature death resulting from transport accidents and ill health. The central Home Office team is planning to undertake similar studies to estimate some of the nonmarketed consequences of crime (e.g., pain and suffering and fear of crime).

Data sources and provisional estimates. Information on the cost of crime has already been drawn from a wide range of sources, from both within and outside the Home Office. Table 6.3 provides illustrative examples of the breakdown of average costs for three crimes that have been calculated to date. These should be regarded as first estimates as they are based on some speculative assumptions and are still being refined.

Distribution of benefits. The same crime may not necessarily have the same cost to all victims. An assault on an elderly or vulnerable person tends to have a greater impact on that individual and on the community than a similar assault on a young adult. Average cost estimates may mask differences in the costs of the same crime to different social, economic, or geographic groups, and the benefits of prevention may therefore be distributed unevenly. This points to the need to treat the results of the cost-effectiveness analysis as part of an overall evaluation of crime reduction initiatives that takes into account subjective valuations of crime.

Comparing Costs with Outcomes and Benefits

The final stage in the analysis is to bring cost and outcome-benefit data together into a cost-effectiveness analysis undertaken by evaluators and ultimately a cost-benefit analysis undertaken by the central Home Office team.

Measuring Cost and Outcome Streams

Input costs will not be incurred uniformly over the intervention period. Greater costs are typically incurred in the initial period because of the need for new capital, recruitment of additional staff, and training and reorientation of existing staff. After the initial start-up period, recurrent costs will be incurred until the end of the intervention period. Evaluators will therefore be recording inputs, outputs, and attributable outcomes on an ongoing basis and reporting them to the central Home Office team periodically.

Measuring the stream of outcomes that result from an intervention is also not straightforward. It involves a series of assumptions that will need to be tested over the course of the evaluation. Assumptions will need to be made about the longevity of the impact of an intervention, the likelihood that the right people or areas were targeted, and the link between intermediate and ultimate outcomes. All costs and benefits will be expressed in real terms.

Risk, Uncertainty, and Sensitivity Analysis

Risk and uncertainty are concepts typically associated with appraisal rather than evaluation. They refer to the relative probability of one or more of the factors not turning out as expected. But an evaluation of the costs and benefits of crime reduction also needs to take into account the uncertainty associated with the calculation of cost-effectiveness. The determining of costs of certain types of crime is a hazardous task, because it invariably relies on a number of untested assumptions. The measurement of input costs may also involve uncertainty. One of the most uncertain aspects of the present analysis will be the assumption underlying the causal link drawn between inputs and outcomes. There may be a number of alternative explanations that cannot be ruled out by the quantitative logic of the research design.

Where appropriate, a sensitivity analysis will be undertaken. Key parameters in the analysis will be varied to test the robustness of results. One such parameter is the assumption of the extent to which observed outcomes are attributable to the CRP intervention. Varying this parameter will yield a range of estimates of outcomes and benefits, rather than a point estimate. The level of variability of results provides a guide to the robustness of findings. The range of variation of parameters used in a sensitivity analysis should take account of known statistical variation.

Testing Replicability

Many of the initial CRP initiatives involve pilot or development projects, with a view to replicating and mainstreaming them if found to be effective and cost-effective. An assessment of the replicability of the intervention, specifying the conditions under which the intervention would be expected to be cost-effective, will form an essential part of the analysis. Evaluators will specify whether an expanded program would be likely to be as cost-effective as the development project, and how and why this might not be the case. They will need to set out the elements and conditions under which mainstreaming would prove cost-effective.

An economic appraisal of mainstreaming will typically need to take into account the following:

- the probability of resources being diverted to outside the target group or area (leakage or net-widening);
- the likely dilution of the quality of intervention through implementation that is more routine and less intensive, focused, or charismatically led;
- the consequences of linkages with related non-crime-reducing initiatives that may give a simple additive boost to impact, or constitute a necessary component of an interactive package; and
- the likely economies of scale of expansion (unit overhead costs are likely to be lower than in the development project).

Conclusion

The "Crime Reduction Programme" is the biggest investment in evidence-based crime reduction initiatives ever undertaken by the U.K. government. It offers the prospect of a real and sustained impact on the level of crime.

Undertaking a comprehensive analysis of the costs and benefits of the various initiatives supported by the "Crime Reduction Programme" is an ambitious and challenging task. However, a sound understanding of the costs and benefits of alternative approaches to reducing crime is fundamental to shaping future policy development. It will help ensure continued improvements in the impact on crime and value for money of policy initiatives both directly, through CRP programs, and by the incorporation of what has been learned into mainstream government programs in the CJS and other areas of social policy.

The CRP will contribute to a better understanding of what works, where, and in what circumstances. Through this understanding, it should help to ensure that crime reduction is viewed less as a series of one-off, discrete projects, and more as a continued and adaptive use of innovative and tailored strategies that can achieve a lasting impact on crime.

The CRP will provide an opportunity to expand interdisciplinary research and development in the area of crime reduction. Constructive contributions have already been made by specialists from a wide range of disciplines. These have included criminologists, economists, criminal justice practitioners, and management specialists. Many of those involved have either not worked in the crime prevention field before or are adopting new perspectives on some familiar problems. This is a particularly exciting aspect of the program, which should, it is hoped, stimulate new approaches to tackling crime.

Notes

1. Investment in the CRP will build over three years: with £40 million in year 1, £100 million in year 2, and £110 million in year 3.

2. Measuring decay requires that monitoring of impact continue beyond the end of a project life.

References

Barr, R., and Pease, K. 1990. Crime placement, displacement and deflection. In Tonry, M., and Morris, N., eds., *Crime and justice: A review of research,* 277–318. Vol. 12. Chicago: University of Chicago Press.

Brown, B. 1995. *CCTV in town centres: Three case studies.* Crime Detection and Prevention Series Paper 68. London: Home Office.

Clarke, R. V., and Weisburd, D. 1994. Diffusion of crime control benefits: Observations on the reverse of displacement. In R. V. Clarke, ed., *Crime prevention studies,* 2: 165–83. Monsey, N.Y.: Criminal Justice Press.

Dhiri, S., and Brand, S. 1999. *Analysis of costs and benefits: Guidance for evaluators.* Crime Reduction Programme— Guidance Note 1. London: Home Office.

Ekblom, P., and Pease, K. 1995. Evaluating crime prevention. In Tonry, M., and Farrington, D. P., eds. *Building a safer society: Strategic approaches to crime prevention.* Vol. 19 of *Crime and justice: A review of research,* 585–662. Chicago: University of Chicago Press.

Ekblom, P., Law, H., and Sutton, M. 1996. *Safer cities and domestic burglary.* Home Office Research Study No. 164. London: Home Office.

Goldblatt, P., and Lewis, C., eds. 1998. *Reducing offending: An assessment of research evidence on ways of dealing with offending behaviour.* Home Research Study No. 187. London: Home Office.

Greenwood, P. W., Model, K. E., Rydell, C. P., and Chiesa, J. 1996. *Diverting children from a life of crime: Measuring costs and benefits.* Santa Monica, Calif.: RAND.

HM Treasury. 1997. *Appraisal and evaluation in central government: The green book.* Treasury Guidance. London: HM Stationery Office.

Hough, M., and Tilley, N. 1998. *Auditing crime and disorder: Guidance for local partnerships.* Police Research Group Crime Detection and Prevention Series Paper 91. London: Home Office.

Jones-Lee, M., Loomes, G., O'Reilly, D., and Philips, P. 1993. *The value of preventing non-fatal road injuries: Findings of a willingness-to-pay national sample survey.* Transport Research Laboratory Contractor Report 330. Crowthorne, England: Transport Research Laboratory.

Karoly, L. A., Greenwood, P. W., Everingham, S. S., Houbé, J., Kilburn, M. R., Rydell, C. P., Sanders, M., and Chiesa, J. 1998. *Investing in our children: What we know and don't know about the costs and benefits of early childhood interventions.* Santa Monica, Calif.: RAND.

Miller, T. R., Cohen, M. A., and Wiersema, B. 1996. *Victim costs and consequences: A new look.* Washington, D.C.: U.S. Department of Justice, National Institute of Justice.

Mirrlees-Black, C., and Ross, A. 1995. *Crime against retail and manufacturing premises: Findings from the 1994 Commercial Victimisation Survey.* Home Office Research Study No. 146. London: Home Office.

Mirrlees-Black, C., Budd, T., Partridge, S., and Mayhew, P. 1998. The 1997 British Crime Survey. *Home Office Statistical Bulletin* 21/98. London: Home Office.

Schweinhart, L. J., Barnes, H. V., and Weikart, D. P. 1993. *Significant benefits: The High/Scope Perry Preschool study through age 27.* Ypsilanti, Mich.: High/Scope Press.

Sherman, L. W., Gottfredson, D. C., MacKenzie, D. L., Eck, J., Reuter, P., and Bushway, S. D. 1997. *Preventing crime: What works, what doesn't, what's promising.* Washington, D.C.: U.S. Department of Justice, National Institute of Justice.

Stockdale, J., Whitehead, C., and Gresham, P. 1999. *Applying economic evaluation to policing activity.* Police Research Series Paper 103. London: Home Office.

Waller, I., Welsh, B. C., and Sansfaçon, D. 1997. *Crime prevention digest 1997: Successes, benefits, and directions from seven countries.* Montreal: International Centre for the Prevention of Crime.

Welsh, B. C., and Farrington, D. P. 1999. Value for money? A review of the costs and benefits of situational crime prevention. *British Journal of Criminology* 39: 345–68.

7

Economic Analysis of Crime Prevention

An Australian Perspective

JOHN CHISHOLM

The perceived or actual (or both) failure of the criminal justice system to reduce levels of crime and criminal behavior has led to the continued search for alternative methods of crime prevention. Crime prevention programs, policies, and practices have been established in both the private and the public sphere, and various institutional bodies have been put in place at the local, national, and international levels. Many reports and initiatives have resulted from these bodies, such as the following:

- A report prepared by the University of Maryland's Department of Criminology and Criminal Justice for the U.S. Congress, *Preventing crime: What works, what doesn't, what's promising* (Sherman et al. 1997).
- The Center for the Study and Prevention of Violence recently reviewed more than 450 delinquency, drug, and violence prevention programs. Of these, 10 were selected as "Blueprint Violence Prevention Programs" (Botvin, Mihalic, and Grotpeter 1998).
- The Washington State Institute for Public Policy has applied benefit-cost analysis to more than twenty-five crime prevention programs (Aos et al. 1999). Following from this research, the Washington State Legislature provided funding for two randomized controlled trials of successful juvenile offender intervention programs.

- The International Centre for the Prevention of Crime has published two crime prevention digests and a review of the one hundred best practices in preventing crime (Waller, Welsh, and Sansfaçon 1997; Sansfaçon and Welsh 1999).
- In July 1998 the United Kingdom's Home Office announced a new crime reduction program that would be supported by £250 million over three years.
- In Australia the federal government established the National Crime Prevention (NCP) in 1996 (formerly known as the National Campaign Against Violence and Crime). NCP is a three-year A$13 million strategic approach to the prevention of violence and crime.
- The Australian Institute of Criminology (AIC) has produced many reports on crime prevention, such as *The promise of crime prevention* (Grabosky and James 1995). The AIC also sponsors the Australian Violence Prevention Awards.

A common goal of these initiatives is to identify best practice in reducing violence, crime, and disorder. Best practice is generally held to be synonymous with effectiveness, which for the present purposes implies the reduction of crime and criminal behavior. However, for those programs that are also concerned with whether the monetary benefits outweigh the monetary costs, best practice also involves efficiency. One method for analyzing the efficiency of a crime prevention program is social benefit-cost analysis.

To date, most of the resources channeled toward the prevention of crime and violence, at both national and local levels, have been invested in untested programs based upon poor research designs and imprecise assumptions. This means that not only do we have very little knowledge about which programs are effective in reducing crime and criminal behavior, but, perhaps more important, we have even less knowledge about which programs use scarce community resources most efficiently. Particularly in the United States, as elsewhere, scientific studies have revealed that many prevention programs are ineffective or inefficient. Nonetheless, these programs continue to attract funding. Although this occurs largely for political reasons, governments must keep in mind that one of their primary goals in allocating resources is that they be used most efficiently. In Australia, most crime prevention programs have never been rigorously evaluated, and though some of these programs may be working (unknown to policymakers), others may not be working yet are absorbing scarce tax dollars that could be redirected toward more effective programs. Without a concerted effort to investigate both the effectiveness and the efficiency of crime prevention initiatives, policymakers will continue to channel scarce resources toward poorly evaluated and unproved programs.

Even where steps have been taken to evaluate the effectiveness of crime prevention programs, typically they exclude any assessment of monetary costs and benefits. However, within the current climate of economic rationalism, built upon the notion of efficient allocation of resources, the determination of monetary costs and benefits is of central importance. Of course, criticism will be, and already has been, leveled at applying benefit-cost analysis to crime prevention programs. Those critical of this approach ask important questions such as: Is it really possible to accurately determine the cost consequences of crime? Can we really place a monetary value on the potential benefits of a program for which the outcome may not be observed for ten years or more? The view expressed in this chapter is that, as funds become increasingly more difficult to obtain, there will be a need to justify financially why one program should be preferred over another. Benefit-cost and cost-effectiveness analysis of crime prevention will become increasingly common, and practitioners must be prepared both to understand these techniques and to position themselves to make use of them.

The main aim of this chapter is to review the use of benefit-cost analysis in crime prevention, with special reference to the Australian situation. The broad categories of crime prevention and intervention programs include: the criminal justice system, developmental and early-childhood intervention, juvenile offender intervention, correctional intervention (treatment), and situational crime prevention. The examples are drawn from across the developed world with a more thorough review of the two identified Australian studies: Clarke and McGrath (1990) and Donato, Shanahan, and Higgins (1999).

The Criminal Justice System, Law Enforcement, and Crime Prevention

Criminal justice agencies—police, courts, and corrections—represent the primary source of crime prevention. It is via these agencies that we as a society attempt to control, apprehend, convict, sentence, and rehabilitate the vast majority of potential and actual offenders. Because of this heavy reliance on the criminal justice system it is hardly surprising that the great bulk of available resources flow to this preventive strategy. Incarceration of known offenders makes society feel somewhat safer. Thus, regardless of whether the process is cost-effective or returns a net benefit, society appears not to be deterred by the enormous amount of government revenue directed to the criminal justice system. Are we as taxpayers justified in this view, or are we getting value for money? If so, how much, and if not, what other alternatives are available?

Walker (1996) estimates that the costs from crime in Australia are roughly between A$11 billion and A$13 billion per year. The crime-countering costs, including money spent on the criminal justice system and private security, are estimated to be around A$8 billion per year. On an individual level, for every A$444 per person spent on the criminal justice system and private security, each Australian endured between A$610 and A$722 in costs from crime. Thus, for every dollar spent on the criminal justice system and private security, Australians endured between A$1.60 and A$1.80 from crime costs. Walker's (1992) corresponding estimates for 1992 show that for every dollar spent on the criminal justice system and private security, Australians endured between A$3.50 and A$1.80 from crime costs. Using the upper-bound estimates, we find that between 1992 and 1996, Australians spent an additional A$2 billion on the criminal justice system and private security costs. Over the same period the costs of crime fell by an estimated A$8 billion. Therefore, according to Walker's figures, individuals saved roughly A$4 from reduced crime costs for each additional dollar spent between 1992 and 1996. However, using the lower-bound estimates, we find that for each additional dollar spent, individuals saved only A$0.35 in reduced crime costs.

There are a number of implications that flow from this extremely crude analysis. First, it shows just how careful one has to be in drawing policy conclusions from any analysis that attempts to estimate the costs of crime and the costs of preventing crime. In a similar vein, it demonstrates the way in which estimates, especially those with broad ranges, can be used to verify a particular policy position. It also demonstrates just how important it is to carry out micro- as opposed to macroanalysis in an area such as this. It is with these cautions that we can now begin to look at more specific benefit-cost and cost-effectiveness approaches to reducing crime. One should always keep in mind that, regardless of whether the benefit-cost ratio of the criminal justice system is 4:1 or 0.35:1, it may prove to be higher or lower for various components of the system. Perhaps more important, the benefit-cost ratio for alternative crime prevention programs may turn out to be significantly higher for either the criminal justice system as a whole or its individual component parts.

Costs and Benefits of Police

Walker (1996) estimates that the financial cost of police and law enforcement in Australia was A$2,858 million in 1996, roughly one-half the total expenditure on the entire criminal justice system. However, this tells us nothing about the cost-effectiveness of police, or the net benefit of extra police. To date, benefit-cost analyses of police in preventing crime have not been carried out. It remains somewhat of a mystery that some work has not been carried out, but nevertheless there are at least two factors that would suggest that such analyses are due to be undertaken. First, given that both substantial and incisive benefit-cost reports have been facilitated for other forms of crime prevention, it seems only a matter of time before police departments must justify their position in order to secure funding. Furthermore, as numbers of private security personnel and police continue to grow, public police may be asked to provide evidence of their cost-effectiveness. Second, as Australian governments continue to maintain budget balances in an environment of increased economic rationalism, Australian police executives may be asked not only to justify their budget requests, but also to illustrate where resources are most effectively and efficiently used (Grabosky 1989). This position is confirmed by the Council of Australian Governments, where there is a general push for police services to include among their efficiency performance indicators a measure of cost per crime, cost per unit of road safety, and cost per response to major automobile accidents.

High among the possibilities for a benefit-cost analysis of police functions would be an analysis of policing hot spots or crackdowns or both. Ideally, this would involve using random assignment of two relatively comparable police districts. Of course, any benefit-cost or cost-effectiveness analysis of such strategies would have to take into consideration any displacement costs that could erode economic efficiency.

There is obviously a paucity of available benefit-cost and cost-effectiveness analyses for either police in general or the various tasks that police carry out. This is not something unique to the Australian situation, as international studies are also scarce. Recently, however, there has been at least one study that has investigated a particular task of day-to-day policing. Crew and Hart (1999) have applied benefit-cost analysis to the police duty of chasing offenders who flee from law enforcement officers in automobiles. Their analysis revolves around the following central question: "On balance, do chases produce benefits that outweigh the associated costs?" (Crew and Hart 1999, 58). Some of the results together with a brief description of the analysis from this study are shown in Table 7.1.

Courts

It has been estimated that the cost of courts and the administration of justice in Australia in 1996 was around A$817 million (Walker 1996). Excluding the High Court, the Industrial Relations court, and the federal and state tribunals, the expenditure on courts was around A$675 million. In all, there were roughly 2.15 million cases, giving a rough estimate of A$300 per case. The 1997 report on government service provision estimated the expenditure per case, civil and criminal combined, at A$382.

Criminal cases account for the majority of this expenditure and are estimated at about A$512. This ranges from an average of A$9,021 per Supreme Court case to A$145 per nonprimary magistrates' court case. Although these estimates represent a useful starting point for any benefit-cost or cost-effectiveness analysis, they fail to take account of all of the costs (e.g., the opportunity cost of time for the plaintiff, defendant, and jury members). Nevertheless, these estimates represent a good possible source for an economic analysis of the Australian court system.

Estimating the costs of courts represents an easier task than estimating the crime reducing benefits. One of the primary difficulties revolves around the issue of what proportion of any possible deterrent effect can be credited to the courts, as opposed to police and prisons. A recent survey of imprisoned adult burglars found that less than one-third thought about the possibility of getting caught, let alone prosecution and punishment (Stevenson and Forsythe 1998). This does not mean that deterrence and incapacitation are not important, but rather that more surveys need to be conducted on a range of offenders for a range of different questions about police capture, court convictions, and prison incarceration.

Considering that courts represent the link between capture and incarceration, there is little doubt about their relative importance. Nonetheless, a comprehensive benefit-cost analysis of the court does not exist within Australia. An interesting study within Australia or international context would involve comparing the costs associated with prosecution in the courts with other strategies such as alternative dispute resolution. Another area of interest is the savings that could be made to criminal court hearings, including the introduction of electronic courts, video and telephone conferencing, remote video recording of court proceedings, and the implementation of electronic document lodgement. It follows that if benefits were to remain constant, then increased cost-effectiveness could be achieved via a reduction in costs.

Prisons

Walker (1996) estimates that the financial cost of correctional services, for both adults and juveniles, is roughly A$750 million per year, or about 12 percent of the total expenditure on the criminal justice system. The 1999 report on government service provision in Australia for 1997–98 indicates the average recurrent cost per prisoner per day (excluding open and periodic detention) to be approximately A$150. As with the court data, this prison cost information has not yet been used to form part of a benefit-cost analysis. Selected international studies are shown in Table 7.1.

TABLE 7.1 Summary of Selected Criminal Justice Programs

Study and Author Location	*Description of Study*	*Economic Analysis Findings*
Zedlewski (1987), United States	Benefit-cost analysis of imprisonment	BC ratio = 17.00
Gray and Olson (1989), Arizona	Benefit-cost analysis of alternative sentences for burglary offenders	BC ratio = 1.70 (probation) BC ratio = 0.24 (prison) BC ratio = 0.16 (jail)
Dilulio and Piehl (1991), Wisconsin	Benefit-cost analysis of imprisonment	BC ratio = 1.84
Greenwood et al. (1996), California	Cost-effectiveness analysis of three-strikes law and early interventions	$16,000 per serious felony prevented (three-strikes law)
Chisholm (1999), Australia	Benefit-cost analysis of imprisonment of burglary offenders	BC ratio = 3.50
Crew and Hart (1999), Minnesota	Benefit-cost analysis of police pursuit for offenses, e.g., driving while intoxicated, traffic violations	BC ratio = 60.20

A strong case can be made that studies of the cost-effectiveness of prisons, such as those by Zedlewski (1987) and DiIulio and Piehl (1991), are largely responsible for sparking initial interest in the area of economic evaluation research on crime prevention programs. Unfortunately, a common problem for benefit-cost analysis for any crime prevention strategy, including imprisonment, is that the costs—in this case of confinement—are quite visible, whereas the benefits are relatively hidden.

Confinement Decisions in Australia

Comparable confinement costs to those found in Zedlewski (1987) are not available for Australia. However, partial cost estimates are available, thus allowing a very crude "Zedlewski-like" analysis of the costs and benefits for Australian prisons to be made. Cost figures for private and public correctional centers are provided by Macionis (1994).[1] The average normalized unit cost per annum per offender (for medium-level security) at two facilities in 1994 was roughly A$47,050. Zedlewski-type benefits for Australia are equally difficult to obtain. The primary difficulty is obtaining data on the frequency of offending. However, a survey conducted by the New South Wales Bureau of

Crime Statistics and Research (Stevenson and Forsythe 1998) of imprisoned adult burglars found that the median number of burglaries per month was 8.7, for an annual rate of 104.4.[2] This figure is comparable with the numbers given by respondents in a survey of both Michigan and Californian jails and prisons (Chaiken and Chaiken 1982). Walker (1992) estimates that the monetary loss from burglary is roughly A$2,340 per commercial burglary and A$1,000 per burglary of other premises. The New South Wales Crime Bureau survey asked respondents what their burglary income was per week. The median level of this income for adult respondents was A$2,500 (A$1,250 per burglary). Obviously, one would expect a considerable difference between offenders' and victims' estimates of the cost of a burglary. Victims would be more likely to inflate the loss for insurance reasons, whereas offenders would be more likely to understate the figures because they are not likely to realize the full value of the stolen property. A very rough approximation would be to simply obtain the average of these three estimates, that is, A$1,530.

Collectively, these very rough estimates suggest that the incarceration of an additional burglar would lead to a cost saving of about A$160,000. Compared with the annual cost of incarceration (A$47,050), which makes no allowance for the various opportunity costs associated with imprisonment, the benefit-cost ratio would be about 3.5 to 1. Again it must be emphasized that at best this represents a rough approximation, and that a more complete analysis would alter these results.

The Criminal Justice System and Economic Analysis: A Concluding Comment

With the exception of imprisonment studies, few benefit-cost and economic analyses have been carried out for either the criminal justice system as a whole or its individual components. Table 7.1 indicates that three of the four benefit-cost analyses of imprisonment are desirable, meaning that benefits outweighed costs. However, the one study that did not show a desirable benefit-cost ratio (Gray and Olson 1989) was by far the most comprehensive. Given the considerable amounts of money that are allocated toward financing the criminal justice system, far more research needs to be performed in evaluating the system financially, both as a whole and broken down to its individual components.

Developmental and Early-Childhood Intervention

The current section is concerned with assessing whether there are more options available to citizens and policymakers at the beginning of the crime prevention time line rather than at the end. In Australia, a recent report by National Crime Prevention (1999) reviews existing developmental and early-childhood interventions. It is unfortunate for the present purposes that the study states: "Certainly in Australia there is no tradition of long term scientific evaluation of any kinds of early intervention designed to prevent crime" (5). The report argues that the pathway by which an individual becomes heavily involved in crime and other antisocial behaviors should be viewed as a series of phases and transitions. Despite the emphasis upon a broader range of prevention and intervention stages, the report suggests "a primary focus on early in life interventions" (101). Specifically, it focuses upon early infancy, the toddler stage, preschool, and elementary school. It also finds that there is no evidence to suggest which early-intervention programs in Australia are working best to prevent crime. The report does, however, make many references to leading North American studies, including the Perry Preschool project (Schweinhart, Barnes, and Weikart 1993).

The report also makes reference to the RAND study by Greenwood et al. in at least three of its recommendations, including the most important one: "Move toward designing a local community based demonstration project" (1996, 99). The authors of the report by the National Crime Prevention suggest that detailed cost-effectiveness analyses, following the methods pioneered by RAND, be embraced. Although the methodology utilized by Greenwood and his colleagues should be applied to early-childhood programs, one should also take heed of the results found using this methodology. The RAND study actually found that the three-strikes law was roughly 5.5 times more cost-effective, and graduation incentives were roughly 23 times more cost-effective, than early-childhood crime prevention in reducing serious crime. This does not undermine the importance of continuing to subject early-childhood intervention programs to economic analysis techniques. In so doing, an effort should be made to include all the benefits, not just those that may stem from the reduction in criminal activity. Furthermore, such programs should attempt to consider any transgenerational benefits. Both these factors are likely to raise the overall cost-benefit findings of early childhood programs.

Developmental and Early-Childhood Intervention Programs: A Concluding Comment

Developmental and early-childhood intervention programs are rarely carried out with the sole intention of reducing criminal behavior. Nevertheless, many of the objectives that these types of programs attempt to satisfy undoubtedly also contribute to reducing criminal involvement.

Two prominent early-childhood programs are the Perry Preschool project and Elmira, New York, Prenatal–Early Infancy Project (Olds et al. 1997). The first of these represents the "gold standard" for benefit-cost analyses of all crime prevention programs, and subsequently should be employed as a guide for the evaluation of future programs. Both programs showed high benefit-cost ratios.

It is important to recognize that, even though these studies have included and quantified a diverse range of benefits, many ancillary benefits remained uncounted. One of the most important is the associated cost of child abuse and neglect that may be overcome by strengthening the parent-child bond. In fact, some programs such as Hawaii Healthy Start (Earle 1995) have focused explicitly on child abuse. Other possible benefits include "spillovers" that siblings may receive from having an older brother or sister in the program. One extremely important factor that is not well discussed in the literature is the possibility of transgenerational or second-generation benefit flows. For example, given the strong link between child abuse victimization and future child abuse offending, a program that is targeted toward protecting a current group of abused children may indirectly reduce the chances of these same children becoming abusive as they grow up.

Juvenile Intervention and Prevention

Potas, Vining, and Wilson (1990) have attempted to estimate the costs of juvenile crime and juvenile crime prevention in Australia. One of the general conclusions of their report is the following: "We have estimated that the direct cost of juvenile crime is at least [A]$610 million. This figure is a rough estimate only and does not include all categories of crime. The need for better costing and reporting of juvenile crime by state agencies is critical especially if juvenile prevention programs are to be successfully evaluated" (Potas, Vining, and Wilson 1990, 3).

Statistically, we know that most criminal careers begin in the juvenile years; we also know that most criminal careers end in the juvenile years as well. In Australia, juveniles account for roughly 15 percent of all arrests for violent offenses and 30 percent of selected property offenses. These proportions remained relatively stable throughout the 1990s (Mukherjee, Carcach, and Higgins 1997). Of course, there are vast differences among the different types of juvenile offenders, both for those who are arrested and for those who are not. Some engage in only a handful of less serious offenses and never come in contact with the criminal justice system. Others are slightly more criminally prone, but cease to be so upon contact with the criminal justice system. For others, initial contact with the criminal justice system marks the start of a cycle of offending and arrest. Those who are arrested five or more times have a very high probability of being arrested again. Given the differences in young offenders, it seems plausible to assume that an array of intervention and prevention strategies is necessary.

Greenwood writes: "Historically, delinquency prevention has been the most widely endorsed and underfunded approach to dealing with crime" (1995, 112). Given the current trend toward early intervention, it is quite possible that juvenile prevention will no longer be the most widely endorsed approach to dealing with crime. Consequently, it is more than likely that it will attract even fewer resources. There are at least two important issues that arise from this observation. First, juvenile prevention and early-childhood programs should not necessarily be viewed as mutually exclusive. In fact, many early-childhood programs may realize their full potential only with a "booster shot" of juvenile prevention, and vice versa. Second, whereas juvenile prevention will still remain relatively well endorsed, if it is to secure increased funding it may require more rigorous evaluation research. The addition of a benefit-cost analysis may serve to further bolster the claims for this increased funding. "[T]he ultimate choice in youth prevention is not just whether some fifteen-year-old mugger should serve an additional year, at a cost to the public of about $40,000 per year, but whether that same $40,000 might be used to hire two staff to run after-school recreational programs for hundreds of youth" (Greenwood 1995, 116–17). Without well-designed research that enables benefit-cost analysis, this type of question will remain unanswered. Fortunately, some juvenile prevention programs, both nonoffender and offender based, have had such an analysis. Table 7.2 presents the results for selected juvenile nonoffender and offender intervention programs.

Juvenile Intervention Programs: A Concluding Comment

Like early-childhood and developmental intervention programs, adolescent programs have also sought to measure their effectiveness in reducing delinquent and antisocial behavior. However, like early-childhood and developmental programs, many adolescent programs do not specify a reduction in crime as the primary objective of the program. Of the three nonoffender programs reviewed in Table 7.2, all were shown to be cost-beneficial. In terms of their effectiveness in preventing crime, it should be recognized that, in contrast to preschool enrichment and home visits, for example, beneficial results are often felt within a few years of the program's implementation. Obviously, the ability to target youths closer to their most crime-prone years is of great importance, especially to governments constrained by fixed short-term election periods.

TABLE 7.2 Summary of Selected Juvenile Nonoffender and Offender Intervention Programs

Study Author and Location	*Description of Study*	*Economic Analysis Findings*
Juvenile Nonoffender Intervention Programs		
Long et al. (1981), United States	Benefit-cost analysis of Job Corps	BC ratio = 1.45
Hahn (1994), United States	Benefit-cost analysis of Quantum Opportunities Program	BC ratio = 3.68
Aos et al. (1999), Washington State	Benefit-cost analysis of Big Brothers Big Sisters of America	BC ratio = 2.12
Juvenile Offender Intervention Programs		
Aos et al. (1999), Washington State	Benefit-cost analysis of multisystemic therapy (Henggeler et al. 1992)	BC ratio = 13.45
Aos et al. (1999), Washington State	Benefit-cost analysis of functional family therapy	BC ratio = 10.99
Aos et al. (1999), Washington State	Benefit-cost analysis of aggression replacement therapy (Goldstein Glick 1987)	BC ratio = 31.40
Aos et al. (1999), Washington State	Benefit-cost analysis of intensive probation supervision (Weibush 1999)	BC ratio = 1.49

NOTE: BC = benefit-cost.

Juvenile offender programs, unlike juvenile programs in general, are designed to treat young people who have already come in contact with the criminal justice system. It follows that, for these programs, practitioners have the clear objective of reducing further delinquent and criminal behavior. Unlike many of the other crime prevention programs that have a range of measurable outcomes, juvenile offender programs are primarily concerned with the gains from reductions in future criminal justice costs or victim costs or both. Of course, this does not preclude the possibility of measuring and including "ancillary benefits," but to date studies have not generally done so. Based upon the objective that these programs are trying to satisfy, namely, to reduce offending behavior, many programs were found to perform particularly well.

Correctional Intervention

This section examines economic analysis research as applied to correctional intervention or treatment programs. It focuses on drugs prevention and sex offender treatment programs.

Drugs Prevention

The financial cost of the illicit drug trade has been estimated to be worth around A$2 billion per year in Australia (Walker 1996). However, there is a vast discrepancy between this financial cost and the true economic cost of drug abuse and drug-related crime (Chisholm 1999). The benefits that stem from drug policies and programs depend upon which link or combination of links between drugs and crime are targeted. Furthermore, the costs and benefits of various drug policies will vary depending not only upon drug type but also on whether the policy is targeted at the supply side or demand side. If we are concerned with drug programs purely as a form of crime prevention, then the objective becomes one of reducing the level of crime. Many benefit-cost analyses of drug treatment programs use an Addiction Severity Index (ASI), which takes into account many potential benefits, such as physical health.

Sex Offender Treatment Programs

The study by Donato, Shanahan, and Higgins (1999) represents a major improvement over earlier works to assess the monetary costs and benefits of sex offender treatment programs, such as the study by Prentky and Burgess (1990). Moreover, the Donato et al. study represents only one of two Australian crime prevention studies that contain any kind of economic evaluation. Unfortunately, this study is not based on a "real-life" program (Welsh and Farrington 2000), but rather represents a hybrid example of a sex offender treatment program.

The report begins with the assumption that although child sex offenders represent a heterogeneous group, it is generally accepted that the best form of treatment for such offenders involves combining cognitive behavioral therapy with relapse prevention. Essentially, the cognitive component of this treatment involves group discussions that aim to isolate causal factors, such as the combination of attributes, beliefs, fantasies, and rationalizations that are used to justify sex offending behavior. Furthermore, it is targeted at reducing deviant arousal, increasing appropriate sexual desires, improving social skills, and modifying distorted thinking. The rationale of such a program is simply that if these factors can be identified and isolated, then attempts can be made to modify them. The representative program involves weekly meetings held over a twelve-month period. Participants discuss victim empathy, social relationships, living skills, sex education, anger management, and alcohol and drug awareness. The other major component of the program, relapse prevention therapy, attempts to teach the offender the appropriate techniques for coping and avoidance strategies required to minimize the chance of relapse.

Based upon the findings by Bakker et al. (1998) and Hall (1995), the most likely reduction in recidivism achieved by the Donato et al. program is between 6 percent and 8 percent. The cost of implementing a generic cognitive behavioral therapy with relapse prevention is estimated to be A$10,000 per offender (in 1998 dollars). The benefits from this program include the cost-savings from lower incarceration, as well as the tangible and intangible costs avoided by potential victims. Tangible victim costs (or costs avoided as benefits) include medical and mental health care, victim services, lost school days, and potentially lost workdays. The study uses an estimate taken from McGurk and Hazel (1998) that combines state and federal services expenditures of A$18,890, together with victim and family out-of-pocket expenditures of A$1,000. This figure is not comparable to that found in the U.S. study by Miller, Cohen, and Wiersema (1996). Foremost, social victim services only amounted to A$1,800, and the remaining tangible costs, including lost productivity and medical and mental health care, were not included. Intangible victim costs include such things as pain, suffering, and loss in quality of life. These costs have been well evaluated, and the sex offender treatment study identifies the following measures. The first measure continues to use the study by McGurk and Hazel (1998), which utilized a willingness-to-pay approach to measure intangible victim costs, for an estimate of A$39,540. The other estimate draws upon the study by Miller, Cohen, and Wiersema (1996). This latter analysis obtained a measure of intangible victim costs by estimating what the average jury award for pain and suffering would be for a particular crime. Unfortunately, Donato, Shanahan, and Higgins (1999) use this estimate in a rather roundabout way. Essentially, they note the ratio of tangible to intangible victim costs (1:10) reported in the Miller, Cohen, and Wiersema (1996) report and apply it to the McGurk and Hazel tangible cost figure to calculate A$198,900 (A$19,890 × 10). The report also calculates intangible victim costs (to tangible costs) by applying an arbitrary ratio of 5:1, because it represents the midpoint between the Miller et al. ratio and zero tangible costs. Given the lack of Australian civil jury award data, the use of these ratios is to some extent acceptable. However, a preferred approach, despite its drawbacks, would be to take the Miller et al. figure for 1993 and convert it into 1998 U.S. dollars by indexing for inflation, and then convert it into Australian dollars for the current period.[3]

Initial results are based upon the assumption that all offenders target only one victim. The report does not express results in terms of benefit-cost ratios, but instead provides results in terms of net benefits (benefits minus costs). For a 2 percent reduction in recidivism and intangible costs set equal to zero, the benefit-cost ratio is 0.32, meaning the program failed to pay back program costs. For a 14 percent reduction in recidivism and intangible costs set equal to A$198,900, the benefit-cost ratio is 4.99. The report, as mentioned above, suggests that the most likely reduction in the recidivism rate is between 6 percent and 8 percent, with the latter figure being derived from the study by Bakker et al. (1998).[4] With an 8 percent recidivism rate the report estimates that the net benefits would range from between A$2,580 to A$18,500. These values translate into benefit-cost ratios of 1.26 and 2.85, respectively. Unfortunately, the net benefits upon which these ratios are based seem inconsistent with the actual recidivism rates from the study by Bakker et al. This study involved a matched control group and revealed that, for those who received treatment, the recidivism rate was 8 percent compared to a recidivism rate of 21 percent for the control group. Therefore, the reduction in recidivism should be 13 percent, not the 8 percent suggested by Donato, Shanahan, and Higgins (1999). Using a 13 percent reduction in recidivism rates, the estimated benefit-cost ratios become even more favorable, ranging between 2.0 and 4.6.

The Donato, Shanahan, and Higgins study relaxes the assumption that there is only one victim per reoffense, and allows for the possibility of two victims per reoffense. Using the same plausible ranges of a 6 percent to 8 percent reduction in recidivism rates, with the assumption of two victims per reoffense, the study finds that the net benefits per one hundred treated offenders range from a loss of A$56,000 to a net gain of A$3.44 million. In terms of benefit-cost ratios, the corresponding values are 0.94 (6 percent reduction in recidivism rate with zero intangible costs) and 4.44 (8 percent reduction in recidivism rate with 10:1 intangible to tangible victim costs and applied to two victims).

There are at least three problems with these estimates. First, as with the single victim case, a 13 percent reduction in recidivism should be used. Second, the tangible victim costs remain constant even though there are two victims rather than one. The report by Donato, Shanahan, and Higgins states that "tangible costs are also unchanged (incarceration costs are held constant) since the basis of calculation was determined at the micro level irrespective of the number of victims" (1999, 77). Although the tangible costs are primarily made up of state and federal government expenditures on services for sexually abused children, the report states this is a cost per victim (59). Moreover, the other component of tangible costs, which totals A$1,000, should be doubled. The third problem with the estimates reported by Donato, Shanahan, and Higgins (1999) is that it is highly unlikely that sentence length, and consequently incarceration costs, would be the same for a multiple-victim child sex offender compared to a single-victim child sex offender. Taking all of these factors into consideration, and keeping incarceration costs constant, a more reliable benefit-cost ratio for this program is 7.47.

Correctional Intervention: A Concluding Comment

The above section has focused upon two important offender-based programs, those concerned with substance abuse and those concerned with sex offending. The former topic is the subject of a heated political debate within Australia. The current Australian government appears to be leaning toward a "zero tolerance" approach. Caulkins et al. (1997) have analyzed the effectiveness of different criminal justice responses to cocaine use in the United States. Their findings suggest that, for each additional million dollars spent, imposing longer sentences would reduce cocaine consumption by only half as much as conventional law enforcement, and only one-eighth as much as treatment of heavy users. The California Drug Treatment program (Gerstein et al. 1994) supports this finding by noting that treatment programs were extremely cost-beneficial. The other primary area of focus regarding drug prevention and intervention is the use of drug courts. The work by the Washington State Institute for Public Policy (Aos et al. 1998, 1999) found that, even for a limited range of benefits, this form of intervention was extremely cost-beneficial.

The work on sex offender treatment programs has been limited. The Australian case (Donato, Shanahan, and Higgins 1999) does not represent a real-life program, but rather draws upon a number of studies to develop a representative program. Nevertheless, even with restrictive assumptions, the representative sex offender treatment program was found to be cost-beneficial. The real-life sex offender treatment program by Prentky and Burgess (1990) was also found to be cost-beneficial; however, the majority of the benefits came from not lower recidivism rates but lower incarceration costs.

Situational Crime Prevention

Situational crime prevention initiatives lend themselves more closely to benefit-cost analysis than any other type of crime prevention strategy. The reasons for this include the comparative ease by which cost estimates of programs' hardware and labor can be obtained, the crime-specific target of many programs, and the reliance on the comparatively inexpensive before-after evaluation design.

Cash Reduction and Robbery Prevention in Australia

Off-track betting facilities in Victoria, Australia, are organized by the Totalizator Agency Board (TAB). Because they traditionally were responsible for the exchange or holding of large sums of cash, they were considered a lucrative target for potential robbers. The situational crime prevention approach (Cornish and Clarke 1986) suggests that the attractiveness of the target could be diminished by changing the expected return. In the wake of this crime prevention approach, the TAB in Victoria introduced various target-hardening schemes from 1980 onward. They included the introduction of time-locking cash boxes and A$500 cash limits on each selling draw. By 1987, a large proportion (400 of the total 425) of off-track betting facilities had been fitted with safes with time-locking devices. The first of these measures, time-locking cash boxes, was assessed using benefit-cost analysis (Clarke and McGrath 1990). The cost of installing time-locking cash boxes in 400 premises was roughly A$360,000. Using a simple before-after evaluation design, it was found that, following the target-hardening exercise, not only did the number of robberies fall over a nine-year period, but the mean value of the dollars stolen fell too. These two factors contributed to an estimated savings of A$614,145.[5] Dividing benefits by costs yields a benefit-cost ratio of 1.71.

There are a number of problems with the simple calculation provided above. The first problem has to do with the evaluation design used to measure program effects. A before-after design is a very weak design. Although Welsh and Farrington (1999) claim that this project had some control, the twenty-five comparative sites that did not receive time locks were not chosen because they represented "very low risk country areas" (Clarke and McGrath 1990, 161); thus, they represented less than ideal sites. Another important issue is crime displacement. Although robberies against Victoria TABs declined significantly, robberies of banks and other commercial premises in Victoria increased during the same period. More precisely, from the data presented calculations can be made to show that over the six-year period following the program's implementation, robbery rates against TABs fell by an average of 67 percent, but at the same time bank robberies increased by an average of 97 percent. A comprehensive benefit-cost analysis would consider the possibility of this geographical displacement and try to estimate the net, rather than gross, reduction in robberies.

Another problem, which is by no means exclusive to situational crime prevention programs, regards the issue of whether the taking of property and cash represents a loss to society or merely a kind of transfer payment. From the perspective of society, it can be argued that a loss in cash or property represents a transfer of resources from victim to offender. There are three main ways of dealing with this notion of social costs. First, a researcher can simply assume that because it is an illegal practice it represents a social loss. Second, one can accept Walker's proposition that social costs represent financial costs "that we intuitively count . . . as costs of crime" (1996, 2). Third, from a victim's perspective, this represents a financial loss.

Situational Crime Prevention: A Concluding Comment

Research into the most cost-beneficial target-hardening, opportunity-reducing (and the like) measures should continue. However, given the smaller range of potential benefits combined with the distinct possibility of "crowding out" private investment, policymakers need to be careful about these types of investment decisions. Having said this, economists need to be careful about applying the concept of crowding out to crime prevention. It could be true that for certain households government-funded initiatives may lower investment in self-protective measures; however, for more socioeconomically disadvantaged households, budget constraints may restrict the purchase of such devices. To overcome this, the government could allow tax rebates on security devices; thus, those who cannot afford to purchase home security devices may have an increased incentive to do so, and any freed-up resources from a reduced need for police in wealthier neighborhoods, for example, could be reallocated to those neighborhoods that cannot afford security devices.

Conclusion

This chapter offers a brief review of crime prevention programs that have been subjected to economic analysis techniques. It covers the broad categories of crime prevention with particular focus on the Australian situation. For the Australian programs a more thorough discussion is provided. The chapter does not go into great detail about the specifics of benefit-cost analysis or related economic evaluation techniques. It focuses more upon possible implications and recommendations with respect to the economic evaluation of the various categories of crime prevention programs, practices, and policies.

Some of the primary recommendations of this chapter include the following: First, there is a real need to investigate the procedures that are presently used to allocate budgets to various crime prevention programs in Australia. Second, it is recommended that all calculations are fully transparent such that results can be replicated. This is important as many bottom-line benefit-cost estimates often mask the process by which these estimates were obtained. Third, it is recommended that a combined scale be developed that would enable policymakers and practitioners to make more informed choices about which crime prevention programs work most effectively and efficiently. The components of this scale should combine benefit-cost ratios, or related efficiency variables, with key characteristics of crime prevention programs, such as sample size, attrition rates, and follow-up period, and, most important, the underlying evaluation research design. Another key recommendation is the need to carry out a full-scale benefit-cost analysis of the entire criminal justice system. Obviously, such an analysis would require enormous effort; however, because it can be used as a basis for comparison for other crime prevention programs and policies—a prerequisite for calculating cost savings for alternative methods of preventing crime—the benefits from such an exercise would most definitely outweigh the costs.

Notes

1. In the course of time it would require only a small leap to obtain a full cost estimate. This analysis would be beneficial for alternative means of crime prevention, as they represent one of the largest cost-savings (benefits) for these types of programs.

2. It is important to note that whereas Zedlewski (1987) used mean crime frequencies, the preferred approach is the one adopted here, that is, the use of median crime frequencies.

3. Strictly speaking, some allowance should also be made for differences in average real earnings between the two countries.

4. The Bakker et al. (1998) study assessed the effectiveness of a sex offender treatment program with 238 offenders in New Zealand. The study showed a recidivism rate of 8 percent after a ten-year follow-up.

5. There is no information on whether costs and benefits were reported in present value.

References

Aos, S., Barnoski, R., and Lieb, R. 1998. Preventive programs for young offenders effective and cost-effective. *Overcrowded Times* 9, no. 2: 1, 7–11.

Aos, S., Phipps, P., Barnoski, R., and Lieb, R. 1999. *The comparative costs and benefits of programs to reduce crime: A review of national research findings with implications for Washington State: Version 3.0.* Olympia: Washington State Institute for Public Policy.

Bakker, L., Hudson, S., Wales, D., and Riley, D. 1998. *And there was light: Evaluating the Kia Marama programme for New Zealand sex offenders against children.* Christchurch, New Zealand: Justice Department.

Botvin, G. J., Mihalic, S. F., and Grotpeter, J. K. 1998. *Blueprints for violence prevention.* Boulder, Colo.: Venture.

Caulkins, J. P., Rydell, C. P., Schwabe, W., and Chiesa, J. 1997. *Mandatory minimum drug sentences: Throwing away the key or the taxpayers' money?* Santa Monica, Calif.: RAND.

Chaiken, J. M., and Chaiken, M. R. 1982. *Varieties of criminal behavior: Summary and policy implications.* Santa Monica, Calif.: RAND.

Chisholm, J. 1999. Benefit-cost and economic analysis of crime prevention. Unpublished report. Canberra, ACT: Australian Institute of Criminology.

Clarke, R. V., and McGrath, G. 1990. Cash reduction and robbery prevention in Australian betting shops. *Security Journal* 1: 160–63.

Cornish, D. B., and Clarke, R. V., eds. 1986. *The reasoning criminal: Rational choice perspectives on offending.* New York: Springer-Verlag.

Crew, R. E., and Hart, R. A. 1999. Assessing the value of police pursuit. *Policing: An International Journal of Police Strategies and Management* 22: 58–73.

DiIulio, J. J., and Piehl, A. M. 1991. Does prison pay? The stormy national debate over the cost-effectiveness of imprisonment. *Brookings Review* (Fall): 28–35.

Donato, R., Shanahan, M., and Higgins, R. 1999. *A benefit-cost analysis of child sex offender treatment programs for male offenders in correctional services.* Child Protection Research Group, University of South Australia.

Earle, R. B. 1995. Helping to prevent child abuse—and future consequences: Hawai'i Healthy Start. *Program Focus* (Oct). Washington, D.C.: U.S. Department of Justice, National Institute of Justice.

Gerstein, D. R., Johnson, R. A., Harwood, H. J., Fountain, D., Suter, N., and Malloy, K. 1994. *Evaluating recovery services: The California Drug and Alcohol Treatment Assessment (CALDATA).* Sacramento: Department of Alcohol and Drug Programs.

Goldstein, A. P., and Glick, B. 1987. *Aggression replacement training: A comprehensive intervention for aggressive youth.* Champaign, Ill.: Research Press.

Grabosky, P. N. 1989. Efficiency and effectiveness in Australian policing: A citizen's guide to police services. In D. Chappell and P. Wilson, eds., *Australian policing: Contemporary issues,* 149–70. Sydney: Butterworths.

Grabosky, P. N., and James, M., eds. 1995. *The promise of crime prevention: Leading crime prevention programs.* Canberra, ACT: Australian Institute of Criminology.

Gray, T., and Olson, K. W. 1989. A benefit-cost analysis of the sentencing decision for burglars. *Social Science Quarterly* 70: 708–22.

Greenwood, P. W. 1995. Juvenile crime and juvenile justice. In J. Q. Wilson and J. Petersilia, eds., *Crime.* San Francisco: ICS Press.

Greenwood, P. W., Model, K. E., Rydell, C. P., and Chiesa, J. 1996. *Diverting children from a life of crime: Measuring costs and benefits.* Santa Monica, Calif.: RAND.

Hahn, A. 1994. *Evaluation of the Quantum Opportunities Program (QOP): Did the program work?* Waltham, Mass.: Center for Human Resources, Heller Graduate School, Brandeis University.

Hall, G. C. 1995. Sex offender recidivism revisited: A meta-analysis of recent treatment studies. *Journal of Consulting and Clinical Psychology* 63: 802–9.

Henggeler, S. W., Melton, G. B., and Smith, L. A. 1992. Family preservation using multisystemic therapy: An effective alternative to incarcerating serious juvenile offenders. *Journal of Consulting and Clinical Psychology* 60: 953–61.

Long, D. A., Mallar, C. D., and Thornton, C. V. D. 1981. Evaluating the benefits and costs of the Job Corps. *Journal of Policy Analysis and Management* 1: 55–76.

Macionis, S. 1994. Contract management in corrections: The Queensland experience. In P. Moyle, ed., *Private prisons and police: Recent Australian trends.* Australia: Pluto Press.

McGurk, H., and Hazel, V. 1998. *The economic cost of child abuse and neglect in South Australia.* South Australia: Office for Families and Children, Australian Institute for Family Studies.

Miller, T. R., Cohen, M. A., and Wiersema, B. 1996. *Victim costs and consequences: A new look.* Washington, D.C.: U.S. Department of Justice, National Institute of Justice.

Mukherjee, S., Carcach, C., and Higgins, K. 1997. *A statistical profile of crime in Australia.* Canberra, ACT: Australian Institute of Criminology.

National Crime Prevention. 1999. *Pathways to prevention: Developmental and early intervention approaches to crime in Australia.* Canberra, ACT: by the author.

Olds, D. L., Eckenrode, J., Henderson, C. R., Kitzman, H., Powers, J., Cole, R., Sidora, K., Morris, P., Pettitt, L. M., and Luckey, D. 1997. Long-term effects of home visitation on maternal life course and child abuse and neglect: Fifteen-year follow-up of a randomized trial. *Journal of the American Medical Association* 278: 637–43.

Potas, I., Vining, A., and Wilson, P. 1990. *Young people and crime: Costs and prevention.* Canberra, ACT: Australian Institute of Criminology.

Prentky, R., and Burgess, A. W. 1990. Rehabilitation of child molesters: A cost-benefit analysis. *American Journal of Orthopsychiatry* 60: 108–17.

Sansfaçon, D., and Welsh, B. C. 1999. *Crime prevention digest II: Comparative analysis of successful community safety.* Montreal: International Centre for the Prevention of Crime.

Schweinhart, L. J., Barnes, H. V., and Weikart, D. P. 1993. *Significant benefits: The High/Scope Perry Preschool study through age 27.* Ypsilanti, Mich.: High/Scope Press.

Sherman, L. W., Gottfredson, D. C., MacKenzie, D. L., Eck, J. E., Reuter, P., and Bushway, S. D. 1997. *Preventing crime: What works, what doesn't, what's promising.* Washington, D.C.: U.S. Department of Justice, National Institute of Justice.

Stevenson, R. J., and Forsythe, L. M. V. 1998. *The stolen goods market in New South Wales: An interview study with imprisoned burglars.* Sydney: New South Wales Bureau of Crime Statistics and Research.

Walker, J. 1992. Estimates of the costs of crime in Australia. *Trends and Issues in Crime and Criminal Justice* 39. Canberra, ACT: Australian Institute of Criminology.

______. 1996. Estimates of the costs of crime in Australia in 1996. *Trends and Issues in Crime and Criminal Justice* 72. Canberra, ACT: Australian Institute of Criminology.

Waller, I., Welsh, B. C., and Sansfaçon, D. 1997. *Crime prevention digest 1997: Successes, benefits, and directions from seven countries.* Montreal: International Centre for the Prevention of Crime.

Weibush, R. G. 1993. Juvenile intensive supervision: The impact of felony offenders diverted from institutional placement. *Crime and Delinquency* 39: 68–89.

Welsh, B. C., and Farrington, D. P. 1999. Value for money? A review of the costs and benefits of situational crime prevention. *British Journal of Criminology* 39: 345–68.

______. 2000. Monetary costs and benefits of crime prevention programs. In M. Tonry, ed., *Crime and justice: A review of research,* 27: 305–61. Chicago: University of Chicago Press.

Zedlewski, E. W. 1987. Making confinement decisions. *Research in Brief* (July). Washington, D.C.: U.S. Department of Justice, National Institute of Justice.

8

Recent Evolution of Governmental Crime Prevention Strategies and Implications for Evaluation and Economic Analysis

DANIEL SANSFAÇON
IRVIN WALLER

Governmental crime prevention strategies, policies, and programs gradually took shape in the mid–1970s in Europe. The British Standing Committee on Crime Prevention, set up in the Home Office in 1966, can be seen as the pioneering coordinating state agency for crime prevention. The first official national crime prevention council was created in Denmark in 1971, soon followed by a similar body in Sweden in 1974. But it was really France, with the creation of the National Crime Prevention Council (NCPC) in 1982 and the establishment of a mechanism to foster the development of local crime prevention councils, that possibly gave the strongest impetus to governmental crime prevention policies. Soon thereafter, England and Wales in 1983 and the Netherlands in 1983 implemented crime prevention programs to tackle specific crimes. Simultaneously, numerous projects were implemented and many evaluated in the United States, although without support from a strong central government policy or strategy.

In recent years, policies, strategies, and programs have been significantly revamped in those countries that had initiated the movement: Such has been the case in Sweden (1998), France (1998), England and Wales (1998), and the Netherlands (1998). Other countries have now adopted crime prevention programs and policies at the central government level: Finland (1988), Estonia (1993), Canada (1994 and 1998), Australia (1995), Hungary (1995), Mexico (1996), New Zealand (1996), the United States (on juvenile delinquency, 1996), South Africa (1998), the Czech Republic (1998), Portugal (1998), Ivory Coast (1998), Hungary (1999), and Bolivia (1999), whereas others such as Argentina, Chili, Nicaragua, and El Salvador are in the process of developing them.

The list is impressive and shows that crime prevention is gaining legitimacy and status as the "fourth pillar" in addition to police, the courts, and prisons in the search to create safer communities. These developments are also in line with directions taken by many international forums since the 1989 Montreal conference on Crime Prevention and Community Safety.

Some commentators have suggested that these developments may be explained by the need for states to find more cost-effective approaches, given the requirement to curtail expenditures and make government services more effective (e.g., Waller and Welsh 1999). Others have suggested that the movement toward community-based crime prevention may represent rather a disengagement by the state and part of a broader trend in the current neoliberal era (e.g., Crawford 1997). Still others interpret it from the perspective of good governance and the reshaping of social solidarity (Habitat 1996; UNDP 1994; Takala 1999).

This paper will show that (1) although there is a degree of convergence among the approaches adopted by governments to sustain crime prevention, (2) the strategies and policies adopted correspond to different preoccupations and (3) are therefore translated into different mechanisms. This will lead, in the second section, to an examination of the place and underlying conception of evaluation and, in particular, cost-benefit evaluation. It will be seen that (4) though all governmental strategies include some evaluation component, they are not articulated in the same manner. The third section will attempt to show that, beyond differences among epistemological and methodological approaches to evaluation, what this reveals is (5) a fundamental difference between policy-driven and project-based approaches to prevention. In conclusion, the paper will identify some issues concerning cost-effectiveness evaluation, especially in the context of large-scale national policies with a view to developing useful approaches in relation to particular objectives and contexts.

Converging Orientations

Governmental crime prevention strategies generally agree on issues such as the need for a more balanced approach to respond to the challenges posed by crime, violence, and insecurity; the importance of developing actions targeting the root causes of crime; and the creation of basic mechanisms to support action. Examples of converging views on each of these issues will be briefly described.

A Balanced Approach to Face the Challenges

Most Occidental nations are experiencing a decline in overall crime rates. The downward trend seems to have started in the early 1990s in the United States and Canada and in the mid–1990s in Europe and Australia. Yet, despite these important reductions in crime rates, a number of concerns remain.

First, overall crime rates are still two or three times higher than in the 1960s. These levels have been reached despite growing criminal justice system expenditures and increased rates of incarceration. In effect, it is estimated that the costs of crime and its control amount to approximately 5 percent of the gross domestic product (GDP) of many Western countries and run as high as 12 percent to 15 percent of the GDP in developing countries (Sansfaçon and Welsh 1999). This level of expenditure eats up limited, in some cases shrinking, resources that could be used for other purposes such as education, health care, and other social development programs. In addition, increases in incarceration rates and stiffer penalties threaten the future ability of governments to invest in these fields. This is revealed, for example, in the projection analysis conducted by the RAND Corporation (Greenwood et al. 1994) on the costs of fully implementing the three-strikes law in California (Figure 8.1).

Concern about the costs of crime is heightened by awareness, whether based on intuition or evaluation studies, of the limited effectiveness of traditional crime control measures. Not only are fewer than 20 percent of delinquents arrested and even fewer prosecuted, but a significant proportion of those who end up in prison will recidivate. Simultaneously, the public is largely dissatisfied with current policies, requesting more safety, stiffer penalties, *and* more investment in preventive measures. Faced with these contradictions, states are indeed looking toward prevention as a complementary means of offering more safety.

This concern is best reflected in the strategies adopted in England and Wales and in South Africa in 1998. For example, in the presentation of the Crime Reduction Strategy, the Home Secretary for England and Wales observed, "For many years, governments have concentrated too much on the consequences of crime, to the detriment of its causes. But we can only make a long-term impact on crime and disorder by concentrating on both" (Home Office 1999, 3). Similarly, in the presentation of the White Paper on Safety and Security, the South African Minister observed, "In keeping with the approach outlined in the National Crime Prevention

FIGURE 8.1 Correctional Expenditures in California as a Proportion of General Revenue, 1994 and 2002

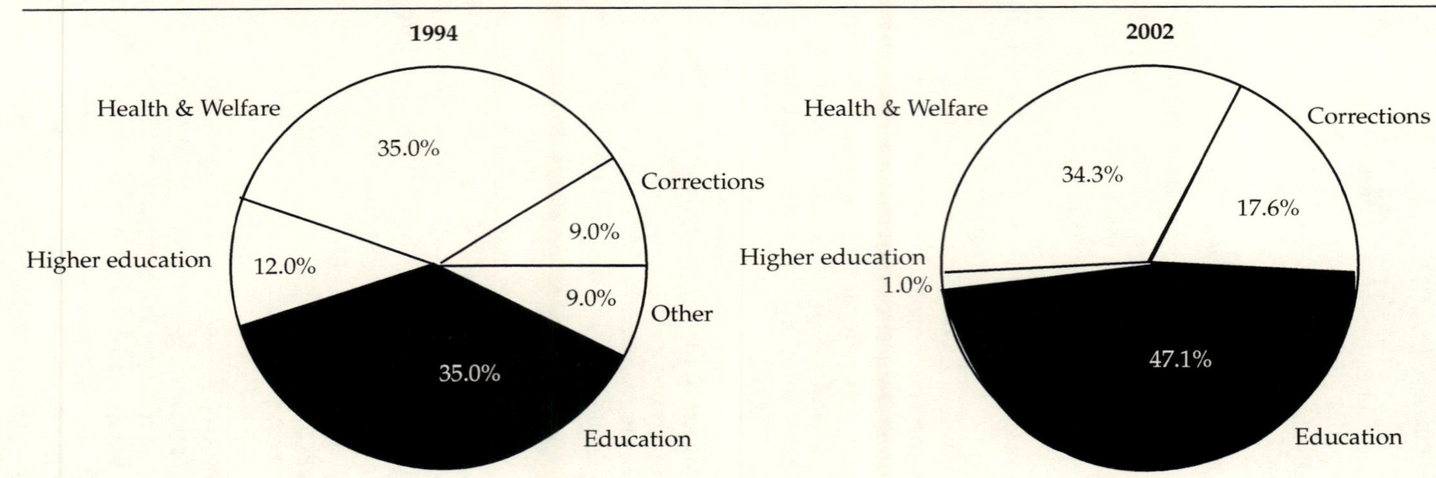

SOURCE: Greenwood et al. (1994).

Strategy, the White Paper advocates a dual approach to safety and security—effective and efficient law enforcement and the provision of crime prevention programs to reduce the occurrence of crime" (Ministry of Safety and Security 1998, n.p.).

In developing countries and emerging democracies, this concern is made more acute by inefficient, if not corrupt, police forces often inherited from previous political regimes. Enacting crime prevention policies becomes one of the means to improve the quality of police services through community-based approaches. This is one of the key elements of national safety policies in South Africa, Bolivia, Argentina, or Chile, for example.

A second concern relates to the fact that decreases in overall crime rates have been counterbalanced by an increase in violent crime, particularly gratuitous or heinous crimes, and an increase in the proportion of juveniles committing crimes, especially violent crimes. In fact, the proportion of juveniles in police recorded crime has increased in most developed countries. In France, for example, the proportion of youths in the criminal justice system was 12 percent in 1978; currently it is 21 percent. In the Netherlands, the proportion of minors involved in all forms of crime rose by 50 percent between 1994 and 1996. Similar trends have been found in England and Wales and in the United States.

Addressing this situation is one of the key objectives of many governmental crime prevention strategies. In the Netherlands, the Integrated Programme on Safety and Security, adopted in 1998, includes a special program of action for young people to better balance preventive and control measures. Among the measures are: improved cooperation at the local level among the various partners in the criminal justice system, improved exchange of information, research on gangs, an action plan on school dropout, a STOP experiment[1] for under twelve-year-olds, implementation of Communities that Care programs, and enhanced cooperation between police and schools.

A third concern deals with underreporting by victims. It is well established through victimization surveys that no more than 50 percent of all crimes are reported to police. This situation is particularly problematic in the area of violence against women. Surveys conducted in various developed countries show consistently that approximately 90 percent of sexual crimes and 80 percent of conjugal violence incidents are not reported. Although overall crime rates are diminishing and despite strong public information campaigns on violence against women (in Canada, for example), nothing indicates that women are anymore willing to report such violence, nor are there indications that this form of crime is abating. A recent report by the Ministry of Public Safety in the Province of Quebec indicates that the incidence of conjugal violence has increased by 20 percent since 1988, despite the implementation of a wide-ranging policy of improved police action, automatic prosecution, and public information (Ministère de la sécurité publique du Québec, 1999). This concern is best exemplified in the strategies adopted in Australia, New Zealand, and Canada, all of which involve action plans specifically targeting violence against women.

Finally, a fourth concern relates to the gap between declining crime rates and an increasing feeling of insecurity in many communities. Obviously, insecurity is generated by factors other than crime itself. It is fueled by precarious living conditions in a changing world, enhanced visibility of itinerants and other deinstitutionalized populations, incivilities, and urban decay. But the public does not necessarily distinguish among these various elements and will be quick to call for more police and stiffer prison sentences. Given the limited effectiveness of these measures alone, in particular to enhance a feeling of public safety, governments are turning to policies that can help build safer communities by increasing public participation.

Tackling the Root Causes

Over the last decade or so, reports from governmental commissions in Australia, New Zealand, England, and France,[2] scientific reports (Donziger 1996; Reiss and Roth 1993; Farrington 1996), declarations from international conferences under the auspices of the United Nations (United Nations 1990, 1995), and syntheses produced by national crime prevention organizations (e.g., Crime Concern 1997; National Crime Prevention Council, Canada, 1996) have identified a number of common, recurring factors associated with delinquency, violence, and insecurity:

- poverty and unemployment deriving from social exclusion, especially for youths;
- dysfunctional families with uncaring and incoherent parental attitudes, violence, or parental conflicts;
- social valuation of a culture of violence;
- presence of facilitators (such as firearms and drugs);
- discrimination and exclusion deriving from sexist, racist, or other forms of oppression;
- the degradation of urban environments and social bonds; and
- inadequate surveillance of places and availability of goods that are easy to transport and sell.

These factors have been further specified by accumulating knowledge from longitudinal studies conducted in many different countries and by numerous evaluations of crime prevention actions targeting specific risk factors for delinquency or victimization. Beyond the specificity of the factors identified, it is fascinating to observe that whether they have been conducted in North America, Western European countries, or Australasia, these studies converge on a similar list of indicators. Furthermore, not only are we now in a better position to identify, with a higher degree of confidence, factors putting children and youths at risk of criminal behavior, and victimization-related factors, but knowledge is also developing on protective factors.

Numerous governmental policies and programs already act on some of the known risk factors for offending. Universal programs for child and family support and specific actions undertaken to improve the living conditions of disadvantaged children or to improve social housing are examples. Not designed to curtail delinquency and victimization per se, these policies respond to other objectives such as solidarity and human rights. However, as Palle and Godefroy observe: "Ultimately, all government expenditures to assist citizens, all actions targeting social problems in the fields of housing, health, education, and the social and professional insertion of people in difficulty contribute more or less to prevention" (1998, 50). Whether as a result of the evolving concept of prevention, the close interrelationships among social problems, or the utilization of crime and delinquency concerns as legitimation tools to mobilize resources behind a policy, it is obvious that many universal programs directly or indirectly include crime prevention among their goals. This being said, the Nordic countries, with their strong welfare state traditions, have not distinguished crime prevention strategies as separate from broader strategies to ensure the equal distribution of wealth and social integration. According to Takala: "Several methods evaluated as effective in crime prevention are implemented in the Nordic countries as routine in ordinary social service systems. Parental advice, free high standard education and so on are, in the Nordic countries, rights of every citizen" (1999, n.p.).

In addition to these universal programs, governments are attempting, through their crime prevention strategies, to implement specific actions targeting some of the known risk factors. This is especially evident in the recent British strategy as well as in the strategies of the Netherlands, Canada, New Zealand, and Australia.

Mechanisms to Support Action

Governmental strategies also converge on a recognition that some form of structure is required to support and strengthen community safety and crime prevention action. These structures generally have some analytical and funding capabilities to enhance coordination among different government departments and cooperation among the police and justice personnel and crime prevention practitioners, and to sustain local action. Indeed, among the key mechanisms for fostering action is the capacity to fund programs and projects locally, whether as pilot projects with an evaluation component or as universal programs.

All countries reviewed in the International Centre for the Prevention of Crime's (ICPC) *Crime Prevention Digest II* (Sansfaçon and Welsh 1999), and many of those mentioned earlier in this paper have created an agency responsible for the implementation of a crime prevention strategy. In Canada, for example, the National Crime Prevention Centre, located in the Department of Justice, was established in June 1998 to (1) promote integrated action of key partners to reduce crime and victimization; (2) develop and implement community-based solutions to problems that contribute to crime and victimization; and (3) increase public awareness and support for effective approaches to crime prevention. Table 8.1 identifies some of these key crime prevention agencies.

Different Preoccupations

Despite common overall orientations, governmental strategies express differing preoccupations. This is best revealed in their underlying vision of crime prevention and the focus and priorities adopted by the responsible agency. A comparison of the French and British approaches will help to clarify these differing preoccupations.

In France, violent events in some cities in the late 1970s prompted the creation of the Mayor's Commission on Security, which in turn led to the creation in 1982 of a National Crime Prevention Council (NCPC), chaired by the prime minister. This council facilitated the creation of local and departmental crime prevention councils throughout France, in particular through a prevention contract mechanism. Participating in the significant decentralization process of the French state, prevention policies were aimed at empowering local authorities and facilitating partnerships among local actors in the resolution of local problems. The focus of action was on social development, renewal of disadvantaged neighborhoods, and the fight against exclusion.

Following a period of uncertainty after the abolition of the NCPC and the relocation of the crime prevention agency within the Interministerial Delegation to the City in 1990, the key characteristics of the French national crime prevention strategy remain its integration into a large urban renewal strategy integrating insertion programs (health, employment, culture, and housing), educative action, and improved criminal justice responses. Today, there are more than nine hundred communal crime pre-

TABLE 8.1 Selected Crime Prevention Agencies

Country	*Agency*	*Under authority of*	*Date created*
Australia	Crime Prevention Unit	Attorney General's Department	1994
Belgium	Permanent Secretariat for Prevention Policy	Ministry of the Interior	1994
Canada	National Crime Prevention Council	Department of Justice	1994–1997
	National Crime Prevention Centre	Department of Justice and Ministry of Solicitor General	1998
England	Crime Prevention Unit	Home Office	1983, modified in 1993
	Crime Prevention Council, now Crime Prevention Agency	Home Office	1993, modified in 1996
France	Council national de prévention de la délinquance	Prime Minister	1983–1988
	Délégation interministérielle à la ville (Pole prévention)	Ministry of Employment and Solidarity	1988
Netherlands	Prevention Directorate	Ministry of Justice	1989
	Prevention, Youth and Sanctions Directorate	Ministry of Justice	1993
	Police Directorate	Ministry of the Interior	1993
New Zealand	Crime Prevention Unit	Prime Minister's Office	1993
Sweden	National Crime Prevention Council	Ministry of Justice	1974, modified in 1993 and 1996
United States	OJJDP Bureau of Justice Assistance National Institute of Justice	Department of Justice	1984, prevention policy defined in 1996

NOTE: Other countries with a crime prevention agency not included in this summary table: Argentina, Bolivia, Chile, Mexico in South America; Czech Republic, Hungary in Eastern Europe; Denmark, Finland, and Portugal in Western Europe; Ivory Coast and South Africa in Africa.

vention councils all over France. In addition to these existing mechanisms, France adopted a new tool to support local action through local security contracts aiming to foster citizenship, bring justice and the police closer to citizens, and enhance effectiveness by improved cooperation among key state agencies.

In England and Wales, in the context of a profound revision of the role of local authorities, prevention policies were largely defined by the central government. Studies conducted by Home Office researchers pointing to rising crime rates and public insecurity led to the creation in 1986 of the Crime Prevention Unit. Action was predominantly focused on situational prevention, particularly to reduce residential burglaries and repeat victimization. Another element specific to the British approach is the sustained research into risk factors and project evaluation, one example being the large-scale evaluation of the Safer Cities Programme.

In 1998, the newly elected British government adopted the Crime and Disorder Act and conducted a Comprehensive Spending Review. This exercise led to the reallocation of substantial sums of money toward more effective and cost-efficient measures to reduce crime. The Crime and Disorder Act requires local authorities and the police to create crime reduction partnerships without additional funding. In addition to this legislative framework, the government adopted a major investment program to implement evidence-based approaches to crime prevention. This investment program is based on research conducted by the Home Office (Goldblatt and Lewis 1998) that, using the work conducted by Sherman and his colleagues in the United States (Sherman et al. 1997) and the ICPC (1997), identified promising programs as well as their effectiveness and efficiency. The British Crime Reduction Programme covers five broad themes: working with families, children, and schools to prevent young people from becoming the offenders of the future; tackling crime in communities, particularly high-volume crime such as domestic burglary; developing products and systems that are more resistant to crime; having more effective sentencing practices; and working with offenders to ensure that they do not reoffend.

Two key differences emerge from this comparison. First, it may be seen that France's strategy was policy driven whereas England's has been more project based. Second, and largely deriving from the first difference, England's strategy focuses on reducing crime whereas France is primarily concerned with increasing social development and improving the quality of life in urban areas.

Crime prevention policies in other countries may be generally considered to reflect one or the other of these approaches. Canada, Sweden, and New Zealand are more concerned with building quality of life through social development, whereas the Netherlands, Australia, and the United

States tend to focus more on reducing specific crimes. Tables 8.2 and 8.3 briefly review differences in vision and priorities among the agencies examined more closely in Sansfaçon and Welsh (1999).

Obviously, these are not contradictory approaches and concerns. Indeed, one may discern a relative degree of convergence whereby governments with policy-driven strategies are now somewhat more concerned with effective actions, whereas governments with project-driven approaches are attempting to develop encompassing preventive policies. The difference in focus, however, has important implications in terms of the means and tools that are required and established.

Diverging Means

Governmental policies and strategies for crime prevention revolve around a clearly identifiable and stable central agency. This agency should be able to provide leadership to foster the preventive agenda, influence other departments' policies that have an impact on crime levels and risk factors, and develop a plan to implement action targeting risk factors to stimulate partnerships and to mobilize citizens.

Given their different underlying concerns, government agencies differ in a number of respects. In most countries, such agencies are located within either the public security or justice ministries, indicating the central focus on reducing levels of crime and insecurity. In France, the agency is under the authority of the Minister for the City, but in New Zealand it is located in the prime minister's office. In these two cases, there is a clear focus on interministerial coordination and improving the quality of life in communities, especially in urban centers. One of the issues for consideration is which of these approaches is better able to influence other departments and play a significant role in decisions on resource allocation.

Where countries focus on reducing crime, the agency directly controls most of the funds allocated to crime prevention. When the agency is more of an interministerial coordinating body, it controls only a limited portion of the money invested in crime prevention. Table 8.4 compares France and England in terms of their crime prevention resources, both specific to the agency and in total. This table shows that the Home Office is directly responsible for about one-quarter of the resources spent on crime prevention ($2.13 per person out of $9.30 per person), whereas the Interministerial Delegation to the City in France is managing less than 1 percent ($0.15 per person out of $33.78 per person).

Countries focusing on reducing crime prioritize crime-specific action. In England and Wales, residential burglary and car theft, and in the Netherlands, youth violence and crimes in public spaces, are examples of

TABLE 8.2 A Vision for Prevention

Country	*Vision*
Australia	The Australian policy has as its central goal to combat the culture of violence by strengthening local communities, protecting vulnerable groups, and modifying attitudes tolerating violence. Some Australian states have also adopted comprehensive community safety strategies.
Belgium	Using both short- and long-term measures, the Belgian policy aims to foster the development and safety of local communities.
Canada	The recently adopted Canadian policy aims at developing safer communities mainly through social development measures targeting children and youth, women's safety and Aboriginal communities.
England and Wales	The Crime and Disorder Act promotes a vision anchored on local communities' responsibility and empowerment through crime reduction partnerships. The evidence-based Crime Reduction Strategy that accompanies this act aims to implement a systematic program of promising action targeting risk factors and based on an analysis of internationally available knowledge.
France	The French policy aims at integrating crime provention at the very center of urban development policies and the fight against exclusion. The newly established local security contracts and the reinforcement of the Intermisisterial Committee of Cities provide a new impetus to prevention policy. In particular, they include the creation of youth employment by hiring local security assistants and social mediators.
New Zealand	The New Zealand policy aims at better coordination of the actions of various government departments and empowering local communities in an effort to effectively reduce delinquency and insecurity by targeting risk factors.
The Netherlands	Largely "pragmatic," the Dutch policy aims at involving citizens, police, public prosecutors, urban managers, and the private sector in order to reduce opportunities and insecurity and foster social integration. The policy rests on a three-phase development cycle: examination, verification, and dissemination.

(*continues*)

TABLE 8.2 *(continued)*

Country	*Vision*
Sweden	The recently revised Swedish policy aims at involving citizens, enterprises, and public and private organizations in reducing the level and costs of crime and is determined to include consideration of crime in all national policies.
United States	Although one can hardly speak of a national crime prevention policy for the entire country, the United States focuses mainly on youth and empowering local communities in order to diminish risk factors and augment protective factors for at-risk groups of the population, in particular at-risk youth.

current priorities. Countries focusing on enhancing social development and improving the quality of life in communities prioritize funding processes best able to bring together the partners at the local level (e.g., the communal crime prevention councils in France and New Zealand) or actions targeting specific groups at risk (e.g., children and youths in Canada).

Another difference between these approaches is the closer link between research and other types of empirical assessment in countries focusing on reducing crime, compared with the generally more tenuous link in countries focusing on improving social solidarity and quality of life. Again, England and Wales currently show the strongest link among strategies and actions on the one hand and research evidence on the other. At the other end of the spectrum, one may say that France's policies have been based more on a political will to enhance social solidarity than on research data. Given these differences in focus and means, where does evaluation stand in these governmental crime prevention approaches, what types of evaluation are conducted, and for what purpose?

A Shared Will to Evaluate

At a recent international conference organized by the ICPC in Montreal in September 1999, which brought together some two hundred people from twenty-six countries, delegates discussed experiences and governmental strategies as well as successful case studies. Among the key conclusions of the conference was a general agreement on the need to further examine evaluation issues in prevention programs and strategies.

TABLE 8.3 Priorities for Prevention in Selected Governmental Agencies

Country	*Priorities*
Australia	residential burglary, fear of crime, youth, family violence, improving prevention practices, Aboriginal communities, and ethnic minorities
Belgium	residential burglary, car theft, drugs, situational prevention, and youths
Canada	children and youths, women's safety, and Aboriginal communities
England and Wales	specific crimes such as residential burglary and car theft; places such as high crime neighborhoods and council estates; and social development for at-risk children, youths and families
France	assisting adults to assume their authority and education responsibilities, prevent drug addiction, prevent recidivism, assistance to victims, and security in selected places (schools, stores, public transportation)
The Netherlands	violence in public places,youths, gangs drug abuse, residential burglary, and insecurity
New Zealand	supporting families at risk, reducing family violence, youths at risk, alternative measures for first-time offenders, drug and alcohol abuse, economic crime, and victims
Sweden	fear and insecurity, drug and alcohol abuse, families and youths, opportunities, and recidivism
United States	youth violence, drug abuse, and high-crime areas

Most governmental strategies currently involve some provision for evaluation. In England and Wales, the Crime Reduction Programme provides that 10 percent of the funds, or approximately $42 million over three years, will be spent on impact evaluation and cost-benefit analysis of preventive action. The chapter by Dhiri and his colleagues more fully describes the key elements of the evaluation strategy developed in England.

The Netherlands has also been relying heavily on evaluation and cost-effectiveness analyses to develop action within its national strategy. A number of examples stand out, such as the Residential Safe Label and the City Guards programs. In both cases, these pilot projects were turned into national programs following evaluation of their results. Further-

TABLE 8.4 Crime Prevention Expenditures Per Capita in England and France (in 1998 U.S. Dollars)

	Specific Prevention Resources	*Total Prevention Expenditures*
England	$2.13 per person	$9.30 per person
France	$0.15 per person	$33.78 per person

more, in 1994, the newly elected government of the Netherlands dedicated an annual budget of 160 million guilders (US$100 million) for local crime prevention efforts to tackle early risk factors for delinquency and later criminal offending. This decision was based largely on research carried out by the Dutch Ministry of Justice (van Dijk 1996, 1997). A simulation model using historical crime and crime control trends was developed to forecast the effects of four hypothetical scenarios on government spending on public safety: (1) extrapolating current trends (doing the same); (2) adding 1,000 extra police officers to a force of 27,620 officers; (3) increasing investment in situational prevention by 30 percent; and (4) strengthening social prevention through interagency cooperation to achieve a 10 percent decrease in crime. As shown in Figure 8.2, over time,[3] social prevention was predicted to have the strongest effect on reducing police or justice spending. The study estimated that after seven years (by the year 2000), adding more police would not reduce crime—in fact, violent crime alone was expected to grow by 6 percent after three years—and to cost the government 100 million guilders (US$63 million) more had they done nothing at all. Situational prevention was estimated to have already begun to pay for itself by reduced crime and modest savings to the government.

In another more recent and influential exercise, the Dutch Social and Cultural Planning Board (1999) examined the capacity of four different scenarios to affect trends in recorded crime over time. They developed a model comparing four crime control strategies. The *reference scenario* is based on an increase in population but unchanged capacity of the police, prosecution, judiciary, prisons, and aftercare. The *police scenario* is based on a desire for a higher-crime-solving percentage. Taken to its extreme, this scenario is equivalent to a "zero-tolerance" police policy. The *sanctions scenario* is based on a more punitive approach whereby the risk of incarceration increases by 3 percent to 3.5 percent. At its extreme, this is a "three-strikes and you're out" approach. Finally, the *prevention scenario* focuses on intensifying situational and offender-oriented prevention. It is based on effective approaches to tackle burglary prevention and to improve upbringing of children, school completion rates, and the supervision of juvenile offenders. The data clearly demonstrate that the prevention scenario is the one best capable of reducing crime rates.

FIGURE 8.2 Results of Dutch Simulation Model

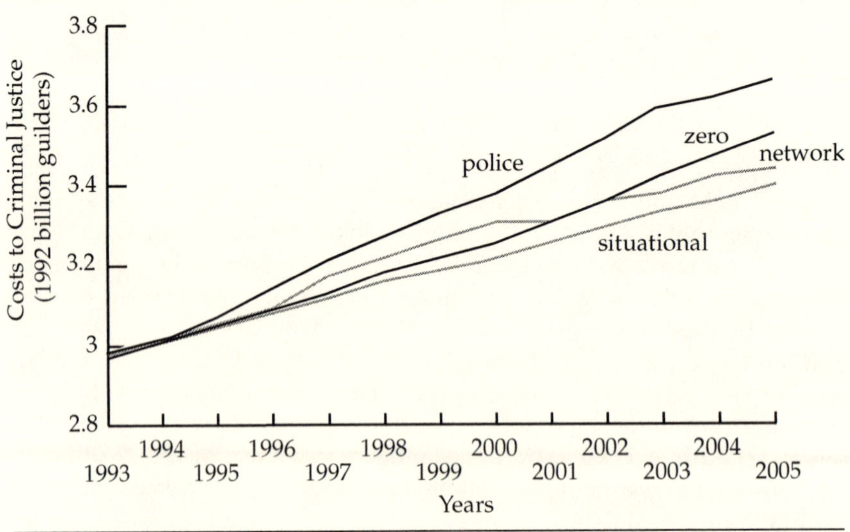

SOURCE: van Dijk (1996, 10).

Other countries have also included specific provisions for evaluation in their national strategies. The Secretariat for Prevention Policy in Belgium has been evaluating local safety contracts since 1996, the National Crime Prevention Centre in Canada will be evaluating model projects as well as its entire initiative, the National Crime Prevention Strategy in Australia provides for the evaluation of specific actions, and the Crime Prevention Unit in New Zealand will evaluate both the contract mechanism and process and the impacts of some model actions. In South Africa, the National Crime Prevention Strategy provides for the evaluation of specific actions undertaken under each of the priority areas. For the most part, these plans for impact evaluations will target specific demonstration and pilot projects; few are intended to be cost-effectiveness analyses.

In France, Sweden, and Denmark, evaluation of specific local action has either remained underdeveloped or been conducted in different ways, as will be seen in the next section.

Different Perspectives on Evaluation

A comparison of governmental strategies to evaluate crime prevention programs and actions is, in many respects, premature. Although significant efforts have been made in recent years to accumulate information about action that has been evaluated in different parts of the world, the picture still remains incomplete.

It is interesting to observe, as did Takala (1999), that two of the three recent reports comparing international "best practices" in crime prevention (ICPC 1997; Graham and Bennett 1995) have generally comparable representation of countries, with the United States, Canada, England, and Wales accounting for approximately 60 percent of the cases proposed. In an American report (Sherman et al. 1997), 96 percent of the cases are from these four countries (with 79 percent coming from the United States alone). These reports remain unquestionably incomplete. The choices they made, however, speak of a particular vision not only of evaluation, but also of crime prevention more generally.

A preliminary comparison nonetheless reveals significant differences among approaches. Some argue that these differences rest on culturally based conceptions of "science," research, and measurement. For example, some set the French scientific tradition in opposition to the British tradition, the former being more phenomenological, the latter more pragmatic. There is certainly some truth to this. But unless one is content with accepting that such differences, ultimately, may be irreconcilable, it is important to look for other explanations for these distinctions with a view to developing better and more useful evaluation practices.

Linking the strategies developed by governments to their respective approaches to evaluation does in fact reveal a picture that may be concerned not so much with different conceptions of what evaluation is as with how strategies are conceived of in the first place, and how actions are in turn implemented.

Evaluation in Project-Based Strategies

Project-based approaches, such as those pursued in the United States, England and Wales, and, to some extent, the Netherlands, have produced the largest number of empirical evaluations using some form of experimental research design. Examining a particular action, these evaluations look at impacts in terms of:

- What actions were implemented and how?
- What were their effects on the specific crime targeted (especially situational crime prevention actions)?
- What were their effects on the targeted group (especially in actions targeting risk factors for youths)?
- In some cases, what were the negative effects (e.g., displacement) or other positive effects apart from reducing crime (e.g., better employment)? and
- In some cases, what was the cost-effectiveness of the action?

Examples such as the residential burglary schemes in England and Wales and the Netherlands (e.g., Safer Cities Programme, Residential Safe Label), social development risk factors for children and youths in the United States (e.g., Perry Preschool, Elmira Prenatal–Early Infancy Project), or actions to develop responsibility in youths (e.g., the HALT diversion program for youth vandals in the Netherlands) have been described elsewhere and are well known (see Goldblatt and Lewis 1998; Sansfaçon and Welsh 1999).

These evaluations are for the most part before and after comparisons, sometimes with control groups, and a few are close to the "true" experimental design as defined for example in Sherman et al.'s (1997) review. As such, they must necessarily select, control, and isolate variables to attribute cause and effect with a relative degree of statistical confidence. Most studies are limited to asking if the intervention caused a reduction in the targeted crime. But the benefits of preventive action are not limited to their capacity to reduce crime or to be cost-effective. Other benefits such as increased cooperation among agencies, enhanced legitimacy for prevention, improved feelings of safety, and increased social solidarity may be just as important. The nature and level of the observed effects must also be examined with care, and largely depend on methodological considerations. Finally, the impacts and cost-benefits of many actions, especially social development action to reduce risk factors and enhance protective factors, may occur only in the medium or long term, long after the evaluation has ended and the expenditure has been made. What is also clear from these evaluations is that they are not so much concerned with the process implemented to achieve the particular results as with the measurement of the impacts.

In most project-based approaches to crime prevention, governmental strategies and policies have either not integrated successful action in a nationwide policy or been slow to do so. The Netherlands is one of the few countries where pilot projects, which have been conducted in some cities and positively evaluated, have been translated into national programs. The Residential Safe Label first tested in the Rotterdam-Amsterdam-The Hague triangle, the HALT project first tested in Amsterdam, and the City Guards project first implemented in Dordrecht have all become universal programs in the country. In England and Wales, though it has a long-standing evaluation practice and strong evaluations of pilot projects (Kirkholt and the Safer Cities Programme in the case of residential burglary, for example) that are recognized around the world, such projects remain isolated examples. Even the Safer Cities schemes, which involved twenty-one cities in a very positive evaluation, were not replicated throughout England. In the United States, where literally hundreds of local projects have been implemented—some of them a long time ago—and where rigorous evaluation has demonstrated effectiveness, few have ever been translated into state- or nationwide programs. Evaluation is not, in other words, any guarantee that a successful project in one location will be turned into a national program to respond to similar problems.

This situation may indicate, among other things, a larger degree of autonomy of local actors, a lesser involvement of the state in building community safety, and a greater tendency to promote a law and order rather than a social inclusion agenda. This may be seen in the fact that in the United Kingdom and the United States in particular, much of the crime prevention effort has traditionally been police driven (whereas in France the police remained only one of the many actors in the mayor-led local coalition), as well as the related fact that many so-called preventive projects (e.g., the "broken windows" and some environmental design approaches) would often be seen as crime control rather than preventive measures in northern European countries.

In other words, whereas evaluating the impacts of local projects is almost run-of-the-mill practice in the project-based approach to prevention, what is not is distilling the key factors leading to success, including knowledge about the elements of the process that led to success, and even less so the reproduction of these actions in other communities through central government intervention and support. In fact, the capacity to conduct strong evaluations is, to a large degree, premised on a project-based model. It is clearly easier to evaluate isolated projects with predetermined objectives and desired outcomes than it is to evaluate national policies and processes that will best support local action. Similarly, it is much easier to evaluate programs' capacities to reduce some specific crime than to enhance local democracy and quality of life in communities.

Evaluation in Policy-Driven Strategies

In countries such as France, Sweden, or Denmark, where the national strategy is overarching and is not based on a project approach, there is much less to say about evaluation. When they are conducted, evaluations—such as that of the communal crime prevention councils in France—will examine such questions as:

- Has the local coalition been implemented?
- Has it successfully brought the local actors together?
- Has it facilitated citizen participation?
- Has it been active and visible?
- What actions have been implemented?

- Has it used the funds made available through the Prevention Action Contract as planned? and
- Is there a qualitatively different perception of community safety locally?

These are entirely different questions from those asked in evaluation of local projects. Because policy-driven strategies have as their goal to enhance quality of life and social equality through establishing regional and local processes capable of redistributing wealth and fighting against exclusion, evaluating impacts, let alone the cost-effectiveness of these measures, will at best prove difficult and at worst appear fallacious. In these countries more concerned with social exclusion in all its forms than with crime as only one form, selecting crime prevention measures will form part of a broader agenda. It becomes difficult to disentangle the effects of this or that action on the particular outcome. In addition, these countries criticize the more project-based countries' approaches for artificially selecting some outcome measures (e.g., the percentage of crime reduced) without proper consideration for other impacts (e.g., how the measures may have reinforced exclusion or heightened fear).

For these reasons, crime prevention strategies in these countries generally do not involve evaluation as do the British or American approaches, and when they do, their orientation and methods may differ considerably. One of the drawbacks of this situation is that there is little capacity to identify the more successful approaches and to export them to other localities in the same country or to translate them into national policies. Furthermore, vast amounts of money may be spent without being able to determine what difference these resources actually make and how they are better investments than other more traditional crime control measures.

What we see, therefore, is a situation where project-based approaches have traditionally led to strong evaluation, but little capacity within the government to turn the more successful projects into large-scale programs, whereas policy-based approaches have not been conducive to strong evaluation, thereby hampering their capacity to direct local action as well as to revise their strategy based on lessons learned. Figure 8.3 is an attempt to depict graphically this situation and the relative lack of interconnectedness among strategies and action.

Conclusion

Beyond the clear indications that more governments are creating coordinating bodies for their crime prevention policies, and that such policies and programs are being developed with a greater preoccupation to make

FIGURE 8.3 Limited Connectedness Between Strategies and Actions

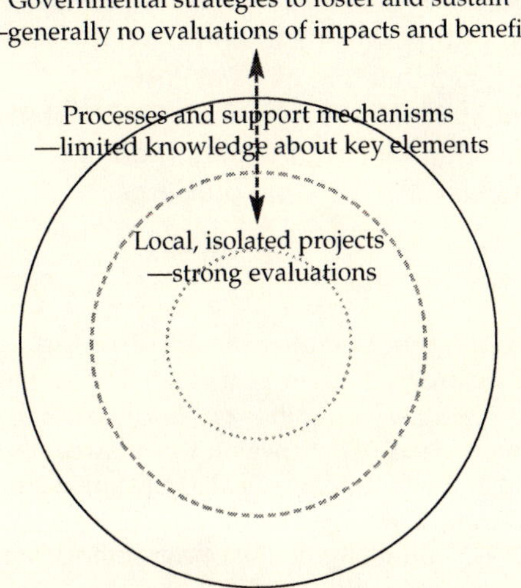

use of lessons learned from other countries, this brief examination of current trends reveals four things with respect to evaluation and cost-benefit analyses.

First, few governments have adopted a cost-benefit approach to their crime prevention policies. It is likely that governments that adopted policy-driven strategies for crime prevention are not as concerned with an "economist" approach to social, health, and quality of life issues as are governments whose strategies are more action oriented. Also, differences in overall objectives pursued by policy-driven strategies imply a different set of "impacts" as outputs. The underlying orientations are different, and so are the conception and practice of evaluation.

Second, there needs to be a closer examination of some of the crucial questions for evaluation, in particular the identification of the impacts measured. Although the capacity to reduce crime is one thing, it may become harder and harder to justify this objective independently of its links to broader social objectives (e.g., enhanced opportunities for disadvantaged children and youths, increased quality of life for disadvantaged neighborhoods). In the same vein, not all approaches are equally preventive in their orientation: providing useful after-school alternatives for youth is very different from excluding them from shopping malls or installing video surveillance cameras.

Third, more thought should be given to the relationship between project-based and policy-based approaches and their respective limitations, to make the best use of accumulated knowledge and "best practices." Insofar as it may be regrettable that strong local actions have remained just that—isolated projects—it is of limited use to have a strong central government policy without the means to know what works best in what circumstances, to produce what and at what cost.

Finally, what is at stake is not so much the exportation of a particular model or vision of evaluation, but the definition of what are useful evaluations, in what contexts, and for what purposes.

Notes

1. The STOP program is modeled after the HALT project, which is a diversion and alternative measure program to prevent vandalism among youth.

2. See, for example: National Committee on Violence (1990) in Australia; Peyrefitte (1977) and Bonnemaison (Commission des maires pour la sécurité 1982) commissions in France; Roper in New Zealand (Ministry of Justice 1987); and Morgan in England (Home Office 1991).

3. The study used 1992 guilders (dfl), hence controlling for inflation. The figure is presented in US$ per household.

References

Commission des maires sur la sécurité. 1982. *Face à la délinquance: Prévention, répression, solidarité.* Paris: by the author.

Crawford, A. 1997. *The local governance of crime: Appeals to community and partnerships.* Oxford: Clarendon Press.

Crime Concern. 1997. *Young people, crime and prevention: A briefing paper for crime prevention and regeneration partnerships.* London: by the author.

Donziger, S. R., ed. 1996. *The real war on crime: The report of the National Criminal Justice Commission.* New York: Harper.

Farrington, D. P. 1996. *Understanding and preventing youth crime.* York, England: Joseph Rowntree Foundation.

Goldblatt, P., and Lewis, C., eds. 1998. *Reducing offending: An assessment of research evidence on ways of dealing with offending behaviour.* London: Home Office Research and Statistics Directorate.

Graham, J., and Bennett, T. 1995. *Crime prevention strategies in Europe and North America.* Helsinki: European Institute for Crime Prevention and Control.

Greenwood, P. W., Rydell, C. P., Abrahamse, A. F., Caulkins, J. P., Chiesa, J., Model, K. E., and Klein, S. P. 1994. *Three strikes and you're out: Estimated benefits and costs of California's new mandatory-sentencing law.* Santa Monica, Calif.: RAND.

Habitat. 1996. *An urbanizing world: Global report on human settlements 1996.* New York: Oxford University Press.

Home Office. 1991. *Safer communities: The local delivery of crime prevention through the partnership approach.* London: HMSO.

______. 1999. *Reducing crime and tackling its causes: A briefing note on the "Crime Reduction Programme."* London: by the author.

International Centre for the Prevention of Crime. 1997. *Crime Prevention Digest 1997: Successes, benefits and directions from seven countries.* Montreal: by the author.

Ministry of Justice. 1987. *Report of the Ministerial Committee of Inquiry into Violence.* Roper Report. Wellington, New Zealand: by the author.

Ministry of Safety and Security. 1998. *White paper on safety and security.* Pretoria, South Africa: by the author.

Ministère de la Sécurité publique du Québec. 1999. *Rapport annuel.* Quebec City: by the author.

National Committee on Violence. 1990. *Violence: Directions for Australia.* Canberra: Australian Institute of Criminology.

National Crime Prevention Council, Canada. 1996. *A sound investment: Preventing crime and victimization.* Ottawa: by the author.

Palle, C., and Godefroy, T. 1998. *Les dépenses de contrôle des infractions en 1996.* Paris: CESDIP.

Peyrefitte, A. .1977. *Réponse à la violence.* Paris: La documentation française.

Reiss, A. J., Jr., and Roth, J. A., eds. 1993. *Understanding and preventing violence.* Washington, D.C.: National Academy Press.

Sansfaçon, D., and Welsh, B. C. 1999. *Crime Prevention Digest II: Comparative analysis of successful community safety.* Montreal: International Centre for the Prevention of Crime.

Sherman, L. W., Gottfredson, D. C., MacKenzie, D. L., Eck, J., Reuter, P., and Bushway, S. D. 1997 *Preventing crime: What works, what doesn't work, what's promising.* Washington, D.C.: U.S. Department of Justice, National Institute of Justice.

Social and Cultural Planning Board. 1998. Views on crime. Unpublished paper. The Hague: by the author.

Takala, H. 1999. Crime prevention in Europe. Unpublished paper.

United Nations. 1990. *Final declaration: Eighth congress on the prevention of crime and the treatment of offenders.* New York: by the author.

______. 1995. Crime prevention strategies, in particular as related to crimes in urban areas and juvenile and violent criminality, including the question of victims: Assessment and new perspectives. Background paper prepared for the Ninth United Nations Congress on the Prevention of Crime and the Treatment of Offenders.

United Nations Development Program. 1994. *International colloquium of mayors on social development.* New York: by the author.

van Dijk, J. J. M. 1996. Assessing the costs and benefits of crime control strategies. Unpublished paper. The Hague: Ministry of Justice.

______. 1997. Towards a research-based crime reduction policy: Crime prevention as a cost-effective policy option. *European Journal on Criminal Policy and Research* 5: 13–27.

Waller I., and Welsh, B. C. 1999. International trends in crime prevention: Cost-effective ways to reduce victimization. In G. Newman, ed., *Global report on crime and justice,* 191–220. New York: Oxford University Press.

PART FIVE

Future Directions

9

Measuring Economic Benefits of Developmental Prevention Programs

DANIEL S. NAGIN

Studies of the economic value of early-prevention programs fall into two broad categories. One compares the effectiveness of early prevention and incarceration in preventing crime. These studies ask the question: Is early prevention a cost-effective alternative to imprisonment in averting crime? The second category asks a conceptually distinct question: Do the benefits of early-prevention programs exceed their costs? The latter question is more ambitious because the scope of benefits considered is more than crime control, but is also less ambitious vis-à-vis crime control policy because it does not compare the costs and benefits of prevention with conventional crime control measures such as imprisonment.

Studies using these alternative analytic strategies for performing economic analysis of early prevention are reviewed and critiqued. Economic analysis of developmental prevention programs is itself in a nascent stage of development. Because of this, in constructing this critique I have steered away from commenting on technical matters of projection and valuation. Instead, the focus is on broader issues of analytic strategy. In particular, I attempt to identify aspects of analytic strategy used to date that should not become the de facto standard for conducting future analyses.

Summaries of Cost-Effectiveness Studies

Two studies have compared the effectiveness of early prevention and prison in averting crime: Greenwood et al. (1996) and Donohue and

Siegelman (1998). In Greenwood et al. the crime control effectiveness of California's "Three Strikes" statute was compared with two types of early-prevention programs—home visit–day care programs and parent training programs. The metric of comparison was serious crimes averted per dollar spent. Serious crimes included murder, rape, and robbery. California's "Three Strikes" statute mandates life imprisonment for the third felony conviction for selected crimes. The home visit–day care prevention alternative was modeled after two well-publicized prevention programs—the Perry Preschool program (Schweinhart, Barnes, and Weikart 1993) and the Elmira Prenatal–Early Infancy Project (PEIP) (Olds et al. 1997, 1998).

The Perry program, which included both day care and home visit components, was designed to improve the target child's cognitive functioning and social development. The target population was low-income, low-IQ African American children. The Perry intervention was conducted in the mid–1960s. The more recent PEIP intervention was conducted from 1978 to 1982 and provided home visits to economically disadvantaged first-time mothers and their children. The visits were made by nurse practitioners who counseled mothers on health-related behaviors during pregnancy (e.g., not using drugs or alcohol). After the child's birth, mothers were coached on effective child-rearing practices. The program also aimed to advance the mother's own personal development by helping her access employment and education programs. The parent training alternative was modeled after programs such as those of Patterson, DeBaryshe, and Ramsey (1989). These interventions aim to train parents in successful approaches for nurturing prosocial behaviors and outlooks in young children. They emphasize the importance of clear and reasonable rules, close monitoring, and firm but not hostile correction for rule breaking.

The Greenwood et al. analysis suggests that the home visit–day care option is not a cost-effective alternative to "Three Strikes" in preventing serious crime. The cost-effectiveness of the "Three Strikes" option is $13,899 per serious crime averted, whereas the counterpart cost for the home visit–day care option is six times greater—$89,035. However, by their calculations, parent training seems to be a promising alternative. Its cost per serious crime averted is only $6,351.

Donohue and Siegelman (1998) took an analytically distinct tact. They compared two states of the world for a contemporary cohort of three years olds: one in which by age eighteen they are incarcerated at the per capita rate as of 1993 and another in which they are incarcerated at a rate that is still 50 percent higher. By their estimate the 50 percent increase would reduce the cohort's index crime rate by 5 to 15 percent. They then compute the present value of the incremental cost of the 50 percent increase in imprisonment fifteen years "down the road." They calculate this cost at about $6 to $8 billion. This sets the stage for the central question of their analysis: Will channeling this $6 to $8 billion of incremental cost into prevention programs now lower the crime rate by at least 5 to 15 percent fifteen years from now? If yes, they argue it is optimal to shift forward this spending because society gets more crime control fifteen years hence at no greater cost in present-value terms.

The Donohue and Siegelman analysis suggests that, without targeting, early prevention is not a competitive alternative to imprisonment for reducing crime. Specifically, for prevention to be competitive it must be targeted "with sufficient precision to encompass all those 3-years-olds who were destined to become the most active 6% of delinquents" (1998, 36). Their analysis suggests that sufficient targeting can be achieved if prevention resources were targeted on black male children—the group who prospectively is the most crime prone of the three-year-old cohort. Specifically, Donohue and Siegelman projected that a Perry Preschool–type program will reduce the crime rate by 9.1 percent to 20.5 percent. They also projected that a similar Syracuse-based pilot program would produce a comparable crime reduction benefit of 7.1 percent to 26.1 percent.

Critique of the Cost-Effectiveness Analysis Strategy

My main criticism of the cost-effectiveness analysis strategy is the difficulty of mounting a convincing argument that early prevention is a cost-effective alternative to imprisonment for averting crime. The favorable conclusion from the Donohue and Siegelman analysis compared prevention to still higher levels of imprisonment than the already historically high rate of 1993. Specifically, two policy options were considered: (1) a 50 percent increase in imprisonment from the 1993 level without a Perry-like program and (2) holding imprisonment at the 1993 level but with a Perry-like program. Had the analysis been conducted in terms of a 50 percent reduction in 1993 imprisonment levels to the rate that prevailed at about 1984, prevention would not have been a competitive alternative to imprisonment for reducing crime. The reason is attributable to their use of a constant elasticity model for measuring the impact of imprisonment on crime. With such a model the increase in crimes attendant to a 50 percent decrease in imprisonment is larger in absolute terms than the reduction in crime from a 50 percent increase in imprisonment. Further, their affirmative conclusion on prevention requires targeting African American males—a strategy that would likely provoke vocal and strident resistance from both within and outside of the African American community.

The Greenwood et al. analysis supported the cost-effectiveness only of parent training, not of home visits–day care. The reason for the difference was entirely due to cost. The present value of the cost of the parent training was estimated at only $3,000 per child, whereas the cost of the home visit–day care alternative was estimated at $26,238 per child. The authors assume both types of programs were equally effective in reducing serious crime, which may not be the case. The home visit–day care alternative includes a parental training component in addition to other measures. Given the difference in the cost and treatment intensity of these two prevention programs, it does not seem plausible to assume equal effectiveness. Finally, the Greenwood et al. estimate of the crime control impact of California's three-strikes law was based solely on crimes averted through incapacitation. If the law also has a deterrent effect, their estimate of the cost-effectiveness of three strikes was conservative.

Reservations about the viability of the cost-effectiveness analysis strategy also involve three generic reservations that extend beyond the specific conclusions and methods of these two studies. One concerns the disjuncture between the timing of the investment and the realization of the reward, the second relates to the rarity of serious criminality in the population, and the third involves neglect of the broad range of benefits that attend to successful early prevention.

The crime reduction benefits of early prevention are not realized for at least ten to fifteen years following the investment. For example, implementation of the Donohue and Siegelman strategy requires investing $6–$8 billion now to reduce crime by perhaps 20 percent fifteen years from now. At $30,000 per person-year of imprisonment, these same resources could be used to increase the current prison population by nearly 250,000 people. If, on average, these individuals commit only two index crimes per year while free, half a million crimes would be averted.[1] Would the political process pass up the opportunity of averting half a million crimes now in favor of an even larger reduction fifteen years hence? Doubtful.

A second reservation concerns the relative rarity of serious criminality in the population—people who murder, rape, rob, or otherwise inflict serious bodily harm on others. To be sure, as a society, we have a collective interest in ensuring the security of our property. However, threats to personal safety are overwhelmingly more important. The priority status of personal safety, for example, is reflected in criminal sentences. Crimes of violence are punished far more severely than property crime.

The rarity of serious criminality is emphasized because it is inherently difficult to measure the impact of an intervention on a rare event. To illustrate, consider the following example. Suppose that in a target population of high-risk two year olds who were not offered intervention, 10 percent were destined to engage in serious criminality, but with intervention the rate of serious criminality is cut to 7.5 percent. Thus, in percentage terms the intervention has a large impact—the rate of serious criminality is cut by 25 percent. However, in absolute terms the change is small—only 2.5 percent. It is this small absolute change that must be statistically identified in an evaluation. Establishing statistical significance at the 0.05 level would require about 700 individuals each in the treatment and the control groups. At the 0.01 level the required sample is even larger, about 1,400 per group. Such large samples are required because, regardless of treatment status, comparatively few from even a high-risk group are destined to be serious criminals. For the above case, with a sample of 700 in both the treatment and the control groups, only about fifty-three and seventy individuals, respectively, would be expected to emerge as serious criminals.

By comparison the sample sizes in prevention pilots are typically far smaller. In the Perry program there were about sixty children in both the treatment and the control groups. In PEIP program samples were larger—about 100 in the experimental group and 150 in the control group—but still far smaller than the 700 per group calculated above.

How then did these programs find significant crime reduction benefits? Consider the Perry program. For the purposes of estimating crime control effects, this pilot intervention has the best data because subjects were tracked until age twenty-seven, a far lengthier evaluation period than most programs. Reduced criminality accounts for the lion's share of the benefit of the Perry program (Barnett 1993, 1996). In this regard, the program evaluation highlights two findings as evidence of this impact. One is that, by age nineteen, a statistically significant difference existed in the percent arrested for any type of crime between the preschool and nonpreschool groups—31 percent versus 51 percent. Compared to the base rates used in the power calculation, these rates are very high. This is because the rates from the Perry evaluation include arrests for nonviolent property offenses and for misdemeanors. The second highlighted finding was a large difference in the percentage of participants with five or more arrests by age twenty-eight. Only 7 percent of the preschool group were chronic arrestees, whereas the counterpart rate for the nonpreschoolers was 35 percent. This implies that the intervention reduced chronic criminality by more than 80 percent. The absolute size of the impact explains why it is statistically significant. More detailed breakdowns of the data reported in Schweinhart, Barnes, and Weikart (1993) suggest that this finding should be interpreted with caution. There is no statistically significant difference in the felony crime arrest rate, personal-violence crime arrest rate, or property crime arrest rate between the treatment and control groups. The only significant difference is for misdemeanor and drug crime arrests. Further, these differences appear to be attributable to the high arrest rates of a small number of individuals.

The third generic concern with crime-based cost-effectiveness is that by construction it ignores other salutary impacts of early prevention programs. The Perry program evaluation found statistically significant impacts not only on crime and delinquency but also on school achievement and employment. PEIP participants not only were less delinquent but also made fewer emergency room visits. Hawkins et al. (1999) implemented and evaluated a school- and home-based intervention targeted at school-age children. They found that the intervention not only lowers violent delinquency, but also reduces heavy drinking and early sexual behavior and improves school performance. Karoly et al. (1998) summarize the variety of benefits of other early-prevention programs and similarly conclude that such programs impact functioning in multiple domains of behavior. This should not be surprising—it is hard to imagine how a program having salutary impacts on social and cognitive development would not have wide-ranging effects on the life course.

Had the analyses of Donohue and Siegelman and of Greenwood et al. been successful in making a compelling case that prevention is a cost-effective alternative to imprisonment for crime control, criticism of the too narrow focus of the crime-based cost-effectiveness approach is arguably moot. However, the case is not compelling. Further, the cost-effectiveness approach frames the question of society's relative use of imprisonment and prevention in a peculiar fashion. It is odd to think of imprisonment as a substitute for prevention. Rather, imprisonment and the criminal justice system (CJS) more generally are a necessary social institution for controlling the behavior of persons for whom socialization has failed. From this perspective the CJS is a backstop for ineffective prevention, not a substitute.

Summary of Cost-Benefit Studies

A small number of valuation studies have considered a broader range of benefits of intervention than crime reduction. Barnett's (1993, 1996) cost-benefit analyses of the Perry program included benefit calculations not only for reduced crime but also for lower schooling costs due to reduced use of special education services, less welfare utilization, and higher earnings. Olds et al. (1993) estimated the impact of the PEIP program on government spending. The costs to the government were the expense of operating the program—paying the nurse practitioners, transportation costs, and so on. The savings to the government came from a variety of sources that were mostly attributable to the mother. These included a small savings from lower Medicaid expenses for childbearing, because the program mothers were less likely to become pregnant, and from reduced utilization of child protective services. The mothers also paid more taxes and made less use of Aid for Dependent Children (AFDC) and Food Stamps because they worked more. Indeed, for the low-income participants, reduced welfare payments accounted for 82 percent of the savings to the government. Karoly et al. (1998) synthesized findings from a number of interventions but gave special analytical attention to the Perry and PEIP programs. Like Olds et al. their analysis focuses on cash flows into and out of the public treasury. For the PEIP program, the cost side of the ledger in their analysis includes the program expense, and the benefit side includes estimates of the dollar value of lowered use of health services, increased employment tax payments, reduced welfare costs, and smaller CJS costs. For the Perry program, savings to government were similar—reduced spending on special education services, welfare, and the CJS, as well as more taxes. The major difference is that, for the Perry program, the savings to the government were attributable to the altered future behavior of the child, whereas for the PEIP program the savings were primarily attributable to changes in the labor-force participation of the mother. In addition, Karoly et al. estimate selected nongovernmental benefits—savings to victims of crimes averted and increases in the child's and mother's future earnings. Aos (1998) is still another analysis that draws from published findings to estimate the costs and benefits of early prevention programs. Unlike Karoly et al., Aos focuses only on crime-related benefits—reduced costs of processing apprehended offenders through the CJS and avoided victim costs.

Critique of Cost-Benefit Studies

With the exception of the Perry analysis, the focus of valuation studies has been on the impact of the program on the public treasury. Specifically, the studies assessed whether the program has a net positive or negative impact on government expenditures. On the debit side of the ledger was the expense to the government of operating the program. On the credit side of the ledger were items such as reduced expenditures for provision of special education and operation of the criminal justice system and increased tax payments from the mother and later the child. This focus is understandable. The argument that a social program will literally pay for itself by generating a net positive flow into the public treasury is very attractive politically. Everyone wins—program beneficiaries are better off, and the net financial burden of running the government for the general public declines.

However, for several reasons this criterion for evaluating developmental prevention programs is fundamentally incomplete. First, and most important, it neglects potential benefits with important consequences for society at large, such as improved public safety, and for the individual who is the target of the program, such as living an effective and productive life. As an example, the principle objective of the PEIP program was to improve the life chances of the target child. Yet, based on the financial analysis reported in Olds et al. (1993), financial justification for the program is based on the effect on the mother—lower welfare use and higher tax payments—not on the child. Second, it suggests that the developmental-prevention public policy option should be evaluated by a different standard than other options such as increased imprisonment or more police. The social desirability of imprisonment and police protection is not judged solely or even primarily by the impact on the public treasury. If this were the case, society would have far fewer police and prisoners because both represent large negative drains on the public treasury. Third, a treasury-based accounting of the impact of developmental prevention depends on other public policies that have no bearing whatsoever on its social and economic value. Returning again to the PEIP example, the reduction in welfare payments and the increase in taxes that attended to mothers' increased earning depended upon current policy governing the generosity of the welfare system and on tax rates. For example, the overhaul of the U.S. welfare system prescribed in the Personal Responsibility and Work Opportunity Act of 1996 placed a limit on allowable time on welfare. Ironically, this change in public policy reduced the value of the PEIP program as measured by its impact on the treasury, while at the same time it increased its value from the perspective of the mother and child.

How then should the broader benefit of developmental prevention be valued, and how well have existing studies measured these benefits? Several studies have included benefits to victims of averted crimes in their analyses (Aos 1998; Karoly et al. 1998; Barnett 1993, 1996). The adequacy of those estimates are discussed in the next section. Here the focus is on the problem of evaluating the noncrime benefits. To date the only broad-based cost-benefit analysis of developmental prevention is of the Perry program, so the critique focuses on this analysis.

First, some important definitions: An economic benefit accrues when something of value is produced. That something might be tangible, like a car or house, but it may also be something intangible, like peace of mind. In economics the metric of value is willingness to pay. If *in principal* someone is willing to pay for this good or service, an economic benefit is produced. Thus, for example, producing pork in a strict Jewish or Muslim society produces no economic value because nobody would be willing to pay for it.

The qualifier "in principal" is emphasized because the fact of an actual transaction to demonstrate such willingness to pay does not affect whether a benefit has been produced or not. For instance, if police foot patrols make members of a community feel safer, then an economic benefit has been produced even though community members did not demonstrate the value of their newfound sense of safety by their purchase of the foot patrol from the police department. To be sure, citizens pay for police services with their tax payments. However, provision of police services to communities is not based on a direct transaction between the citizens of the community and the police department. Instead allocation of policing resources is determined administratively.

An economic cost is incurred when something of value is consumed or exhausted. That something may be tangible, like food or a natural resource, but it may also be intangible, like a person's time and energy. The value of a resource is measured by its opportunity cost—its value in its best alternative use. Most commonly, opportunity cost is measured by the price that resource commands in the marketplace.

Are not the tax dollars used by the government considered costs? In an economic sense the answer is no. Taxes transfer purchasing power from individual citizens to the government. The government in turn uses these funds to achieve collective goals. In some cases achieving the goal may involve incurring economic costs. An example is providing police services. The police officers themselves could be working to provide some other valued good or service, and the equipment they use to provide public safety has valuable alternative uses. However, other uses of tax funds do not involve the purchase and use of valuable goods and services. Instead their use simply represents a transfer of purchasing power from one group of citizens to another group of citizens. Examples of such transfer are welfare and Social Security payments.

The critique of the Perry cost-benefit analysis focuses on the benefit side of the ledger. Although a number of tricky technical problems attended the estimation of costs, the real technical hurdles pertained to benefit estimation. Barnett's (1993, 1996) analyses valued four domains of impact: education effects, employment effects, crime effects, and welfare effects. Here the focus will be on the education and employment effects. As noted, valuing crime effects will be discussed separately. Welfare effects are not included in the discussion because welfare is a transfer payment, not an economic cost.

The evaluation of education effects focused on valuing the cost of educating the experimental and control children. The primary source of benefit in this regard was that the children in the preschool program made less use of special education services throughout primary and secondary school. Such services included separate education for mentally handicapped children, speech and language support, compensatory education, and disciplinary education. There were two benefits to decreased use of such services. One is that special education services were more expensive to provide than general education services. The second is that treated children were less likely to suffer from the cognitive or behavioral problems that trigger the provision of these compensatory services. Barnett's analysis measured only the benefit of the former impact and left unvalued what was surely the more important impact, especially for the child.

The importance of capturing and valuing impacts on personal development is exemplified by the program's impact on postsecondary education outcomes. The program had no statistically significant impact on the educational attainment of male participants. However, for the female participants, impacts were large: 84 percent of female program participants achieved a high school education or the equivalent, whereas only 35 percent of the control females achieved the same. As a result, far more of the female participants enrolled in postsecondary education than their control counterparts. Consequently, the valuation of postsecondary education impacts resulted in a debit, not a credit, to the Perry program benefit ledger. To be sure, education, postsecondary or not, is costly, but to take account of that cost without valuing the benefits of education is to miss the point of cost-benefit analysis. Still another example of this valuation problem is reflected in the salutary impacts of the program on female participants' high school graduation rate. On the margin, this impact also increased the cost of educating program participants, so in this respect it was a cost and not a benefit.

To be fair, Barnett examined one outcome domain in which education pays large returns—earnings. Whereas program evaluations reported statistically significant earnings impacts for both male and females (Schweinhart, Barnes, and Weikart 1993), Barnett's projections of impacts for lifetime earnings show that only program females had higher earnings than their control counterparts. The present value of the difference, however, was modest, $27,000 for a 3 percent discount rate. For males the estimated impact was actually negative, although small.

How well does the Barnett analysis capture the full benefits of developmental prevention? Should it serve as a template for future analyses? In my judgment the answer to both these questions is no. Karoly et al. in their discussion of the importance of early childhood observe, "Research and clinical work have found that the experiences of the infant and young child provide the foundation for long-term physical and mental health as well as cognitive development. The period of early childhood development is thus unique—physically, mentally, emotionally, and socially. It is a period of both opportunity and vulnerability"

(1998, 2–3). They go on to conclude that, on the whole, developmental programs result in "gains in the emotional or cognitive development, improvements in educational process and outcomes, increased economic self-sufficiency, reduced levels of criminal activity, and improvements in health-related indicators" (xv). In my view programs having such potentially far-reaching impacts must be valued in broader terms than savings on special education services, increased earnings, or lower welfare payments.

Further, the limitations of Barnett's valuation strategy are not easily remedied by including a broader sampling of outcomes such as lower medical costs for treating mental illness or accidents, reduced expenditures for child protective services, and saving for remedial job training in the benefit calculations. The problem with the broad-based, itemized valuation approach is at least threefold. First, it is difficult and expensive to assemble data to demonstrate such discrete impacts. Many potential impacts such as improved performance in the labor market or lower criminality require years of follow-up to document. Second, valuing discrete impacts is tedious and inevitably highly speculative. The valuation methods used to place a monetary value for discrete events such as an arrest or a year of special education services have not been critiqued, but not surprisingly such cost estimates are highly imprecise. Lengthening the list of items so valued only increases the speculative content of the analysis. Third, and most important, this approach still does not begin to capture the far-reaching impacts of an effective intervention as reflected in the observations of Karoly et al. An alternative, more consciously holistic approach is required.

An Alternative Approach for the Future

The main criticism of the broad-based, itemized valuation strategy is that it falls very short of appropriately valuing benefits of effective preventive intervention. A related criticism is that important components of tangible benefits such as higher earnings are hard to value in a theoretically sound fashion. As a possible remedy to these two problems, I next consider a valuation strategy from the economics literature on valuing a human. Under this approach an effective developmental intervention is treated as tantamount to saving a human life.

Criminality is rarely a desirable life-course option. Not only are the "wages" of crime meager (see Reuter, MacCoun, and Murphy 1990; Levitt and Venkatesh 1998), the lives of criminals are typically dissipated by long periods of penal confinement, drug addiction, conflict-ridden personal relationships, and impoverishment. An intervention that is effective in diverting an individual from a such a life path to the sort symbolized by the left side of the figure may literally save a life by averting a premature death due to violence, drugs, or disease. More commonly, the impact will not be so literal. Instead it will affect the quality, not the quantity, of life. However, the difference in quality may be so profound that it is equivalent to saving a life and, therefore, should be evaluated accordingly. Economic-based estimates of the value of a human life typically range from $2 to $4 million (Viscusi 1993).

Viscusi begins his review of the economics-based value of life literature with the observation: "Health and safety risks comprise one aspect of our lives that we all like to eliminate" (1993, 1912). Like all economics-based methods to valuation, economists search for evidence of the value individuals place on their lives by examining individual willingness to pay to avert life-threatening risks, or alternatively, in their requirements for compensation to take on such risks. The former valuation strategy uses evidence on people's willingness to pay for safety devices such as seat belts or smoke detectors to draw inferences about value of life. Most commonly, however, value-of-life estimates are inferred from what economists call "compensating wage differentials." Compensating wage differentials refer to the wage premiums that in theory are required to lure people into taking risky jobs such as construction or coal mining. For example, if persons demand $1,000 in compensation to take on a task with a 1-in–1,000 risk of death, the inference is that the 1,000 such persons would collectively pay $1 million to avert this risk. Such an investment would be expected to save one of their lives. It is by this logic that economists would surmise from this hypothetical that the value of human life is $1 million.

Making a determination of the amount of a compensating wage differential is a tricky task both statistically and conceptually. Wages for jobs depend on much more than the life-threatening risk attending to their performance. Some jobs are more onerous or unpleasant. Most people would prefer to work aboveground than underground in a cold and wet coal mine. As a result, wages for coal mining undoubtedly reflect a premium for the unpleasant work environment in addition to any premium for its physical dangers. Alternatively, one of the downsides of vocations with high intrinsic satisfaction, such as art or the ministry, is that wages may be lower because part of the compensation comes in the form of job satisfaction. Moreover, other factors determining wages reflect the supply and demand for people with certain skills. In contemporary society, wages for draftsmen are low because of the availability of computer-aided drafting software. On the other hand, wages for the software developers who create such software are high because of the booming demand for their services.

For our purposes the technical complexities of parceling out the size of the compensating wage differential for incurring life-threatening risks are of secondary concern. Instead, two key features of this valuation strategy are of central concern. The first is that the amount of the compensation is based on choices made by the individual at their own volition. Second, value is inferred "on the margin." In the example above, the margin was defined in terms of the $1,000 compensation for accepting the 1-in–1,000 risk of death. From this it was inferred that 1,000 people would pay a total of $1 million to avert one of their deaths, not that any single individual would forfeit his life for $1 million.

Economists look for value in choices made by individuals themselves, not in choices made in their behalf. Sometimes choice may be limited to poor options, like taking a dangerous and unpleasant job or having no job at all. Still the act of choosing reveals preferences even if only between unattractive states. Volitional choice reveals individual preferences, which in economics is the ultimate source of value.

Young children do not make choices about their life course. Their developmental course is largely determined by forces beyond their control—their biological inheritance, their household income, the social and economic stability of the country in which they live. The early life course is also heavily affected by the choices of others—whether mothers choose not to use drugs and alcohol during pregnancy, whether parents choose to invest their time and energy into building a child's personal capital rather than fulfilling their own needs, whether teachers intervene with help if they observe a developmental delay and respond with encouragement when they detect a special talent, and so on. Of course, as time goes on, individuals increasingly take greater control over their lives, but in profound ways life-course outcomes are determined, not chosen.

Consider the life-course choices of persons who follow the "antisocial" pathway. The observation that life-course outcomes are substantially affected by forces beyond an individual's control does not mean that persons who follow the antisocial pathway lack free will—that they have no capacity to abstain from the temptations of drug and alcohol, that they are unable to control the impulse to abuse their partners and children, and that they are driven to commit crimes by forces beyond their control. Such a conclusion would require the wholesale rejection of research showing that the price of alcohol and drugs affects consumption even among the addicted (Cook and Moore 1993), that criminals strategically chose targets (Cook 1986; Clarke 1995), and that the threat of punishment deters crime (Nagin 1998). Nor does it follow from this line of reasoning that individuals on the antisocial pathway are incapable of making life-course choices that improve their condition. John Laub and Robert Sampson show that life-course trajectories are not immutable. Instead their research shows that social institutions such as work, family, and the military can materially deflect an antisocial trajectory (Sampson and Laub 1993; Laub and Sampson 1993; Laub, Nagin, and Sampson 1998). Nonetheless, the choices made by individuals with a history of antisocial behavior are tightly circumscribed. They are made within the narrow confines of the trajectory in which they find themselves, not within a trajectory that they chose. Except in unusual circumstances, the alternative to a career of crime is a low-wage menial job, not a career in medicine. John Irwin's assessment is even more pessimistic: "Most of those who stay out of prison are 'successes' in only the narrowest, most bureaucratic meaning of the term *non-recidivism*. Most ex-convicts live menial or derelict lives and many die early of alcoholism or drug use, or by suicide" (1987, viii).

If life-course trajectories are not chosen, how then can the choice-based valuation strategies of economics be applied to evaluating developmental prevention? The answer is that the antisocial life-course trajectory is plainly not a life anyone would willingly choose. Retrospective assessments of criminals themselves are testimony to this proposition. Neal Shover's book *The Great Pretenders* reports an ethnographic study of career criminals. By the subjects' own accounts their lives are pathetic and wasted. One of Shover's older subjects confided: "I saw myself for what I really was . . . I could see it just as plain as I'm looking at you now. And I know that what I looked at was a sorry picture of a human being" (1996, 131). Or as Gottfredson and Hirschi observe about a career in crime, it will "start at the bottom and proceed nowhere" (1986, 218). There is also economic evidence that is directly on point. In an unusual and innovative study, Levitt and Venkatesh (1998) obtained the accounting records of a drug-dealing gang in Chicago. Drug dealing is a very dangerous occupation. Using the economics-based, risk-compensation approach, they calculate that the gang's drug dealers valued their lives at no more than $100,000.

Consider the following thought experiment. Suppose people were confronted with two lotteries and asked how much they would be willing to pay to avoid each. In one there is a 1-in–1,000 chance of death, and in the other there is a 1-in–1,000 chance of following the antisocial life course. Based on the ethnographic evidence and on the quantitative evidence, a plausible prediction is that there would be no material difference in willingness to pay to avert these two lotteries. By this reasoning, it seems reasonable to value an intervention that successfully diverts a child from a life of antisocial behavior to one in which he or she functions as an effective citizen at the standard economic estimate of the value of a human life—$2 to $4 million.

Although this saving-a-life approach avoids fundamental problems with the broad-based, itemized valuation strategy, some formidable conceptual and measurement problems must be overcome before it can be considered the dominate alternative. Just how to measure the number of successes remains a problem. This question has conceptual and technical components. The conceptual component concerns how to think about a success rate in the context of an actual intervention. The technical component concerns how to measure it.

Consider the conceptual issue. Even highly touted programs such as Perry Preschool did not have a 100 percent success rate—some of its graduates followed the criminal life course. By age eighteen, 51 percent of the control group and only 31 percent of the experimental group had been arrested. How should the 20 percent improvement in the success rate be interpreted? One interpretation is that Perry somehow moved its participants 20 percent closer to the effective life course. Based on the lower-bound economic estimate of the value of a life, $2 million, should Perry be valued at $400,000 per participant (or 20 percent of $2 million)?

The discussion of life-course outcomes has been framed in terms of two stylized life states, one with high intrinsic value and the other with low intrinsic value. What does it mean to be 20 percent closer to the high intrinsic state? In the jargon of economics, the utility of life varies qualitatively between these two states, so it makes no sense to interpolate utility between them. However, an alternative conceptual interpretation of the 20 percent shift does have a meaningful interpretation. If the program increases the proportion of individuals following the high-value life course from 49 percent (100 percent minus 51 percent) to 69 percent (100 percent minus 31 percent), then for every hundred individuals enrolled in the program, on average, twenty "lives will be saved" by diverting them from the low- to high-utility life course.

Although this interpretation avoids the problem of valuing intermediate states between the two life-course extremes, it leaves open the problem of measuring the success rate. A properly conducted evaluation of a developmental intervention will measure success in multiple behavioral and social domains, not just in criminality. How does one go about combining these measurements in a conceptually meaningful fashion? For example, in the Perry program the treatment group had a significantly higher high school graduation rate than the control group, 71 percent versus 54 percent. How to combine the 17 percent improvement in the graduation rate with the 20 percent reduction in the juvenile arrest rate to create a meaningful metric of improved life chances is not self-evident. Further, the depiction of the life course as a lottery between two stylized life states is a gross simplification. In reality there are many states with varying degrees of personal and social value.

A successful developmental intervention not only benefits the individual by improving the quality of his life chances, but also benefits society by averting the social harms the individual might otherwise have imposed. Among these is crime. Cohen (1998) estimates that the value of saving a high-risk youth from a career in crime and the heavy drug use commonly associated with such criminality is in the range of $1.7 to $2.3 million. Such savings are in addition to the social and personal value of averting a life of crime that I have discussed here.

Conclusion

For too long crime policy has been formulated without careful assessment of economic costs and benefits. Recent work has moved toward filling this important gap in policy analysis. The focus of this essay has been economic evaluation of developmental prevention programs. Just as Lewis and Clark demonstrated that overland passage to the Pacific Ocean was possible, the nascent literature on valuing developmental prevention has demonstrated the feasibility and utility of such analysis. However, just as those who succeeded Lewis and Clark found better routes to the Pacific Northwest, future economic valuations of developmental prevention should use different analytic strategies.

The recommended changes in analytic strategy can be summed up in terms of the answers to a two-part question: What is the appropriate unit of analysis—individuals or criminal events, society or government? In both cases I have argued for the first alternative. The argument that developmental prevention is a cost-effective alternative to criminal sanctions for averting crime is attractive, but it cannot be convincingly sustained. Instead, a more holistic approach is necessary that values benefits across multiple domains of individual functioning. Here it was argued that successful intervention is tantamount to saving a human life and should be valued accordingly. Analyses that have valued more than crime benefits have, by and large, measured financial impact on the public treasury. Here again it was argued that this was too narrow a focus. Although impacts on the public treasury are important, such an impact analysis should be viewed as a complement to, not a substitute for, a society-wide cost-benefit analysis.

Notes

1. An alternative approach to calibrating this crime impact is to employ the elasticity strategy used by Donohue and Siegelman (1998). Assuming a low-end elasticity of the index crime rate with respect to the imprisonment rate of 0.15 yields an identical crime reduction impact of 500,000 index crimes.

References

Aos, S. 1998. Costs and benefits: Estimating the "bottom line" for crime prevention and intervention programs: A description of the cost-benefit model, version 2.0. Unpublished manuscript. Olympia: Washington State Institute for Public Policy.

Barnett, W. S. 1993. Cost-benefit analysis. In *Significant benefits: The High/Scope Perry Preschool study through age 27*, by L. J. Schweinhart, H. V. Barnes, and D. P. Weikart. Ypsilanti, Mich.: High/Scope Press.

______. 1996. *Lives in the balance: Age–27 benefit-cost analysis of the High/Scope Perry Preschool program.* Ypsilanti, Mich.: High/Scope Press.

Clarke, R. V. 1995. Situational crime prevention. In *Building a safer society: Strategic approaches to crime prevention*. Vol. 19 of *Crime and justice: A review of research*, ed. M. Tonry and D. P. Farrington. Chicago: University of Chicago Press.

Cohen, M. A. 1998. The monetary value of saving a high-risk youth. *Journal of Quantitative Criminology* 14: 5–33.

Cook, P. J. 1986. The supply and demand of criminal opportunities. In *Crime and justice: A review of research*, ed. M. Tonry and N. Morris. Vol. 7. Chicago: University of Chicago Press.

Cook, P. J., and M. J. Moore. 1993. Economic perspectives on reducing alcohol-related violence. In *Alcohol and interpersonal violence: Fostering multidisciplinary perspectives*, ed. Susan E. Martin. Washington, D.C.: National Institutes of Health.

Donohue, J. J., and P. Siegelman. 1998. Allocating resources among prisons and social programs in the battle against crime. *Journal of Legal Studies* 27: 1–43.

Gottfredson, M., and T. Hirschi. 1986. The true value of Lambda would appear to be zero: An essay on career criminals, criminal careers, selective incapacitation, cohort studies, and related topics. *Criminology* 24: 213–34.

Greenwood, P. W., K. E. Model, C. P. Rydell, and J. Chiesa. 1996. *Diverting children from a life of crime: Measuring costs and benefits*. Santa Monica, Calif.: RAND.

Hawkins, J. D., R. F. Catalano, R. Kosterman, R. Abbott, and K. G. Hill. 1999. Preventing adolescent health-risk behaviors by strengthening protection during childhood. *Archives of Pediatrics and Adolescent Medicine* 153: 226–34.

Irwin, J. 1987. *The felon*. Berkeley: University of California Press.

Karoly, L. A., P. W. Greenwood, S. S. Everingham, J. Houbé, M. R. Kilburn, C. P. Rydell, M. Sanders, and J. Chiesa. 1998. *Investing in our children: What we know and don't know about the costs and benefits of early childhood interventions*. Santa Monica, Calif.: RAND.

Laub, J. H., and R. J. Sampson. 1993. Turning points in the life course: Why change matters to the study of crime. *Criminology* 31: 301–26.

Laub, J. H., Nagin, D. S., and Sampson, R. J. 1998. Trajectories of change in criminal offending: Good marriages and the desistance process. *American Sociological Review* 63: 225–39.

Levitt, S. D., and S. A. Venkatesh. 1998. Drug selling gang's finances. Working Paper No. 6592. Cambridge, Mass.: National Bureau of Economic Research.

Nagin, D. S. 1998. Criminal Deterrence research: A review of the evidence and a research agenda for the outset of the 21st century. In *Crime and justice: A review of research*, ed. M. Tonry. Vol. 23. Chicago: University of Chicago Press.

Olds, D. L., C. R. Henderson, C. Phelps, H. Kitzman, and C. Hanks. 1993. Effects of prenatal and infancy nurse home visitation on government spending. *Medical Care* 31: 155–74.

Olds, D. L., C. R. Henderson, R. Cole, J. Eckenrode, H. Kitzman, D. Luckey, L. M. Pettitt, K. Sidora, P. Morris, and J. Powers. 1998. Long-term effects of nurse home visitation on children's criminal and antisocial behavior: Fifteen-year follow-up of a randomized controlled trial. *Journal of the American Medical Association* 280: 1238–44.

Olds, D. L., J. Eckenrode, C. R. Henderson, H. Kitzman, J. Powers, R. Cole, K. Sidora, P. Morris, L. M. Pettitt, and D. Luckey. 1997. Long-term effects of home visitation on maternal life course and child abuse and neglect: Fifteen-year follow-up of a randomized trial. *Journal of the American Medical Association* 278: 637–43.

Patterson, G. R., B. D. DeBaryshe, and E. Ramsey. 1989. A developmental perspective on antisocial behavior. *American Psychologist* 44: 329–35.

Reuter, P., R. MacCoun, and P. Murphy. 1990. *Money from crime: A study of the economics of drug dealing in Washington, D.C.* Santa Monica, Calif.: RAND.

Sampson, R. J., and J. H. Laub. 1993. *Crime in the making: Pathways and turning points through life.* Cambridge: Harvard University Press.

Schweinhart, L. J., H. V. Barnes, and D. P. Weikart. 1993. *Significant benefits: The High/Scope Perry Preschool study through age 27.* Ypsilanti, Mich.: High/Scope Press.

Shover, N. 1996. *Great pretenders: Pursuits and careers of persistent thieves.* Boulder: Westview Press.

Viscusi, W. K. 1993. The value of risks to human life. *Journal of Economic Literature* 31: 1912–46.

10

Improving Confidence in What Works and Saves Money in Preventing Crime

Priorities for Research

BRANDON C. WELSH
DAVID P. FARRINGTON
LAWRENCE W. SHERMAN

This chapter brings together the main conclusions on the economic costs and benefits of crime prevention from the chapters in Parts 2, 3, and 4, and identifies gaps in knowledge and priorities for research and policy development. Central to this chapter is a discussion of the key issues that need to be addressed in working toward a standard manual for carrying out benefit-cost analyses of crime prevention programs.

Methods and Perspectives of Economic Analysis

Mark Cohen's chapter on the monetization of the cost of crime to victims illustrates the importance and feasibility of assessing crime victim costs, both tangible and intangible, as part of benefit-cost analyses of crime prevention programs. Unfortunately, costs to crime victims are seldom measured in benefit-cost analyses of crime prevention programs. This was found by Welsh and Farrington in Chapter 3, which reviewed existing benefit-cost studies of crime prevention programs. Of the twenty-six studies identified by Welsh and Farrington, only a handful included an assessment of costs to victims of crime, and only one—the Perry

Preschool program of Schweinhart, Barnes, and Weikart (1993)—assessed intangible costs (e.g., pain, suffering, lost quality of life).

As noted in Chapter 3, much of the reluctance to include intangible victimization costs is attributable to the lack of existing estimates of these costs, which first appeared in the published literature in Cohen (1988), and the doubts that many researchers have about the validity of these costs or the underlying theory used in their calculation or both (Zimring and Hawkins 1995, 138). In defense of the inclusion of intangible victim costs in benefit-cost analyses of crime prevention programs, Cohen notes that the main methodologies used to calculate these costs—jury compensation and willingness-to-pay methods—have been shown to be valid and are endorsed by various U.S. government regulatory agencies (e.g., the Consumer Product Safety Commission).

In Chapter 1, Cohen identifies a number of key aspects of the costs to crime victims that, in his words, "would benefit most from further work." These issues include:

> refinement and agreement on the "statistical value of life," studies that directly elicit the public's willingness-to-pay for reduced crime (especially for property crimes where intangible losses are difficult to estimate), a better understanding of how to incorporate public perceptions into policy decisions, agreement on the proper discount rate for policy analysis involving long-term benefits, and measures of community wellness that go beyond individual crime victims.

Research is also needed on many other important methodological issues of economic analysis, including using average versus marginal costs, measuring capital costs, particularly in those cases that require the borrowing of money to pay for a program (e.g., improved streetlighting), discounting costs and benefits over different time periods, and projecting costs and benefits of crime prevention programs (beyond the time frame of the most recent assessment; see Barnett 1996; Karoly et al. 1998).

In the context of a randomized controlled experiment of institutional-based interventions for substance abusing offenders, Chapter 2 by Faye Taxman and Brian Yates reports on a planned economic approach that is characterized by a systematic analysis of the relationships among program resources used (costs), treatment procedures, psychological and related processes, and outcomes. The authors term this approach "Cost → Procedure → Process → Outcome Analysis" (CPPOA). This approach allows for a detailed examination of how relationships between program resources and outcomes (benefits) may be enhanced or diminished by a variety of programmatic, community, interpersonal, and psychological variables. In the absence of research findings, the authors speculate that CPPOA will provide a better understanding—compared to traditional benefit-cost and cost-effectiveness analyses—of how treatment resources should be allocated to match treatment needs and achieve desired outcomes.

Economic Analysis Findings

Chapters 3, 4, and 5 present evidence of the economic efficiency of different programs to prevent delinquency and crime, ranging from early childhood to correctional rehabilitation programs. A number of important findings are common to these three chapters. First, few crime prevention programs have been the subject of benefit-cost analyses to assess economic efficiency. This is true both for programs that have carried out benefit-cost analyses as part of the original research design (prospective) and for programs that were later the subject of benefit-cost analyses (retrospective), the latter being similar to secondary analysis of published research studies.

A second finding common to the three chapters is that different types of crime prevention modalities can be cost-beneficial, and can produce substantial benefits per dollar of cost. The majority of the studies reviewed in the three chapters were found to be economically efficient. It is acknowledged, however, that this finding may be partly because it is namely programs with demonstrated effectiveness in reducing crime that have been the subject of benefit-cost analyses. The logic behind this is that not much is gained, at least from a policy perspective, from performing a benefit-cost analysis of an ineffective program.

A third finding common to Chapters 3, 4, and 5 is that crime prevention programs can provide important monetary benefits beyond reduced crime. (Chapter 5 acknowledged the importance of measuring noncrime benefits, but did not examine them.) These noncrime or spin-off monetary benefits can take the form of, for example, increased tax revenues from higher earnings, savings from reduced usage of social services, and savings from less health care utilization. It is important to note that many early developmental prevention programs, for example, are designed to impact on other important life-course outcomes such as educational achievement, health, and parent-child relationships, and, therefore, any benefits accruing in these areas should not be seen as spin-off benefits. These noncrime benefits can account for a substantial portion of a program's total benefits.

A fourth important finding common to these chapters is that benefits tended to be estimated conservatively, whereas costs were often taken account in full. This has much to do with researchers' doubts about monetizing certain outcomes such as intangible victimization costs, and uncertainty about the perspective (e.g., government/taxpayer, society) to be adopted in benefit-cost analysis. Overcoming this tendency to "undervalue" or "assume away" benefits will require a program of research to develop and perfect better estimates of unit costs (since benefits are usually costs avoided) of outcomes relevant to crime prevention programs. Regarding the cost of crime to victims, for example, a number of recent studies by Mark Cohen and his colleagues (Miller, Cohen, and Wiersema 1996; Cohen 1998; Cohen and Miller 1998) have provided important data for benefit-cost analyses of crime prevention programs.

There are a number of priorities for research for improving upon the existing state of benefit-cost analysis of crime prevention programs, in terms of both the robustness of findings and the quantity of studies. First, there is a need for greater use of experimental research designs, particularly randomized experiments, in evaluating program effects. As a benefit-cost analysis (or any other type of economic analysis) is only as strong as the evaluation upon which it is based, the stronger the research design of the outcome evaluation, the more confidence that can be placed in the findings of the benefit-cost analysis. Weimer and Friedman recommend that benefit-cost analyses be limited to programs that have been evaluated with an "experimental or strong quasi-experimental design" (1979, 264). As discussed in the Introduction, the most convincing method of evaluating crime prevention programs is the randomized experiment (Farrington 1983).

On the well-known "scientific methods scale," developed by Sherman and his colleagues (1997) to assess the methodological quality (i.e., overall internal validity) of outcome evaluation studies, benefit-cost analyses should be restricted to programs with evaluation designs of level 3 or higher. The scientific methods scale is as follows, with level 1 being the lowest and level 5 the highest:

1. Correlational evidence (low offending correlates with the program at a single point in time).
2. No statistical control for selection bias, but some kind of comparison (e.g., program group compared with nonequivalent control group, program group measured before and after intervention, with no control group).
3. Moderate statistical control (e.g., program group compared with comparable control group, including pre-post and experimental-control comparisons).
4. Strong statistical control (e.g., program group compared with control group before and after, with control of extraneous influences on the outcome, by matching, prediction scores, or statistical controls).

5. Randomized experiment: units assigned at random to program and control groups prior to intervention.

The scale represents a shorthand means of summarizing well-established and agreed-upon rules for "assessing the level of certainty that a conclusion in any one test is correct" (Sherman et al. 1998, 3). Levels 3 to 5 permit valid inference about cause and effect: The program produced the observed change in outcome.

Another priority for research should be the development of a standard list of costs and benefits that should be measured as part of benefit-cost analyses of crime prevention programs. This was an important issue that was addressed in all three chapters in Part 3. In Chapter 3, the noncomparability of the costs and benefits of the different crime prevention programs prohibited comparisons of the programs' economic efficiency. This is because for valid comparisons "like" needs to be compared with "like" (Knapp and Netten 1997).

In Chapter 4, Greenwood and his colleagues note that the net savings figures of the two programs they analyzed (the Perry Preschool program and the Elmira Prenatal–Early Intervention Project) should not be compared to determine which program represents the best investment. This is because the program outcomes measured (and valued) differed between the two programs. For Elmira, the outcomes measured were health, employment, welfare, and crime, whereas for Perry the outcomes measured were education, employment, welfare, and crime.

In Chapter 5, Aos and his colleagues were able to overcome the problem of noncomparable benefits and costs of programs, thus allowing for like-with-like comparisons of the economic efficiency of the different crime prevention programs. This was possible because a standard methodology was used to measure program costs and benefits. Program costs were measured by choosing Washington State as a reference point. This allowed the researchers to carry out a detailed cost analysis of the costs the state would incur to pay for the prevention programs they analyzed had the programs been implemented in the state (some programs were based in Washington State). Program benefits were limited to the outcome of crime in the form of financial costs (or savings) to Washington State taxpayers (e.g., from police arrests, court processing, prison) and tangible costs (or, rather, costs avoided) to victims of crime. More efforts of this kind are needed, including a wider range of program benefits. Two implications of the research by Aos and his colleagues are very important: (1) There is greater scope for a program to achieve a high benefit-cost ratio if subjects are chronic offenders (e.g., in the case of multisystemic therapy programs; Henggeler, Melton, and Smith 1992) rather than community samples; and (2) it is difficult to have a benefit-cost ratio greater than 1.0 if the program is very costly (e.g., in the case of the Syracuse Family Development Research program; Lally, Mangione, and Honig 1988).

In developing a standard list of program costs and benefits that should be measured in crime prevention programs, key outcome variables should include crime and delinquency, substance abuse, education, employment, health, and family outcomes. Table 10.1 provides a summary of the relevant (potential) benefits on these outcome variables. For crime, an assessment of benefits should focus on affected agencies within the criminal justice system (e.g., police, courts, probation, corrections) and crime victims and their families. Many of the same benefits assessed for crime can also be examined in relation to substance abuse. For education, an assessment of benefits should focus on educational output and schooling expenses. For employment, benefits should be assessed for increased wages (tax revenue for government) and decreased use of welfare services. Decreased use of public health care and improved mental health are two of the potential benefits that should be examined in relation to health. For family issues, a number of potential benefits should be assessed, including fewer childbirths to at-risk women and increased parental time spent with children.

For program costs, both operating and capital costs should be included (although not all programs have capital expenditures). For operating costs, all of the human and physical resources consumed in administering and running the program should be assessed. These typically include staff salaries and benefits, overhead, supplies, and transportation. For capital costs, all of the resources consumed by fixed items should be assessed. These typically include program facilities and technical hardware. Where applicable, payments on capital expenditures and debt charges on loans also need to be included.

Policymakers and researchers also need to play a greater role in ensuring that crime prevention programs include, as part of the original research design, provision for an economic analysis, preferably a benefit-cost analysis. Prospective economic analyses have many advantages over retrospective ones. However, it would also be desirable, as part of a program of research, to carry out a number of retrospective economic evaluations of crime prevention programs, particularly for programs shown to be effective in reducing delinquency and crime. Programs could be selected according to criteria that would increase confidence in the benefit-cost findings, including high-quality research designs (preferably randomized experimental designs), large samples, and long-term follow-ups with low sample attrition. There is no shortage of high-quality crime prevention programs that could be the subject of retrospective benefit-cost analyses. For example, from our review of the twenty-four highest-qual-

TABLE 10.1 Summary of Program Benefits to Be Measured

Outcome Variable	*Benefits*
Delinquency/Crime	—savings to criminal justice system (e.g., police, courts, probation, corrections) —tangible and intangible costs avoided to crime victims (e.g., medical care, damaged and lost property, lost wages, lost quality of life, pain, suffering) —tangible and intangible costs avoided to family members of crime victims (e.g., funeral expenses, lost wages, lost quality of life)
Substance Abuse	—savings to criminal justice system —improved health
Education	—improved educational output (e.g., high school completion, enrollment in college or university) —reduced schooling costs (e.g., remedial classes, support services)
Employment	—increased wages (tax revenue for government) —decreased use of welfare services
Health	—decreased use of public health care (e.g., fewer visits to hospital and clinic) —improved mental health
Family Factors	—fewer childbirths to at-risk women —more parental time spent with children —less divorce and separation

ity family-based crime prevention programs (Farrington and Welsh 1999), only two had carried out a benefit-cost analysis (both prospective).

International Policy Perspectives

Chapters 6, 7, and 8 discuss the general trend toward and importance of countries reorienting their national crime prevention (and criminal justice) policies around an evidence- and efficiency-based model, aiming to put in place programs with demonstrated effectiveness and economic efficiency. As discussed in the Introduction, this has occurred for many reasons, including rising criminal justice costs—particularly in the area of prisons—evidence of the magnitude of the financial costs of crime and victimization to society, governmental fiscal restraints, a movement toward general efficiency practices in government, and growing evidence of the effectiveness of alternative, noncriminal justice approaches to preventing crime.

Efforts to advance an evidence- and efficiency-based approach to preventing crime require two main elements: policy guidance and funding. The United Kingdom, as discussed in Chapter 6, has already initiated these two elements, and other countries such as Australia (discussed in Chapter 7), Canada, and the United States show promising signs of achieving these ends in the not-too-distant future. Chapter 8 suggests that benefit-cost analysis is more feasible in countries with project-driven strategies (e.g., the United States, the United Kingdom) than in countries with policy-driven strategies (e.g., France, Sweden), where rigorous impact evaluation is rare.

Policy guidance to aid researchers in conducting outcome and economic evaluations of crime prevention programs needs to take account of much of the preceding discussion of key research issues (e.g., use of high-quality research designs to evaluate program effects, need for comprehensive and rigorous assessment of monetary costs and benefits). A central coordinating body—in the form of a governmental agency or university-affiliated policy and research center—is also needed to support field research efforts and compile and synthesize research findings nationally. A computerized registry of research findings modeled on the Cochrane collaboration[1] in the United Kingdom needs to be established.

Funding bodies must be prepared to finance economic evaluation research. Governmental agencies with responsibility for the prevention of crime should commit a percentage of their research budgets to support benefit-cost analyses of a number of new and existing prevention programs. Also, governmental agencies, foundations, private sector organizations, and other groups that fund crime prevention programs need to make future funding conditional upon a built-in evaluation component that includes an assessment of monetary costs and benefits.

Each country should set up a national crime prevention agency whose mandate is prevention, including high-quality evaluation and economic analysis research. This agency could provide technical assistance and funding to local crime prevention programs and could foster the large-scale implementation of programs shown to be effective in small-scale experiments.

From the standpoint of future research on the economic costs and benefits of crime prevention, there appears to be no shortage of possibilities; mobilizing the necessary funding and identifying the priorities for research seem to be the most pressing issues. Concerted efforts to improve confidence in what works and saves money will go a long way toward creating a more effective and efficient program of preventing crime and promoting safer communities throughout the world.

Notes

1. For information, contact the U.K. Cochrane Centre at Summertown Pavilion, Middle Way, Oxford, OX2 7LG.

References

Barnett, W. S. 1996. *Lives in the balance: Age–27 benefit-cost analysis of the High/Scope Perry Preschool program.* Ypsilanti, Mich.: High/Scope Press.

Cohen, M. A. 1988. Pain, suffering, and jury awards: A study of the cost of crime to victims. *Law and Society Review* 22: 537–55.

______. 1998. The monetary value of saving a high-risk youth. *Journal of Quantitative Criminology* 14: 5–33.

Cohen, M. A., and Miller, T. R. 1998. The cost of mental health care for victims of crime. *Journal of Interpersonal Violence* 13: 93–110.

Farrington, D. P. 1983. Randomized experiments on crime and justice. In M. Tonry and N. Morris, eds., *Crime and justice: A review of research,* 257–308. Vol. 4. Chicago: University of Chicago Press.

Farrington, D. P., and Welsh, B. C. 1999. Delinquency prevention using family-based interventions. *Children and Society* 13: 287–303.

Henggeler, S. W., Melton, G. B., and Smith, L. A. 1992. Family preservation using multisystemic therapy: An effective alternative to incarcerating serious juvenile offenders. *Journal of Consulting and Clinical Psychology* 60: 953–61.

Karoly, L. A., Greenwood, P. W., Everingham, S. S., Houbé, J., Kilburn, M. R., Rydell, C. P., Sanders, M., and Chiesa, J. 1998. *Investing in our children: What we know and don't know about the costs and benefits of early childhood interventions.* Santa Monica, Calif.: RAND.

Knapp, M., and Netten, A. 1997. The cost and cost effectiveness of community penalties: Principles, tools and examples. In G. Mair, ed., *Evaluating the effectiveness of community penalties,* 133–50. Aldershot, England: Avebury.

Lally, J. R., Mangione, P. L., and Honig, A. S. 1988. The Syracuse University Family Development Research program: Long-range impact of an early intervention with low-income children and their families. In D. Powell, ed., *Parent education as early childhood intervention: Emerging directions in theory, research and practice,* 79–104. Norwood, N.J.: Ablex.

Miller, T. R., Cohen, M. A., and Wiersema, B. 1996. *Victim costs and consequences: A new look.* Washington, D.C.: U.S. Department of Justice, National Institute of Justice.

Schweinhart, L. J., Barnes, H. V., and Weikart, D. P. 1993. *Significant benefits: The High/Scope Perry Preschool study through age 27.* Ypsilanti, Mich.: High/Scope Press.

Sherman, L. W., Gottfredson, D. C., MacKenzie, D. L., Eck, J. E., Reuter, P., and Bushway, S. D. 1997. *Preventing crime: What works, what doesn't, what's promising.* Washington, D.C.: U.S. Department of Justice, National Institute of Justice.

______. 1998. Preventing crime: What works, what doesn't, what's promising. *Research in Brief* (July). Washington, D.C.: U.S. Department of Justice, National Institute of Justice.

Weimer, D. L., and Friedman, L. S. 1979. Efficiency considerations in criminal rehabilitation research: Costs and consequences. In L. Sechrest, S. O. White, and E. D. Brown, eds., *The rehabilitation of criminal offenders: Problems and prospects,* 251–72. Washington, D.C.: National Academy of Sciences.

Zimring, F. E., and Hawkins, G. 1995. *Incapacitation: Penal confinement and the restraint of crime.* New York: Oxford University Press.

About the Editors and Contributors

Steve Aos is Associate Director of the Washington State Institute for Public Policy (Olympia).

Robert Barnoski is a Research Associate at the Washington State Institute for Public Policy (Olympia).

Sam Brand is an Assistant Economist at the United Kingdom Home Office (London).

James Chiesa is a Communications Analyst at RAND (Santa Monica, Calif.).

John Chisholm is a Research Analyst at the Australian Institute of Criminology (Canberra).

Mark A. Cohen is an Associate Professor of Management at the Owen Graduate School of Management and Director of the Vanderbilt Center for Environmental Management Studies, Vanderbilt University (Nashville).

Sanjay Dhiri is an Economic Adviser at the United Kingdom Home Office (London), currently on sabbatical at the London Business School.

Susan S. Everingham is a Policy Analyst and Director of the Forces and Resources Policy Center, RAND (Santa Monica, Calif.).

David P. Farrington is Professor of Psychological Criminology at the Institute of Criminology, University of Cambridge, and Jerry Lee Research Professor of Criminology at the Department of Criminology and Criminal Justice, University of Maryland (College Park).

Peter Goldblatt is Chief Medical Statistician at the Office of National Statistics (London).

Peter W. Greenwood is a Senior Research Scholar with the Criminal Justice Program and Director of Cyber Assurance, RAND (Santa Monica, Calif.).

Jill Houbé is an Assistant Professor with the Division of Developmental Pediatrics, Department of Pediatrics, University of British Columbia, and Research Fellow with the Centre for Community Health and Health Evaluation Research, British Columbia Children's and Women's Hospital (Vancouver, Canada).

Lynn A. Karoly is a Senior Economist and Director of the Labor and Population Program, RAND (Washington, D.C.).

M. Rebecca Kilburn is an Economist at RAND (Santa Monica, Calif.).

Roxanne Lieb is Director of the Washington State Institute for Public Policy (Olympia).

Daniel S. Nagin is Teresa and H. John Heinz III Professor of Public Policy at the H. John Heinz III School of Public Policy and Management, Carnegie Mellon University (Pittsburgh).

Polly Phipps is a Senior Research Analyst at the Washington State Institute for Public Policy (Olympia).

Richard Price is Head of Economics and Resource Analysis at the United Kingdom Home Office, on loan from Her Majesty's Treasury (London).

C. Peter Rydell was a Senior Social Scientist at RAND (Santa Monica, Calif.).

Matthew Sanders was a Graduate School Fellow at RAND (Santa Monica, Calif.) and is now at the John F. Kennedy School of Government, Harvard University (Cambridge).

Daniel Sansfaçon is Coordinator at the International Centre for the Prevention of Crime (Montreal).

Lawrence W. Sherman is Albert M. Greenfield Professor of Human Relations and Director of the Fels Center of Government, University of Pennsylvania (Philadelphia), and Jerry Lee Research Professor of Criminology at the Department of Criminology and Criminal Justice, University of Maryland (College Park).

Faye S. Taxman is an Associate Research Professor at the Department of Criminology and Criminal Justice, University of Maryland (College Park), and Director of the Bureau of Governmental Research.

Irvin Waller is Director General of the International Centre for the Prevention of Crime (Montreal) and a Professor of Criminology at the Department of Criminology, University of Ottawa.

Brandon C. Welsh is an Assistant Professor at the Department of Criminal Justice, University of Massachusetts–Lowell.

Brian T. Yates is a Professor at the Department of Psychology, American University (Washington, D.C.).

Index

Note: Bold page numbers indicate definitions